PERSPECTIVES IN ENTREPRENEURSHIP

Perspectives in Entrepreneurship

A Critical Approach

Edited By

Kevin Mole

Associate Professor, Centre for Small and Medium Sized Enterprises, Assistant Dean (Ph.D.) Warwick Business School, University of Warwick, UK

with

Monder Ram

Director, Centre for Research in Ethnic Minority Entrepreneurship (CREME) De Montfort University, UK

First published 2012 by
PALGRAVE MACMILLAN

Palgrave Macmillan in the UK is an imprint of Macmillan Publishers Limited, registered in England, company number 785998, of Houndmills, Basingstoke, Hampshire RG21 6XS.

Palgrave Macmillan in the US is a division of St Martin's Press LLC, 175 Fifth Avenue, New York, NY 10010.

Palgrave Macmillan is the global academic imprint of the above companies and has companies and representatives throughout the world.

Palgrave® and Macmillan® are registered trademarks in the United States, the United Kingdom, Europe and other countries.

ISBN 978–0–230–24110–7

This book is printed on paper suitable for recycling and made from fully managed and sustained forest sources. Logging, pulping and manufacturing processes are expected to conform to the environmental regulations of the country of origin.

A catalogue record for this book is available from the British Library.

A catalog record for this book is available from the Library of Congress.

10 9 8 7 6 5 4 3 2 1
21 20 19 18 17 16 15 14 13 12

Printed in China

Table of Contents

List of Figures and Tables   vii
Preface   viii
Foreword   x
Notes on Contributors   xii

1   Introduction   1
    Kevin Mole

Part I   Micro Perspectives

2   The Rational Choice Approach to Entrepreneurship   13
    Kevin Mole and Stephen Roper

3   The Psychology of the Entrepreneur   27
    Lars Kolvereid and Espen J. Isaksen

4   Undertaking Interpretive Work in Entrepreneurship Research   40
    Denise E. Fletcher

Part II   Macro Perspectives

5   Feminism, Gender and Entrepreneurship   59
    Susan Marlow

6   An Introduction to Network Approaches and Embeddedness   75
    Sarah Drakopoulos Dodd

7   Entrepreneurship and Neo-Institutional Theory   93
    Paul Tracey

8   Evolution and Entrepreneurship   107
    Dermot Breslin

9   Entrepreneurship in the Context of the Resource-Based
    View of the Firm   120
    Nicolai J. Foss

Part III   Integrating Micro and Macro Perspectives

10 Critical Realism and Entrepreneurship   137
    Kevin Mole

11 Critical Theories of Entrepreneurship   149
    André Spicer

12   Pragmatism, Reality and Entrepreneurship: Entrepreneurial
      Action and Effectuation Perspectives   161
      Tony J. Watson

Conclusion   175
Kevin Mole

Bibliography   178
Author Index   202
Subject Index   209

List of Figures and Tables

Figures

2.1   UK self-employed income vs wages, 1968–93   15

2.2   Most important sources of finance over three decades   19

10.1   The Morphogenetic Cycle   139

Tables

6.1   Entrepreneurial network functions, benefits and drawbacks   78

6.2   Contrasting strong and weak ties   80

6.3   Networking characteristics across countries   82

6.4   Development of networks through the entrepreneurial process   84

Preface

This book was written for two reasons. Firstly, because it seemed that it was about time that entrepreneurship and small business embraced perspectives in the discipline and secondly because this meant that the teaching of entrepreneurship and small business should do the same. So this book is not directly about the topics of finance, opportunity, growth and so on; instead it takes the reader through different ways of understanding entrepreneurship and enterprise.

As a reader you might be interested in just one perspective; however, we suggest starting with the introduction which gives an overview of the perspectives, with the strong suggestion that each deserves a place in the understanding of entrepreneurship. Then dip into one of the chapters, they certainly can be read on their own. As someone who wants to broaden their knowledge of perspectives there is the opportunity to sample several. On the other hand, you might treat the text like a course, as it is suitable for either more advanced undergraduates or masters level students.

In fact, a course that this text supports is taught at Warwick Business School and has been for several years. Students are exposed to perspectives in much the same way that students in other social science disciplines would be. This course begins with debates surrounding the definition of entrepreneurship (see the introduction). It then discusses three perspectives based on the individual: the rational choice or economics perspective (Chapter 2) the psychological perspective (Chapter 3) and the interpretivist perspective (Chapter 4). The next few weeks see the students examine topics influenced by more than one of these perspectives, such as entrepreneurial learning. Students would endeavour to understand how academics working within each of these perspectives would view the topic and to understand the relationship between perspectives and topics, and methods. In the second term, more of the perspectives at a societal level are included: feminism, networking, organizational ecology, the resource-based view (RBV) and institutional theory. In later weeks, a selection of topics are discussed, identifying how different authors had used different perspectives to write about the same topic, such as internationalization or innovation. If you are an individual and not a student following this course, try viewing work on internationalization, because you should be able to identify different approaches like networks or the RBV.

Our students were assessed on presentations about a paper and had a choice of assignment questions, all of which were designed for them to compare and contrast perspectives. This course endeavours to provide evidence of the range of entrepreneurship studies; it is not a course that leads students to become entrepreneurs. Nonetheless, some students did comment that it made them look at their enterprises in a different light. It also helped to reinforce their critical thinking and engage more with the subject. It also demonstrated that some situations require an understanding of what others assume or take for granted. Entrepreneurship is being researched using a wide repertoire of approaches. This book seeks to embrace this breadth of perspectives as it sees this as enriching our understanding of entrepreneurship.

There are a number of further benefits to be had by laying out the rich variety of perspectives available to study entrepreneurship. First, the divergent approaches catalogued in this text serve simultaneously to highlight the comparatively narrow range of theoretical resources utilized with the domain of entrepreneurship (for example, strategy-based disciplines), while at the same time flagging up real opportunities for a richer exchange with standpoints hitherto at the margins of the field. We hope that researchers and students take up this invitation to engage in the creative application of approaches from a variety of fields. Second, the rigorous articulation of the features of different perspectives sketched out in the contributions to this text facilitates the kind of contextualized theory building that leading scholars, notably Zahra (2007), have suggested is necessary if the field is to develop greater coherence. This 'would require researchers to delve deeply into the underlying logics and structures behind them, not simply to catalog them' (Zahra, 2007, p. 445). The reflexive enterprise engaged in by our various contributors affords an opportunity to 'delve' in some depth into theoretical antecedents of particular approaches. Finally, the interrogation of disciplinary perspectives offers the prospect of providing a measure of 'discipline and structure' (Chua, Chrisman and Steier, 2003) to a field of study characterized by complexity, heterogeneity and eclectism; this too can enhance theoretical development.

We'd like to thank all the contributors to this volume, Martin Drewe at Palgrave Macmillan for his support through the process and finally Kevin would like to mention a big thank you to Miranda.

Kevin Mole and Monder Ram

Foreword

The subject domain of entrepreneurship has grown spectacularly over the past 20 years and has become one of the most popular and topical of all the management subjects. This was not always the case; until relatively recently, the study of entrepreneurship was met with some scepticism from practitioners and scholars from the more established management domains. Entrepreneurship has developed from a parvenu into one of the most rigorous and respected of all the management subjects. To a large extent, the legitimization and growth of the subject domain has been due to the quality and rigour of the theorizing and the empiricism that has been undertaken within the field. High-quality research attracts others into the field, and a growing number of scholars now focus their attention on issues related to entrepreneurship. The current size and strength of the subject domain is seen most obviously in indicators of the number of academics working in the domain and the quality of their outputs. The Entrepreneurship Division of the Academy of Management has become one of the largest and fastest growing interest groups within the academy, with over 2700 members. Scholarly journals specializing in entrepreneurship have grown in number and quality, and mainstream management journals, such as the *Academy of Management Journal* and the *Journal of Management Studies* are increasingly publishing entrepreneurship articles. Indeed, the domain has developed to such an extent that entrepreneurship scholars are becoming increasingly concerned with ensuring that their theoretical contributions not only advance understanding of entrepreneurship but also give something back to the established domains.

While the entrepreneurship domain has enjoyed great success for its research, it has paid less attention to its pedagogy, and the development of entrepreneurship as a teaching subject has been much slower. While most universities now offer one or two modules relating to enterprise and new venture creation, few have developed their entrepreneurship curriculum to the extent of creating entire subject pathways, especially at undergraduate level. This is in stark contrast to other management domains, such as marketing, where research and teaching have matured simultaneously. The comparison between marketing and entrepreneurship as taught subjects on the business and management curriculum is instructive. When the marketing domain emerged in the 1970s, many sceptics argued that marketing was a glorified label for selling, and selling could not be taught – you either have the gift of the gab or you haven't. Forty years on, marketing has become long-established as a core subject within the business and management curriculum, producing several thousand graduates each year, and has encouraged widespread appreciation of the importance of marketing both as a set of competencies and as a social phenomenon. Entrepreneurship is unlikely to fulfil its potential as a subject domain until it develops the pedagogic maturity evident within other well-established university subject departments. While many sceptics contest whether it is possible to teach entrepreneurship, they overlook the identical arguments that were posed to other 'new' subjects in their early years, such as marketing 40 years ago, psychology 40 years earlier and medicine a century before that. The continued development of entrepreneurship as a subject domain will depend on its ability to develop effective pedagogy and sustain its relevance and appeal to generations of students.

This book makes an important contribution to the development of entrepreneurship pedagogy. It makes no claims to teach people how to start a business – this functional information can be gained from any number of sources – its aims are much wider than this. Entrepreneurship is a phenomenon that focuses on the emergence of new economic activities. These take place in a variety of contexts, including new firms, corporate ventures, social organizations and even governmental institutions. In their attempts to understand and explain entrepreneurship, researchers have approached the subject from many different perspectives, all of which illuminate different facets of the phenomenon but none of which explain the whole. Understanding the contributions that many different research perspectives offer, the analysis of entrepreneurship is the best possible introduction to the subject, and Kevin Mole and Monder Ram have brought together an impressive collection of work that provides a complete overview of the entrepreneurship domain.

Sara Carter OBE

Notes on Contributors

Dermot Breslin is a Lecturer in Enterprise and Entrepreneurship at the University of Sheffield. The specific focus of his research has been a Generalized Darwinian approach, drawing on related fields from within both organization science and the natural sciences, to develop a theory-led approach to the study of changing behaviour in organizations. Recent publications have been in the *International Journal of Management Reviews*.

Sarah Drakopoulos Dodd is Associate Professor of Entrepreneurship at ALBA Graduate Business School, Greece and the Academic Director of AHEAD-ALBA Hub for Enterprise and Development. With more than 50 journal articles, book chapters and conference papers, Dr. Dodd's research concentrates on the social side of enterprise. She has studied extensively the structure, composition and exchanges of entrepreneurial networks, both in Greece and Scotland.

Denise E. Fletcher is Professor of Entrepreneurship and Innovation at the Luxembourg Business Academy, University of Luxembourg and Vice President of practice for the Institute of Small Business and Entrepreneurship. Her work focuses on the contribution that narrative, ethnographic and social constructionist ideas have for deepening understandings of how and why entrepreneurial practices occur. She edited the book 'Understanding the Small Family Business' (2002) published by Routledge, and has published in a variety of entrepreneurship and organization journals. Her current research focuses on two areas: the entrepreneurial aspirations of cohabiting couples or sibling partners in the creation of new business ventures, and the absorptive nature of entrepreneurial occupations.

Nicolai J. Foss is Professor at Copenhagen Business School. He is affiliated with the Danish Research Unit for Industrial Dynamics His research is mainly concerned with firm strategy and economic organization. He is particularly interested in the intersection between these two fields. He has published in a wide variety of economics and strategy journals. He is the author of *Strategy, Economic Organization, and the Knowledge Economy: The Coordination of Firms and Resources* (2006) published by Oxford University Press.

Espen J. Isaksen is currently an Associate Professor and teaches entrepreneurship at the Bodø Graduate School of Business, Bodø, Norway. He received his doctorate in economics from Bodø in 2006. His research interests include entrepreneurial intentions and action in addition to an interest in the performance of new ventures and advice to the entrepreneur. He has published widely, including international conferences, in book chapters and in international journals.

Lars Kolvereid is Professor of Entrepreneurship and a former Dean of Bodø Graduate School of Business. His interests concern the psychology of entrepreneurship, including entrepreneurial intentions, start-up attempts and new businesses. He has published many articles in international journals and several books on the entrepreneurial process from a psychological perspective. He has supervised more than 14 doctoral students and is on the editorial boards of *Entrepreneurship Theory and Practice* and *Entrepreneurship and Regional Development*.

Susan Marlow is Professor of Entrepreneurship at De Montfort University. Her research interests are in gender, incubation and labour management in small firms. She is the editor of the *International Small Business Journal* and the VP Research for the UK's Institute for Small Business and Entrepreneurship (ISBE). Her recent work on gender performance in high tech is published in *Entrepreneurship Theory and Practice* and the work on formality is published in the *British Journal of Management*.

Kevin Mole is an Associate Professor at Warwick Business School and Assistant Dean (PhD programme). His research interests include business advice, evaluation and critical realism. He is an international authority on business advice, has influenced UK government policy and is cited in government and OECD reports. He is a member of, and has presented to, the Critical Realism in Action Group. His recently published work includes a paper on the morphogenetic approach to critical realism in the *Journal of Business Venturing* (2008).

Monder Ram is Professor of Small Business and Director of CREME at De Montfort University. He has extensive experience of working in, researching and acting as a consultant to ethnic minority businesses. He is a leading authority on ethnic minority entrepreneurship research and has published widely on the subject. His work has been supported by grants from a full range of research funding bodies; including research councils, government departments, regional and local agencies and the private sector. He has been awarded an OBE in recognition of his services to enterprise.

Stephen Roper is Professor of Innovation and Enterprise. He is an economist with major research interests in enterprise growth and development, diversity and business performance, innovation, regional development, and industrial policy evaluation. He has published extensively in international journals and has a number of recent articles on the innovation value chain. He is the Director of InnovationLab (Ireland) Ltd.

André Spicer is Professor in Organizational Behaviour at Warwick Business School. His research interests are in power and resistance, institutional change, entrepreneurship, social movements, workplace architecture and space. He has published a variety of articles in highly regarded journals. His recent publications include *Unmasking the Entrepreneur* (2009). He is an editor of the *Journal of Management Studies*.

Paul Tracey is a Reader in Human Resources and Organizations at Judge Business School, University of Cambridge. His research focuses on entrepreneurship, institutions and institutional change regional innovation and social innovation. He is the author of over 24 publications in highly rated international journals focussing on institutional theory and social entrepreneurship. He has published innovative work on institutional aspects of entrepreneurship, such as the institutionalization of social venture franchises, the institutionism of new organizational forms and the institutional impact of dining rituals of Cambridge colleges.

Tony J. Watson is Professor of Organizational Behaviour at Nottingham Univeristy Business School. He is interested in Realist Pragmatism. His research is on organizations, managerial work, strategy-making, entrepreneurship, HRM and industrial sociology. He has published numerous articles in both sociology and in organizational studies including *Organising and Managing Work* (2002) and *Sociology, Work and Industry* (5th edition 2008).

CHAPTER 1

Introduction

Kevin Mole

This book introduces the way that scholars within entrepreneurship carry out their studies. The book aims to fill a gap in the courses offered to entrepreneurship students within business schools. Its aim is to make students aware of the different perspectives taken within this particular academic discipline. While, there are studies and issues that are covered within the book, it does not provide a comprehensive coverage of entrepreneurship and small business. There will be gaps and issues not covered; even where the book does discuss an issue, it may not discuss it with sufficient depth to satisfy the student. The book claims to provide an overview and context for the different approaches taken by authors who study entrepreneurship. In addition, the book aims to provide a balanced assessment of the approaches and the claims made within each approach.

The book is divided into three parts. Each part examines a group of approaches to entrepreneurship. These approaches are significant for the study of enterprise and entrepreneurship and are expected to continue to have important impacts upon the field. There are eleven chapters that consider each approach (perspective). Each of the chapters is proposed by an expert and covers not only the approach but also explores how the approach has been critiqued and evaluates the responses made by those within the approach. The first part maps out three approaches to entrepreneurship that take as their starting point the individual entrepreneur: interpretivism, rational choice and psychology.

The second part of the book examines perspectives that are concerned with more macro influences on the entrepreneur: feminist views of entrepreneurship, whether the entrepreneur has appropriate networks, the institutional influences on the entrepreneur, the resource-based view of the entrepreneur and critical approaches to entrepreneurship are all represented in this second part.

The third part of the book examines perspectives that are concerned with trying to fit the micro view of the entrepreneur with the macro context. A new set of perspectives are represented in this section: evolutionary views of entrepreneurship, critical realist views of entrepreneurship, the pragmatic view are represented in this third part.

It is always a judgement as to where each of the perspectives fit. Cases could be made to make all of the micro perspectives featured in the early part of the book as macro. Psychology has its social psychology side, economics concerns large scale changes and interpretivist views involve ideas from outside the entrepreneur. It should be added that which section the perspective occupies has no bearing on its validity.

By way of introduction, we here offer a broad overview of issues in the study of entrepreneurship. Entrepreneurship and small business is relatively young as a 'discipline'. In 1970 there were just eight articles written on small business within the social science citation index; by 2008 this had increased to 398. Within that period a number of small business and entrepreneurship journals had joined the social science index. This is an academic endeavour that is about 40 years old. There has been some debate in entrepreneurship and other management sub-disciplines about whether entrepreneurship and small business is a distinct 'discipline' with its own approaches or whether it is simply a site of interest for scholars (Sorenson and Stuart, 2008). The other facet that has changed over the 40 years has been the emphasis on small business versus entrepreneurship. Entrepreneurship conjures up images of powerful buccaneering individuals wheeling and dealing and in command of their world. Small business is defined in opposition to the more powerful larger businesses. Over time, the academic discussion has shifted away from small business and towards entrepreneurship. One indication of this was that the 'American Journal of Small Business' changed its name to 'Entrepreneurship Theory and Practice' between 1998 and 1989.

The introduction addresses itself to four questions that those who are new to the discipline might want to ask. In this sense the book acts as a field map of the terrain. We ask:

- What is meant by entrepreneurship and small business?
- Is there a best way to study entrepreneurship and small business?
- Is there a scientific approach to entrepreneurship and small business?
- How does the study of entrepreneurship link to entrepreneurs?

Answering these questions will provide us with a useful introduction to the issues that are contained in the book and a useful introduction to the chapters. However, even before that there are two concepts that need to be explained: ontology and epistemology.

Ontology and epistemology

The differences between academic perspectives are often rooted in differences between ontology and epistemology (Lewis, 2002). Many academic disputes are clearer once their assumptions about ontology and epistemology are revealed (Marsh and Furlong, 2002). Therefore, a book that examines different perspectives needs to equip students with the understanding of these two building blocks of research, starting with ontology (Grix, 2004).

Ontology concerns what we think the world is like (Blaikie, 2000). Thus ontology relates to 'claims and assumptions that are made about the nature of social reality, claims about what exists, what it looks like' (Blaikie, 2000, 8). Different traditions of scholarship have very different views of the world. To make these assumptions clear it is useful to distinguish two very different assumptions about the nature of the social world made by foundationalists and anti-foundationalists.

Foundationalists believe that there is a world outside of our socially derived concepts. There is a world out there independent of our knowledge of it. True knowledge is found when we get closer to knowing this world (Grix, 2004). The opposite view of the anti-foundationalist says that the world is socially constructed (Marsh and Furlong, 2002). This means that the world in made up of our concepts of the world and the meanings we share.

Different views of ontology tend to imply different ways of finding out about the social world (epistemology). If you believe that there is a world outside of your existence you are more likely to want to find out objectively about it. If you believe that the world is constructed from shared meanings then you are likely to want to understand the interpretations that people make about their world.

Epistemology concerns how to find knowledge about the world (Blaikie, 2000). Crudely, there are two main ends of the spectrum on epistemology: a positivist view versus a interpretivist view (Marsh and Furlong, 2002). The positivist view tends to try to use scientific methods in a value-free way to conduct objective research (Grix, 2004). The interpretivist view seeks to understand the meanings that people place upon events. Interpretivists are sceptical of the capacity to be value-free and therefore do not see that it is possible to conduct objective research (Grix, 2004).

Having defined these two 'ologies' the introduction turns to a discussion of what is entrepreneurship.

What is entrepreneurship?

When people say they study entrepreneurship they are making a statement about something that exists and that we might be able to agree on, at least to some extent. In this case it is a concept that we have used to describe a complex set of behaviours. We might expect that an academic discipline would at the very least be able to define what it studies. In the case of entrepreneurship this is not the case. The discipline has emerged from the studies of small firms that focused on a definition by size. Even this was not settled, with some scholars using turnover or employment measures, and others using characteristics where small firms had little market power (Greene and Mole, 2006). Entrepreneurship is even more contested.

There are presently two general approaches to defining entrepreneurship. One is broadly identified with innovation and Joseph Schumpeter and the other with business creation and Isreal Kirzner. The two are not mutually exclusive yet there has been a shift towards the business creation view in recent years (Shane and Venkataraman, 2000).

The Schumpterian view identified the entrepreneur as an lynchpin of economic development (Schumpeter, 1934a). Schumpeter identified five methods through which the entrepreneur could innovate: new products (product innovation), new markets (market innovation), new methods (process innovation), creating a new type of organization (administrative innovation) and 'conquering' a new source of supply of raw materials or half-manufactured goods. Schumpeter saw these five types of innovation as stemming from the actions of entrepreneurs. At the same time as the new innovations were brought in older industries suffered; accordingly Schumpeter called the process 'creative destruction'. A Schumpeterian entrepreneur can bring in disruptive technology that makes older ways of doing things obsolete.

A Schumpeterian entrepreneur can be anywhere. She does not have to run a company, she can work for an old established company or she can work for a government department. She can change the practices of doing business and create new institutions (Tolbert and Zucker, 1983; Tracey, Phillips and Jarvis, 2011).

The second approach identifies the Kirznerian entrepreneur as someone who is alert to opportunities and creates the vehicle to exploit them (Kirzner, 1973; Shane, 2000; Shane and Venkataraman, 2000). Here the entrepreneur may be someone who moves the economy towards equilibrium through arbitrage. The focus is less on the entrepreneur as a innovator and more on the entrepreneur as a carrier of knowledge that diffuses practices (Audretsch and Keilbach, 2004). Thus, Kirznerian entrepreneurs have faith in their ability to spot opportunities (Dimov, 2010). In this approach the distinct focus is on the formation of new enterprises and the conditions which facilitate them (Delgado, Porter and Stern, 2010; Romanelli and Schoonhoven, 2001).

At this point the reader may have a sinking feeling. If experts cannot agree on a definition of what entrepreneurship is how can the reader know how to study it? It seems fair to say that both of the defined Schumpeterian and Kirznerian views of entrepreneurship have their positive attributes. Each of the definitions involves change, albeit more incremental for the Kirznerian entrepreneur. Each entrepreneur mobilizes resources. The Kirznerian entrepreneur is more everyday whereas the Schumpeterian entrepreneur is a hero figure.

Following Shane and Venkataraman (2000) it is the Kirznerian view of the entrepreneur that appears to be the dominant view of entrepreneurship in the literature at present. That is, the issue of how entrepreneurs are alert to opportunities which are out there in the environment.

Nonetheless, entrepreneurship encompasses more than what entrepreneurs do (Dodd and Anderson, 2007). It involves the circumstances that enable entrepreneurs to start their businesses (Blanchflower and Oswald, 1998; Gnyawali and Fogel, 1994) and the processes that enable some places to be more 'entrepreneurial' (Armington and Acs, 2002; Bennett, Bratton, and Robson, 2000; Bennett and Smith, 2002; Keeble, 1997; Keeble, Lawson, Moore, and Wilkinson, 1999; Romanelli and Schoonhoven, 2001).

Connecting to the world of entrepreneurs

If you say you are a professor of entrepreneurship, one of the questions you might reasonably expect to be asked is whether you have run a business yourself or whether you think entrepreneurship can be taught. The majority of textbooks and entrepreneurship courses are intended for those who are interested in starting their own business or are part of the support infrastructure (Bygrave and Zacharakis, 2010). Some textbooks recommend their contributors as 'tireless campaigners for entrepreneurship' (Bygrave and Zacharakis, 2010) or reflect the public policy in favour of more entrepreneurial economies, the latter being more common in European texts (Carter and Jones-Evans, 2006; Deakins and Freel, 2006).

In practice, many teaching entrepreneurship do take the view that it is a positive phenomenon whether it is defined as being innovative, either in economic or institutional terms, or founding new organizations. Many teaching entrepreneurship try to involve practising business owners to give a flavour of the life-world of being an entrepreneur. Some hold a more 'objective' view that distances them from entrepreneurs. This may be because their discipline emphasizes a detached view that analyses secondary data for patterns that can be predicted (Blanchflower and Oswald, 1998). They may suggest occasions where forming more new businesses is detrimental (Greene, Mole and Storey, 2004; Van Stel and Storey, 2004). This particular viewpoint is often identified with the economists approach.

There is of course a critique of value-free social science (Hollis, 1994). Besides, the critical approach may be positively hostile to more new firm formation, seeing it as detrimental to society and as a reflection of a continuing dominance by particular groups in society (Jones and Spicer, 2005; Karatas-Ozkan and Murphy, 2010; Ogbor, 2000; Ram and Trehan, 2010). They might argue that the use of 'enterprise culture' is ideological and was meant to induce self-reliance and move people away from a 'dependency culture', and hence individualize problems such as unemployment (MacDonald and Coffield, 1991).

The discipline of entrepreneurship

Read many of the reviews of entrepreneurship and you might find a discussion about a dominant approach to research, often labelled quantitative or positivist, and a set of alternative approaches (Jennings, Perren and Carter, 2005). These articles showcase entrepreneurship as out of step with mainstream management because the alternatives to positivist social science are more marginalized. There are fewer qualitative studies in the major entrepreneurship journals, for example (Grant and Perren, 2002), while a pluralist view of research is quite evident in disciplines such as organization behaviour (Eisenhardt, 1989). This book is clearly within the pluralist camp. In recent times, the pluralist view has been given a boost by its use by subject specialists within the entrepreneurship journals: associate editors of these from economics and sociology are evidence of an acceptance of pluralism.

Beyond agreeing with the case for pluralism, the book emphasizes two further points. First, there is a wide variety of approaches to entrepreneurship. In the chapters to come eleven distinct approaches are discussed; even then, there are perhaps notable omissions, such as effectuation. Nonetheless, the approaches to entrepreneurship range from the rational choice approach adopted by mainstream economics to the interpretive approach adopted more by management scholars and influenced by sociology. These different approaches beget a richer knowledge of the subject matter, since there are some perspectives, by their assumptions, that avoid some issues. In using an interpretive approach, one can understand the way that entrepreneurs make meaning of their situation.

From the rational choice perspective, one can assess the potential for finance gaps in funding and the call for public policy intervention.

This leads to the second point. There is a tradition of strong paradigms within the sciences (Aldrich and Ruef, 2006). Economics takes a mainstream approach to problems: see Chapter 2. In the search for legitimacy in academia one approach has been to call for a mainstream approach to the subject, in which the discipline has a coherent understanding of the subject matter and a consistent methodology (Arauzo and Manjon, 2004). This is not the only view; the counter is that if entrepreneurship remains as a field for interdisciplinary work, then it can attract a wider set of interested scholars who might enhance our knowledge of entrepreneurship (Sorenson and Stuart, 2008). Clearly, the line of attack taken in this book is the latter: many perspectives are represented from economics, psychology and sociology. The intent is to showcase these different perspectives and highlight the advantages and disadvantages of each.

The book begins with the rational choice or the economists' style of approach. This approach has been involved in entrepreneurship because entrepreneurship provides a way in which economies develop. Writers such as Schumpeter (1948) and Knight (1921) were concerned about innovation and risk respectively. Economists tend to see entrepreneurs as making a rational choice to start a business given their alternatives. Kevin Mole and Stephen Roper discuss the rational choice approach in Chapter 2.

The second approach that the reader will meet is the psychological approach. This is an approach that has a long involvement in entrepreneurship since early examples that stressed the psychological needs of those who became entrepreneurs (McClelland, 1961). The psychological approach takes the view that the attitudes and beliefs of the entrepreneur are the key to explaining entrepreneurship. The psychological view has been quite important in the United States. Psychologists share with economists, the attention towards beliefs and attitudes but their methodology is more quantitative, at least in the mainstream. Lars Kolvereid and Espen J. Isaksen discuss the individual psychology of the entrepreneur in Chapter 3.

The third style of approach is the interpretivist view. The interpretivist view is a challenging one to the more dominant approaches that have hitherto held sway within entrepreneurship and small business (Dodd and Anderson, 2007). Interpretivists argue that to understand entrepreneurship and entrepreneurs, researchers have to be aware of the meanings and interpretations that those engaged in entrepreneurial activities put on their situation and behaviour. Moreover, these interpretations and meaning cannot be simply read from the objective situation within which a person finds themselves (Audretsch and Keilbach, 2007). Consequently, two people might have similar backgrounds and education, be subject to the same experience in a job environment and one might start their own firm and the other move to another firm as an employee. Because interpretivists claim that there is no objective truth but that we construct our social world together in our social lives, it has also become known as social constructionism (Marsh and Stoker, 2002). This book uses the two phrases interchangeably. The chapter is written by Denise Fletcher.

These first three perspectives examine entrepreneurship and small business management from perspectives that emphasize the individual agent. Either the agent interprets their surroundings and makes meaning, or has certain attitudes or beliefs, or rationally chooses from competing ends. However, the wider societal issues and cultural aspects are not the focus of this work. Psychological attitudes may be formed within a context. Accordingly we turn to more macro approaches that situate the entrepreneurs within a context.

Macro views

What we have termed macro views – where macro refers to population or societal level explanations – impact entrepreneurship. At the empirical level controls for gender, prior income and social capital are almost obligatory; yet these controls reflect a view that societal influences are important (Turner, 2005). Gendered relationships reflect the processes that are evident within the wider society.

Accordingly, the first approach in this section examines feminist theory. Feminist theory sets out a context for the study of female entrepreneurship under conditions of patriarchy. The chapter begins by situating the gendered role of women as inferior and discusses the challenges to that structured position. The chapter builds upon Ahl's critique of feminist studies (Ahl, 2006) to argue that feminist studies are important not just for women's entrepreneurship but that 'entrepreneurship cannot be adequately analysed from a gender neutral perspective'. Sue Marlow discusses feminist theory and entrepreneurship in Chapter 5.

The second approach in the macro section introduces networks. This chapter brings in the local context to the entrepreneur. It is not so much that macro influences like patriarchy are critical; within networks it is the local opportunities to get information that are important (Clark, Palaskas, Tracey and Tsampra, 2004; Kenney and Patton, 2005). This view takes the perspective away from the individual entrepreneur and situates or embeds them within their social groups (Uzzi, 1997). Your membership of social groups enables and constrains your ability to find information. This suggests that there are trade-offs within networks. Strong, close-knit ties can be influential (Anderson, Jack and Dodd, 2005; Karra, Tracey and Phillips, 2006) but too many close ties in your network can leave it unable to hear of new ideas (Uzzi, 1997). Sarah Dodd discusses network approaches and embeddedness in Chapter 6.

When people are embedded in social groups they become subject to social norms. It is relatively easy to demonstrate the impact of group norms on behaviour. Some behaviours are legitimated and others are not, and the influence of legitimation and conformity has attracted the attention of organizational scholars such as Meyer and Rowan (1977). They studied the way that managers mythologized what they were doing and created rituals. The approach was called neo-institutional and examined the processes by which managers and entrepreneurs legitimate their actions in the eyes of others. This has also brought the idea that entrepreneurs conform to patterns of expected behaviour. Paul Tracey discusses the institutional approaches to entrepreneurship in Chapter 7.

So far the social aspects of entrepreneurship have been stressed. At this point the book turns towards more competitive aspects of entrepreneurship. In the evolutionary approach authors have discussed the ways in which new firms can be selected by the operations of the market (Aldrich and Wiedenmayer, 1993). Researchers in this tradition have used biological metaphors to study new firm founding, rather like they were animal populations (Aldrich and Ruef, 2006; Carroll and Hannan, 2000). Authors have argued that this approach has revealed patterns of entrepreneurial behaviour that have previously been hidden. They suggest that individual firms reflect their early years and are 'imprinted' and show that there are cultural aspects of entrepreneurship where business models are widely understood. More recently, a generalized Darwinian approach has examined the processes of variation, selection and replication among populations. Dermot Breslin discusses the evolutionary approaches to entrepreneurship in Chapter 8.

Carrying on with the more competitive theme we turn to the key question of what makes firms able to out-compete their rivals. In Chapter 8 the answer would have been that they were better adapted to the environment. In Chapter 9 the notion is that the competitive firm has resources that others cannot match. If this is the case, the question becomes how did the firm get them. This chapter looks at the intersection between the resource-based view and entrepreneurship. This has become known as strategic entrepreneurship. Nicolai Foss discusses how entrepreneurs create competitive advantage in the resource-based view in this chapter.

These four chapters, from feminism to networks and neo-institutionalist views, from the Generalized Darwinian view to the resource-based view of the firm, form our macro view. They emphasize the social context and the strategic competitive elements of entrepreneurship. From this point there are a number of approaches that try to integrate both the micro emphasis on the entrepreneur with the macro emphasis of those elements that enable and constrain one's actions.

Integrating macro and micro

The first approach that attempts to integrate macro and micro is the critical realist approach. For critical realists the macro is structure and the micro is agency. They are interested in how both interrelate. Critical realism derives from the philosophy of Roy Bhaskar and the developments within social science to outline a cycle of change (Archer, Bhaskar, Collier, Lawson and Norrie, 1998; Bhaskar, 1975, 1979). Since entrepreneurship is all about change the critical realist approach fits with the subject matter (Mole and Mole, 2010). Kevin Mole discusses the critical realist approach to entrepreneurship in Chapter 10.

The sense of challenge also emerges in the next chapter as we might think about what the study of entrepreneurship means in the wider sense. What is the concept of entrepreneurship and what is it used for? What does this concept take for granted? Critical approaches to management are concerned to expose the implications of using terms such as the entrepreneur. In doing so they can alert us to the way that entrepreneurship can be used to push forward some projects at the expense of others. Andre Spicer discusses a critical approach to entrepreneurship in Chapter 12.

The final element in the macro and micro is a pragmatic one. Critical realism is not the only way to integrate macro and micro. The way in which pragmatist philosophers like Charles Dewey framed the world has inspired a pragmatic realism. This approach which draws on the work of Max Weber is interpretive while accepting the realist view of a world outside of our senses. Human action represents creative responses to the situation that one finds oneself in. Consequently, human action is in the potential of all human beings given the circumstances. This is not simply rational action such as the rational choice economists advocate because an interpretivist element is also involved in the situation. The call in this chapter is to associate entrepreneuring within everyday life, rather than with exceptional individuals such as Bill Gates. Entrepreneuring is a verb. Tony Watson discusses a pragmatic realism in Chapter 11.

Finally we conclude with an exploration of the future of perspectives in entrepreneurship. How can we balance competing demands to have enough variety to understand each of the perspectives and to explore the topics that different perspectives emphasis while at the same time creating a coherent body of work. Kevin Mole discusses the future of entrepreneurial perspectives in a concluding chapter.

Reconciliation is not a theme that the book supports. There is little prospect of a new paradigm that will enable us all to migrate to one approach (Grant and Perren, 2002; Kuhn, 1996) or indeed be able to combine approaches (Burrell and Morgan, 1979). Each approach emphasizes topics that may have been overlooked by others, but there are barriers to combining approaches. Economists do not recognize meanings and want to predict, interpretivists want to understand and critical realists want to explain but not predict. There is no rapprochment likely.

So to answer the first question there is no one best way to study entrepreneurship. Instead we offer a diversity of approaches to the study of entrepreneurship and being enterprising. The key for the study of entrepreneurship is to celebrate diversity and to enable those of different positions to take cognizance of each other's work and to build our knowledge together. Hence, we endorse the project to keep the disciplinary boundaries of entrepreneurship porous to enable scholars from outside disciplines to contribute to our understanding of the entrepreneur in society (Sorenson and Stuart, 2008).

What is a scientific approach to entrepreneurship?

If there are differences in the approach to studying entrepreneurship, and differences in the way that entrepreneurship is defined, it will come as no surprise that there are debates about what a scientific approach to entrepreneurship consists of – indeed whether it is of use. There are clear differences in the subject matter between natural sciences and social sciences. In particular, the ability of those in the natural sciences to conduct experiments in closed controlled environments is often difficult to achieve in social science and therefore in the study of entrepreneurship (Bhaskar, 1979).

There have been extensive debates concerning the whys and wherefores of the scientific methods within economics, psychology and sociology (Hollis, 1994). It is not the intention of this book to enter into this debate. Nonetheless, the issue of methodology is significant in our chapters. Within each chapter is a 'classic' study that serves to illustrate how those who work within the perspective operate. The methods that each of the perspectives use are thus a sub-theme that is not explicitly recognized.

The studies shown in the book are examples of how to work within their respective traditions. In the interpretivist approach, interviews and case studies are the predominant form of research methods (Eisenhardt, 1989; Miettinen, Mazhelis, and Luoma, 2010; Perren and Ram, 2004). For psychologists and (rational choice) economists the survey method and positivist approaches dominate, with statistical analysis being the norm (Capelleras, Mole, Greene and Storey, 2008; Dimov, 2010; Fraser, Storey, Frankish and Roberts, 2002; Wren and Storey, 2002).

There has been a great deal of debate concerning the dominance of positivist work in the journals (Jennings et al., 2005). While, this is a side-issue for the present book, there may be agreement that high quality work from every tradition is required. The differences occur within the implementation of this, although there are plenty of examples of how to do high quality qualitative work (Chell and Tracey, 2005; Eisenhardt, 1991; Eisenhardt and Graebner, 2007; Jack and Anderson, 2002; Ram, 1991, 1999a; Tracey et al., 2011).

There may be a basic agreement that each tradition has its own approach. The psychological and (rational choice) economist approaches are positivist, on the whole. The interpretivist approaches, perhaps including the neo-institutional approaches, are more anti-positivist. The approaches towards the end of the book such as critical realism and pragmatic realism are different again. Suffice it to say there is no one scientific method that all authors within the book would agree was the most appropriate.

So, we know that there is not one best way to approach the theory of entrepreneurship and small business. We suggest that there is some dispute about what entrepreneurship means, although we believe that it is connected to innovation and change. And we accept that the scientific methods associated with entrepreneurship also depend upon one's point of view. The last issue with which we conclude this section concerns the relationship between theory, academia and practice.

Conclusion

Once again, we see the differences between disciplines and perspectives, this time over their values towards practitioners. As the reader may have guessed by now difference between disciplines and perspectives is a leitmotif of this book.

The purpose of the introduction has been to introduce the conflicting approaches to entrepreneurship, to introduce a flavour of the controversies between different approaches to entrepreneurship and to assure the reader that there is no reconciliation on the horizon. Thus, we are just going to have to deal with the issues surrounding perspectives and entrepreneurship and to embrace them. 'Vive la différence'.

Part I
Micro Perspectives

The Rational Choice Approach to Entrepreneurship

Kevin Mole and Stephen Roper

Economics has played a large role in the development of entrepreneurship and small business studies, particularly in the earlier stage of the development of the discipline. Entrepreneurship is not alone in benefiting from the economists' approach to studying problems. Economics has 'exported' its approach to other social sciences, including management, politics, sociology and human geography. These other social science disciplines have defined the economics approach as 'rational choice'. This label is useful because it points out a basic stance of mainstream economics: faced with a set of circumstances, people (economic agents) make rational choices. The chapter tends to use 'economists' and 'rational choice theorists' interchangeably as both describe the methods and assumptions of mainstream economists. At the time of writing, the success of 'Freakeconomics' showed economic methods to be capable of explaining everyday activities from the crime rate in America to the incentives to cheat in exams (Levitt and Dubner, 2007). This chapter will explore the way that economists think about and study entrepreneurship.

Economics offers a rigorous, mathematical and empirically robust account of entrepreneurship. It potentially offers an analytically precise way to approach entrepreneurship that is valued within academic circles. At the outset, we need to distinguish between the macro-economy, which is concerned with interest rates, unemployment, inflation and the like and the micro-economy, which focuses on production, costs and market mechanisms. Entrepreneurship may play a part in the macro-economy but this chapter, like most work on the economics of entrepreneurship, focuses on the micro-economy.

Micro-economists focus on individuals and firms. Micro-economics concerns how households allocate resources; that is, what we spend our time and effort working on and what we consume. Micro-economics is also concerned with the aggregate of these decisions within markets, such as the market for labour or for a particular product. In addition, the micro-economist is concerned with the behaviour of firms in the economy. Entrepreneurship, therefore, is of interest to a micro-economist in terms of how it affects consumers and workers, how it affects choices in the labour market and how it influences the economic behaviour of firms.

How economics makes sense of the world is through models. Economic models are generally mathematical. A model attempts to show the workings of a market or the parameters of some decision made by people in the economy (economic agents). For example, why does someone start a business? A mathematical model depicts a system through a set of variables and relationships between the variables. The variables that matter for starting a business might include: your access to finance, your previous experience and your attitude to risk. However, the colour of your hair, your attitude to foreign food and your sense of direction are variables that probably do not matter. Thus, modelling requires researchers to identify those aspects of the situation that are important in the real world.

In their view, economists study a real phenomenon outside of an agent's interpretation. Material goods and services make up the real economy. Not only that, but mainstream economists are wary of interpretive approaches; they practice 'positive economics' (Friedman, 1953).

Positive economics refers to economics as a value-free social *science*, within a positivist approach. This means that theory should make testable hypotheses that are confronted with the data. Economic theories ought to be judged for their ability to predict, rather than describe. Positive economists are not interested in good descriptions of a phenomenon. They are interested in a parsimonious model that can predict outcomes. A positive statement might read, 'If business taxes are reduced then more people will start businesses'. Martin Robson's data showed that during the 1980s both the cost of hiring workers and the tax burden on small businesses fell and the number of entrepreneurs increased (Robson, 1997). The positive statement was used to predict the number of entrepreneurs and the result worked, offering support for the theory. In a flippant view, economists are interested in how eight out of ten people behave.

Testable hypotheses are derived from the assumptions underlying economics. The starting point for mainstream microeconomics is an agent's preferences. People have preferences for goods, services and activities that contribute to their happiness (utility). For example, wine-makers may decide to produce higher quality products because they prefer to identify themselves with a high quality product, even if it is less profitable (Morton and Podolny, 2002). Being aware of their preferences, people act to maximize their happiness. If working for myself would add to my happiness then I might work for myself for less money than my alternative paid work; however, different people (economic agents) have different preferences. As well as being aware of their preferences, economists expect that agents can order their preferences by rank. An agent might prefer wage-employment to self-employment and self-employment to unemployment. If there are few jobs available, this agent may become self-employed, but if the economic situation improves they might take a waged job and end their self-employment (Foreman-Peck, 1985). Given these preferences, the issue for rational choice theorists is how the agent maximizes their utility; hence, another term for the mainstream economics approach is utilitarianism.

Since the agent is choosing options that maximize their utility, what matters are the incentives that they face. If the effort required to start a business is reduced by cutting the formal requirements, then more people can be expected to start businesses, at least in the formal economy (Capelleras et al., 2008). If the tax on entrepreneurs' incomes falls then more people maybe expected to start businesses (Robson, 1997). On the other hand, if the way to improve your social standing is to join the state bureaucracy then the economy is unlikely to be entrepreneurial (Baumol, 1990).

When constructing models, economists start with the rational self-interested maximizing agent and then try to develop rational responses to the particular economic problem that they face. Consider the problem of whether an entrepreneur stays in business or becomes a waged employee. The choice is one of utility. An economic agent will remain an entrepreneur if their utility is higher as an entrepreneur:

$$\text{Remain Entrepreneur if } U_{entrepreneur} > U_{waged}.$$

This explanation can be added to by suggesting that the U_{waged} is equal to the wages earned from that employment (W) and that the income from being an entrepreneur may proxy for the utility of being an entrepreneur ($Y_{entrepreneur}$). Working as an entrepreneur can make some people happier (Blanchflower and Oswald, 1998), so we must add this effect in too ($H_{entrepreneur}$)

$$\text{Remain Entrepreneur if } Y_{entrepreneur} + H_{entrepreneur} > W.$$

Now we have a model and a testable hypothesis that entrepreneurs will choose to start their business even if they would lose some income from so doing. In addition, the decision to become an entrepreneur depends upon the available alternatives.

Now we need some evidence to support the model. Martin Robson set out to discover why there was a rise in self-employment in the 1980s. His first hypothesis was that the earnings from self-employment had risen and this incentivized more people to become self-employed. As you can see from the graph this was not the case.

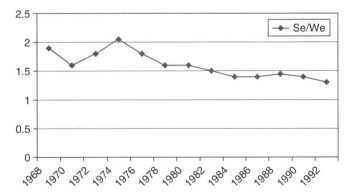

Figure 2.1 UK self-employed income vs wages, 1968–93
Source: Adapted from Robson (1997)

So Robson dug deeper to incorporate this finding that the average return from self-employment fell over the 1980s. He assembled a large data set and then estimated a regression model. The numbers of self-employed swelled throughout the period. Robson argued that the average income from self-employment came from people starting businesses with less capital, but his evidence suggested that this was offset by the lower taxation of the self-employed. So more people were self-employed, reducing their income, but they got to keep more of it. Since we can only utilize what we keep the incentives did encourage self-employment (Robson, 1997).

Hence, economists are interested in the rational choices made by agents who face structures of incentives. The approach taken by rational choice is formal and empirical. Many rational choice papers will use a simplified model of reality to make formal mathematic models (Jovanovic, 1982). Rational choice is interested in topics such as entrepreneurial ability, finance, entry and exit to the industry, growth and productivity, and finally public policy.

One more assumption in rational choice is that everyone has equal access to all information. However, following groundbreaking work by George Akerlof (1970), economists have examined the implication of relaxing this assumption, most notably in work on entrepreneurial and small firm finance and public policy.

Asymmetric information and small firm finance

The key assumption made in the discussion of small firm and entrepreneurial finance is that owners and managers have 'inside information' about their firm, to which 'outsiders' are not privy; technically this is known as asymmetric information. With internal sources of finance, there are no asymmetric information issues, so this is wholly a problem for external finance. Most theorists agree that the entrepreneur knows better than an outsider the likely effort that she will put in and her capability. The asymmetric information leads to two problems: adverse selection and moral hazard.

Adverse selection

Adverse selection describes a situation where the people who choose to deal with you are biased in a way that is unhelpful to you. Akerlof's seminal paper on adverse selection examined the market for used cars (Akerlof, 1970). Consider that there are two types of used cars: good used cars and bad used cars ('lemons'). Assuming you cannot easily tell the difference then used car buyers face the risk that they might get one of the lemons; this risk is an extra cost of dealing in this market. Acting rationally, buyers offer a price less than the value of the car to price in the extra cost to them of this risk. Looking at the problem from the sellers' point of view you would be offered less than the fair value of a good car. If you had a bad car then you would get more than fair value. Therefore, this is an attractive market for bad car sellers and an unattractive market for good car sellers. As a result, the 'good car sellers' may withdraw from the used car market. The inevitable result, said Akerlof, was a used car market filled with 'lemons'. The market is seen to be 'failing'. Adverse selection applies to a wide variety of markets: including finance, where a financier wants to work with those businesses that have high entrepreneurial ability and not with those who have low (Evans and Jovanovic, 1989), but cannot distinguish between the two. As well as adverse selection, the financier will have to deal with 'moral hazard'.

Moral hazard

While, adverse selection concerns the person with whom you contract, moral hazard occurs after two parties have agreed a contract. We think of the contract as between a 'principal' and an 'agent'. The principal wants someone to act on his or her behalf and the agents do so. In bank finance, the principal is the bank that wants to put their capital to work and the agent is the entrepreneur who puts the bank's capital to work in their business and thus provides a return for the bank. Having given the agent the money, the bank wants to know that the money will be 'wisely' and that the agent will put in all the effort necessary to repay their debt. However, the bank finds it too expensive to monitor the effort of the agent: asymmetric information again. The *agent* can put in a level of effort that only they observe, so it might be that the agent puts in less effort than the banker might expect!

Bank lending to small firms does not produce high rewards (Storey 1994).

Algebraically the expected profit for the bank might be expressed thus:

$$E(\pi B) = p[K(1+i)] - K(1+r)$$

where $E(\pi B)$ is the expected return to the bank, p is the probability of repayment, K is the amount borrowed, $(1+i)$ is the interest rate from the repayment and $(1+r)$ is the risk-free rate of interest (possibly from Treasury Bills). The return then depends on the difference between the interest rates and the probability of repayment. If the probability of repayment is low then the bank will start to lose money in lending to small firms – as happened in the UK recession of the 1990s. If the banks were losing money because the risk of lending was high, they could increase their interest rates. However, there might be a problem here too.

Credit rationing

Stiglitz and Weiss (1981) argued that the banks could not charge higher rates of interest because the rates of interest themselves change behaviour. Stiglitz and Weiss assume that the bank has less information than the entrepreneur about the likely success of the project. The success of the project leads to the repayment with interest; the failure of the project is very costly for the bank (Stiglitz and Weiss, 1981). There are two types of projects. One is low-risk, low-return and the other is high-risk, high-return. Again the bank finds it difficult to distinguish between the two types of project. Given these assumptions, the argument follows that of Akerlof (1970). As the interest rates are raised then the borrowers with low risks and low returns will find it more difficult to repay their loans, and so the loans become unattractive for them and they leave the market. Thus, as interest rates rise bad risks drive out the good risks. As fast as the bank gains from increasing the interest rate (i), it loses by a decrease in the probability of repayment (p), leaving the bank with a portfolio of highly risky projects. So the bank can end up losing.

If the entrepreneur has more than one project or can make choices about the project then something akin to moral hazard occurs. As the bank interest rates increase i↑, the entrepreneur might switch projects; hence the riskiness of the projects that the entrepreneur controls also increases and, once again, the probability of repayment falls p↓. Again, the bank can be worse off by increasing interest rates because of its impact on the behaviour of the entrepreneur. Consequently, the bank will prefer to ration credit and keep interest rates below the point at which the projects being brought forth are too risky.

Credit rationing is still controversial. Whether the availability of finance deters new businesses is hotly contested (Hurst and Lusardi, 2004). In a comprehensive survey of small firm finance, Stuart Fraser concluded that the capacity to fund a UK business is much improved compared with the 1980s (Fraser, 2009). Other contributors to the debate suggest that banks can design lending policies using collateral to encourage the entrepreneur to reveal themselves as low and high risk (Bester, 1985).

So, the bank needs to distinguish between the bad and the good risk and may use induce the small firm to use signals. The firm wants to tell the bank what a good business it is, and may want a better deal from the bank next door. Banks cannot fully price risk – to do so will increase the risk. However, the good project may not be able to signal that it is a good project, due to lack of equity finance, or collateral. Consider the case of a new innovative business led by a young entrepreneur who has debt from her student days and no home. She cannot signal to the bank that she is a good business because she lacks the collateral; thus, she may be unlikely to get debt finance. This is the most likely example of a market failure. It occurs because of asymmetric information that distorts the market and in this case leads to some good projects being rationed for credit.

Has credit scoring changed things?

Credit scoring is the relationship of a number of quantitative variables to the likelihood of repayment. Banks are increasingly doing this for businesses as well as customers (Deakins and Freel, 2006; Fraser, 2009). Thus your occupation, postcode, previous payment records and family commitments can all be part of the decision to grant a loan to buy a computerized CNC lathe, for example. The role of the bank manager has changed from the one who makes lending decisions to one who oversees the process.

Is credit scoring on the whole a positive development? On the positive side, it has reduced a perhaps biased qualitative decision process that may in part depend on the personal chemistry of the lender and borrower; this may have beneficial impacts in terms of reducing any possible discrimination (Fraser, 2009). Further, it has enabled fewer requests for collateral to be made (Deakins and Freel, 2006).

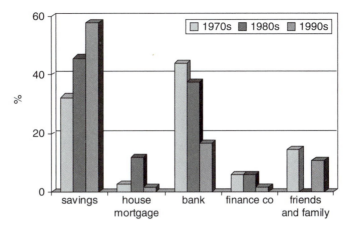

Figure 2.2 Most important sources of finance over three decades
Source: Derived from Greene, Mole and Storey (2008)

However, the use of credit-scoring for start-up firms has not been developed as yet (Deakins and Freel, 2006). Consequently, the technique may not help banks lend to new start-up businesses unless they credit score the individuals concerned. In this sense, there has been a switch to evaluating the borrower rather than the project. The Leverhulme-sponsored research into three decades of enterprise policy in the Teesside area around Middlesbrough shows how the role of personal savings has increased over the period and how the role of the banks has reduced (Greene, Mole and Storey, 2008). A comparative study of England and Spain showed that Spanish banks were more involved in start-up finance (Capelleras and Mole, 2011).

In 1990s Teesside, the most important source of finance for new business was the personal savings of the potential entrepreneur, but this was not always the case. In the 1970s the most important source of finance was the bank. The graph shows how, over this time period, banks have become less important, whereas personal saving has become more important. This also represents a shift from external finance to internal finance, perhaps in response to the issues of asymmetric information.

Also note from the graph that bank finance is the most important external finance for start-up businesses. However, recent attention has focused on equity finance, which is another form of external financing subject to asymmetric information.

Equity finance

The sources of private equity finance can be informal in terms of family and friends or more formal in terms of business angels or very formal, venture capitalist partnerships. *The Economist* (2007) defined private equity as:

When a firm's shares are held privately and not traded in the public markets. Private equity includes shares in both mature private companies and, as venture capital, in newly started businesses. As it is less liquid than publicly traded equity, investors in private equity expect on average to earn a higher equity risk premium from it. (*Economist*, 2007)

Theory of venture capital

The theory of venture capital (VC) also derives from asymmetric information, but the solutions differ. Three conditions are required for the venture finance market to thrive (Baygan and Freudenberg, 2000).

1. Supply of investors – there has to be a willingness to finance high-risk projects with a high return.
2. Demand from entrepreneurs – there has to be the sorts of entrepreneurial projects and ideas that can satisfy the requirements of VC funding. These have to be fast growth businesses.
3. Expertise in evaluating and assisting high-risk firms.

A fourth condition of a thriving stock market where investors can realize their assets might also be added to this list.

The supply of investors is normally from large institutional investors such as pension funds and insurance companies, even prestigious Ivy League universities like Yale's endowment fund.

Demand from entrepreneurs requires a certain type of opportunity to be developed. Some have argued that the media plays an important role in positive stories of entrepreneurial buccaneers like Bill Gates, Steve Jobs or Richard Branson. Venture finance requires 'scalable opportunities' where the project has a realistic, if uncertain, chance to become a listed public company, with returns on capital employed of up to 60 per cent (Mason and Harrison, 1999). This represents a very small proportion of very ambitious firms.

The venture capitalist's role is to be the institution that can identify the 'best' projects to fund (adverse selection) using more institutional money and thus help the recipient better to implement the project (moral hazard) in order that they might realize the profits from it. Now venture capitalists 'solve' the information asymmetries by performing 'due diligence', which is a process of researching the proposal.

Venture capitalists solve the problem of asymmetric information in the equity finance world. However, questions remain concerning whether the market works efficiently and effectively. The idea that there is an 'equity gap' for the smallest amounts of risk capital has been received wisdom since the 1930s MacMillan report, which brings us to another use of asymmetric information and market failure: public policy.

Public policy: Market failure

While outwardly eschewing normative statements like 'should' or 'ought', rational choice theorists are very interested in public policy. Rational choice provides a rationale for government intervention. The fundamental case for policy intervention is that there is market failure in the allocation of goods and services. Goods and services are allocated efficiently through the price mechanism in the presence of competition in the product market, informed consumers, an absence of externalities (i.e. the private and social costs and benefits are the same) and when willingness to pay reflects demand (Storey, 2003). For the market to fail, some of these assumptions must fail. The most likely assumptions to fail in the case of small firms are the informed consumers (asymmetric information) and the presence of externalities or 'spillover' effects.

Storey (2003) suggests three likely information problems:

1. The benefits to individuals of self-employment may be unknown to them.
2. The benefits to small business owners of expert advice from outside the firm may be unknown to them.
3. Financial institutions are unable to assess the risks and rewards of lending to small firms, which has been discussed.

These three problems have justified government intervention, in support for new firms (Chrisman, McMullan and Hall, 2005), support for advice to existing firms (Bennett and Robson, 2003) and support for finance (McGuinness and Hart, 2004). You can see the justification outlined clearly in some UK government publications such as *A Government Action Plan for Small Business* (SBS, 2004). For example, the lack of knowledge of the benefits of business advice means that businesses are likely to purchase a less than optimal amount of such advice, with a consequent negative impact on the development of the business. One of the ways to overcome the uncertainty surrounding the benefits of advice is for the state to subsidize information and advice, which happens in almost all developed countries, like the US Small Business Development Centers (SBDC). SBDCs involve the private sector, education, federal, state and local government to offer training and counselling (Chrisman et al., 2005; Mole and Bramley, 2006).

The rational choice approach to public policy is only in response to market failures. The more clearly policy makers identify these alleged failures the better. Having identified the problem, Herbert Simon argued that the task of the decision maker was to:

- List all the available alternative strategies.
- Determine the outcomes from each strategy.
- Compare the outcomes. (Simons 1957)

This has become known as the means–ends rational model. In the comparison of outcomes economists have bequeathed another tool the 'cost, benefit analysis'. In addition to policy addressing a market failure, the benefits of the policy should outweigh cost. It would be foolish to produce a policy that cost more than its benefits to society. For example, a recent study of the UK's Business Link found that for every £1 Business Links spent the gain to the economy was £2.11 (Mole et al., 2009). Thus, appraisals of policy ascertain whether the benefits outweighed the costs. Of course, this did stop further debate about whether the system cost too much (Bennett, 2008).

Economists and rational choice theorists have used asymmetric information extensively in their analysis of entrepreneurship. There are many implications for financing and public policy to be drawn from Akerlof's seminal article. Economists are concerned about such topics but they are also concerned about how entrepreneurial the economy has become (Baumol, 1990). In this aspect, the approach of rational choice is to try to explain the proportion of entrepreneurs and the factors that make people more likely to enter entrepreneurship. A classic study was by Blanchflower and Oswald (1998).

The classic study

Blanchflower and Oswald (1998) set out to ask who makes the choice to be an entrepreneur. In addition, they investigated the possibility that potential entrepreneurs were held back by a lack of capital.

Blanchflower and Oswald develop a mathematical model based on the demand and supply of entrepreneurs. This model shows that the number of entrepreneurs in an economy depends upon

- The number of people with the ability to see good projects.
- The utility from self-employment.
- The probability of loans to those without the capital to set up in business.
- The average cost to set up in business.

If the capital constraints bind, then the more people who have the capital to set up in business the less the difference in the utility from self-employment. In the modelling we might consider this as an extra measure of capital constraints.

Evans and Jovanovic (1989) consider the issue of whether an inheritance will increase the likelihood of being self-employed. They argued that this was like 'manna from heaven'. If an inheritance increased the likelihood of being self-employed this was considered a test of financial constraints. Blanchflower and Oswald argued that this was as near as an economist could get to the randomized controlled trials of medical studies. Hence, the authors wish for the methodology to be scientific and robust, although Blanchflower and Oswald accept that the sample is not truly random. The sample was from the National Child Development Study, which traces a birth cohort of British children born in 1958. In a regression equation holding constant personal, family and geographical factors, the impact of inheritance was large and significant. They found an inheritance effect at both age 23 and 33. There was a larger effect on the younger age group.

Secondly, Blanchflower and Oswald (1998) used the British Social Attitudes Survey to investigate what deterred people from becoming self-employed. The main explanation was that raising the start-up capital discouraged respondents. Further, data from the UK National Survey of the Self-Employed suggested that obtaining start-up capital was the biggest concern for potential entrepreneurs.

Third, Blanchflower and Oswald find that the self-employed report that they are happier than the employed. This imperfect indicator of utility is a further indicator of capital constraints within their model. It also indicated that women are generally happier than men.

The debate surrounding capital constraints is contested (Hurst and Lusardi, 2004). Hurst and Lusardi argued that the inheritance test used previously (Blanchflower and Oswald, 1998; Evans and Jovanovic, 1989) was flawed because inheritance was not simply money but also involved non-pecuniary aspects.

The critique

The critique of rational choice rests on three points: the first is the requirements rational choice makes of its agents; that is, the ability to calculate how to maximize. The second criticism of rational choice concerns preferences. A third criticism concerns the measurement of constructs.

The first criticism suggests that people do not maximize their behaviour. Most undergraduate psychology students could quite easily devise experiments that would falsify the assumptions of rational choice. Tversky and Kahnemann show that 'people rely on a set of heuristic principles which reduce the complex tasks of assessing probabilities and predicting values to simpler judgmental operations' (Kahneman, Slovic and Tversky, 1982). While these heuristics are useful, they lead to three common systematic errors. The errors concern estimates of the representativeness of their sample, availability of the event, and being tied to an anchor. Representativeness describes the bias that afflicts even experienced researchers, who believe their samples are more representative of the general population than predicted by sampling theory. If two people that you know started new businesses then you would be likely to overestimate the numbers of people starting new businesses.

Availability refers to the frequency of events. This suggests that more newsworthy events are recalled more easily, and are therefore overestimated. If successful entrepreneurs have a high media profile then people are likely to overestimate the likelihood of being a successful entrepreneur. Newsworthy events, like crime or disasters are overestimated. Conversely, people underestimate mundane events.

Anchoring describes the occasions where estimates are too close to an initial value because estimators are reluctant to leave it behind. For example, a recent study asked business owners to estimate the numbers employed by the firm today and then the numbers employed three years ago. By asking the question in that order the question set up an anchor and, unsurprisingly, business owners systematically underestimated the change (Fraser, Greene and Mole, 2007).

These three heuristics show that people behave irrationally: they make irrational choices. This is particularly marked in respect to risk. Just as the assumptions of rational choice about information have been relaxed, it may be necessary to relax the assumptions surrounding making rational choices.

A second problem is that rational choice theorists pay scant attention to how preferences may be formed (Grix, 2004). Sociologists argue that the norms and values involved in the society and the group to which an individual belongs are at least as important as their choices. These effects can be seen in the impact of expectations of behaviour by entrepreneurs. For example, Paul Tracey's chapter on neo-institutional theory in the current volume shows how expectations and conformity influences behaviour (Tracey, 2011). In addition, individual preferences are often unstable (Stinchcombe, 2005). Granovetter considered the case of whether an economist at a conference who was eating in a restaurant to which he is unlikely to return should leave a tip. Whether an economist leaves a tip in that restaurant owes more to norms than to rational maximizing behaviour (Granovetter, 1985).

A third problem for economists and rational choice theorists in entrepreneurship is the measurement of constructs. Within entrepreneurship other quantitative disciplines, such as psychology, have a method by which to design measures (Lumpkin and Dess, 1996). Thus the entrepreneurial orientation measure uses several ways to measure the same underlying construct. Single statements of attitudes are said to be contaminated with other influences and therefore constitute a poor measure, whereas several statements will collectively measure a construct more effectively (Procter, 2001). Since entrepreneurship has a mix of disciplines then the practices may blend together. Hence when economists have used estimates of one variable to measure risk they have often fallen foul of this more careful construction of concepts.

Nonetheless, rational choice has a number of strengths. Because we are talking about the situation within which the rational actor finds themselves in, it focuses the attention on the significant parts of the situation; for example, what is central to the decision to be self-employed (Ward, 2002).

The methodology gives a clear positivist approach. This emphasizes the ability to generalize from the findings. More importantly, there is a strong theoretical base in mathematics to show hypotheses that follow logically from assumptions. Even when irrational behaviour is evident, rational choice provides a standard against which action can be judged.

The future development

Dropping the assumption of perfect information and embracing the interesting implications of asymmetric information provided a strong impetus to economics, leading to our standard view of finance and public policy. Today, one feature of economics is its embrace of the interesting possibilities of irrational decision-making through a rapprochement with psychological theories. There are commonalities between rational choice and psychology: both are foundationalist in believing that there is a world needing to be explained, by which they mean predicted; both share methodological individualism; and both share the same penchant for statistical analysis and a scientific approach.

The outcome is Behavioural Finance or Behavioural Science. The role of optimism in the choice to enter self-employment is an early example of this rapprochement (Fraser and Greene, 2006).

The implications for entrepreneurs

Economists, though their approach starts with the individual, tend to focus on industrial and policy implications. Nevertheless, they suggest interesting outcomes for entrepreneurs. New business founders might think about what alternatives they have. The type of opportunity an entrepreneur seeks depends on the opportunity cost of that opportunity. If the alternative is unemployment or under-employment then a 'lifestyle' business may be useful. If the alternative is a highly paid job, only an opportunity with high potential will suffice. In addition, further investment in the business needs to be assessed against other opportunities that will be foregone. Owner-managers may invest in their business at a lower return on capital employed then they could get from the bank (Reid, Jacobson and Anderson, 1993)! Economists have shown the role of signalling in the search for venture finance. The entrepreneur can use signals to reassure investors that they will treat outsiders' money as well as they would treat their own. Jovanovic has shown entrepreneurs that their ability makes a great difference to their business performance but that they need to spend time in business in order to find out (Jovanovic, 1982).

Economists have discussed new venture strategies. The industrial economist Gavin Reid has shown that the low cost strategy is a poor one for an SME. Successful small firms manage their customer base. Quite conservative marketing strategies can enable a company to survive, but both to survive and prosper the firm must manage the product profile, improve their product range and improve the quality of their products (Reid et al., 1993). In this study, firms in decline took the fewest steps to improve their competitiveness and, when they did, they concentrated on cost cutting rather than quality improvements. Thus, SME managers should pay attention to developing added value for customers if they want to grow.

Conclusion

Rational choice theorists and economists have offered a mathematical and empirically robust account of entrepreneurship. It describes the aspects of the situation most likely to incentivize people to become entrepreneurs. Economists derive mathematical models to highlight the significant parts of a situation. They can then use econometric statistics to assess whether the data agrees with the model. In entrepreneurship, rational choice highlights the links between finance and enterprise. It shows the problems of asymmetric information and so the sense in rationing credit rather than pricing risk. It offers a rationale for public policy within entrepreneurship. While it has its critics, the rational choice approach to enterprise provides us with some guidance for developing new enterprises, through the progressive reduction of the cost of setting up in business and the cost of hiring labour (Robson, 1997; Robson and Wren, 1999). While economists do not claim to be able to identify who becomes an entrepreneur they do claim to be able to identify the levers to pull if government wants to increase enterprise. Thus for economists the incentives surrounding entrepreneurship, compared with other activities, are what make an economy entrepreneurial (Baumol, 1990).

Further reading

In the journals, there are a number of reviews of the economics of entrepreneurship, for example by Mirjam Van Praag (van Praag and Versloot, 2008). As well as the articles referenced, books using the economists approach by David Storey and Simon Parker are available (Storey, 1994; Parker, 2006). Classic articles include Baumol (1990) and Blanchflower and Oswald (1998). A number of Bank of England reports on finance and small firms are of interest (www.bankofengland.co.uk/publications/financefor smallfirms/index.htm). There are two chapters on finance in Deakins and Freel (2006). SBS (2004) gives a series of market failure justifications for public policy intervention.

Questions for discussion

Discuss the role of incentives in the decision to become an entrepreneur.
To what types of new firm is the government most justified in providing finance?
Economic agents find it difficult to assess risks rationally. Discuss how this might impact on the decision to start a business.

CHAPTER 3

The Psychology of the Entrepreneur

Lars Kolvereid and Espen J. Isaksen

Introduction

There are a vast number of different psychological approaches to the study of entrepreneurship. Far more than can be comprehensible discussed in a short book chapter like this. We have therefore chosen to give a broad overview of different psychological approaches with a special emphasis on entrepreneurial intention models. For more detailed coverage to the psychological approach to entrepreneurship, see for example The Psychology of Entrepreneurship (Baum, Frese and Baron, 2007a).

The individual entrepreneur is of great importance when understanding and explaining entrepreneurship. Since it is the individual who perceives opportunities, forms intentions and actually decides to start new ventures, the entrepreneur should be recognized as a key element when studying entrepreneurship. As pointed out by Shaver and Scott the creation of new companies is dependent upon focused and sustained entrepreneurial behaviour (Shaver, 2003; Shaver and Scott, 1991). The entrepreneur and a new business are closely linked (Chandler and Hanks, 1994; Cooper, Gimenogascon and Woo, 1994), hence the use of theoretical perspectives that appropriately illuminate the entrepreneur's contribution to new business formation is important. Moreover, theoretical frameworks within the domain of psychology have the potential to increase the knowledge base with regard to business start-ups as well as growth of new businesses.

The psychological approach to the study of entrepreneurship concentrates on three main questions (Baron, 2004): (1) Why do some persons but not others choose to become entrepreneurs? (2) Why do some persons but not others recognize opportunities for new products and services that can be profitably exploited? (3) Why are some entrepreneurs more successful than others? Among these three questions, we find the last one most interesting. We can distinguish between two different broadly defined psychological approaches to entrepreneurship (Littunen, 2000; Gilad and Levine, 1986): the trait approach and the cognitive approach.

The trait approach

A number of early entrepreneurship studies focused on psychological characteristics or traits that characterized the entrepreneur in distinction to non-entrepreneurs. According to Gartner (1988, p. 12), a basic research question was concerned with 'who is the entrepreneur?' Moreover, Gartner (1988) labelled this search for entrepreneurs' characteristics or traits as the trait approach. He suggested that instead of asking who the entrepreneur is, one should focus on what the entrepreneur does. Hence, a behavioural approach that takes into account that the entrepreneur is a part of a complex process should be a more fruitful approach. In line with this, Shaver and Scott (1991, p. 39) suggested that a psychological approach including three elements – person, process and choice – is needed.

In the trait approach the entrepreneur is assumed to be a particular personality type, a fixed state of existence (Gartner, 1988). The emphasis is put upon individual characteristics that are static and do not change over time. Central concepts in the trait approach include achievement motivation (McClelland, 1961), locus of control (Rotter, 1966), risk taking, creativity and innovation, extrovert versus introvert personality (Lee and Tsang, 2001), and self-assertion (Brandstätter, 1997).

Research on tracking or role models and family background of entrepreneurs is somewhat related to the trait approach. These models suggest a connection between the presence of role models and the emergence of entrepreneurs (Brockhaus and Horwitz, 1986; Cooper, 1986; Cooper, Woo and Dunkelberg, 1988 ; Shapero and Sokol, 1982; Timmons, 1986). Empirical evidence for the relationship between parental role model and preference for a self-employment career has been reported (Matthews and Moser, 1995; Scherer et al., 1989; Scott and Twomey, 1988). However, research has generally failed to find any connection between the presence of parental role models and entrepreneurial performance.

The cognitive approach

The cognitive approach is concerned with how entrepreneurs think and behave. Some models focuses on attitudes or psychological values as predictors of the emergence of entrepreneurship (Katz, 1992; Robinson et al., 1999).

Cognitive style refers to an individual's preferred and habitual approach to organizing, representing and responding to information and situations (Mitchell et al., 2002; Streufert and Nogami, 1989), a built-in and automatic way of responding to information and situations (Riding and Rayner, 1998). According to the cognitive style index (Allinson and Hayes, 1996), individuals are viewed as falling along a continuum between two poles, labelled intuitivists and analysts. Initivituists tend to be relatively nonconformist, prefer an open-ended approach to problem solving, rely on random methods of exploration and work best with ideas requiring a broad perspective. On the other hand, analysts tend to be more compliant, favour a more structured approach to problem solving, prefer systematic methods of investigation and are especially comfortable with ideas requiring sequential analysis (Allinson and Hayes, 1996).

While analysts represent a normative/rational model of decision making, the intuitivists represent people who take shortcuts in the decision-making model. Some of these shortcuts can be beneficial and produce superior results. In other situations they can lead to wrong evaluations and decisions.

The shortcuts or simplifying strategies that individuals use to carry out evaluations and to make decisions are called 'heuristics'. The heuristic based logic approach argues that individuals and situations do not vary in the extent to which these shortcuts are used (Busenitz and Barney, 1997). While research on cognitive style is in a very early state of development, it has been found that people who use heuristics are more likely to become entrepreneurs and more likely to succeed as such because of reduced exposure to certain other cognitive biases like the avoidance of sunk costs (Baron, 2004).

Intention models

Intention models can be placed within the social psychology domain. According to Shaver (2003) social psychology can be distinguished from psychology and sociology by the level of analysis. Hence Shaver explained that 'social psychology concentrates on the *socially meaningful actions* of an individual person (actions for example, like those associated with starting a new venture)' (2003, p. 331). Since entrepreneurship is concerned with social actions, Shaver (2003, p. 353) argued that the theories and methods of social psychology seem particularly appropriate to understanding processes such as new venture creation.

A key assumption linked to intention models is that individuals form intentions towards behaviour prior to the decision to act (Krueger, 2003). Further, a key concept relating to intention models is perception. As Krueger (2003, p. 109) argued, 'our brains grasp external phenomena through processes of perception. We are unlikely to pursue an opportunity we do not perceive'. Therefore, it is not necessarily an entrepreneur's 'objective' competences that are the main drivers of initiating and continuing a entrepreneurial process. According to intention models it is how the entrepreneur perceives her or his own capability as well as the external environment that is of importance. Moreover, assuming that entrepreneurial actions, such as starting new businesses, can not be appropriately explained by stimuli-response models (Krueger, 2003), intention models seem an invaluable alternative.

In recent years the theory of planned behaviour (TPB) has become one of the most widely used psychological theories to explain and predict human behaviour. TPB postulates three conceptually independent determinants of intentions (Ajzen, 1991; Ajzen, 1988). The first is the attitude towards the behaviour and refers to the extent to which a person has a favourable or unfavourable appraisal of the behaviour in question. The second factor is the subjective norm, which refers to the perceived social pressure to perform or not perform the behaviour. The third antecedent of intentions is the degree of perceived behavioural control, which refers to the perceived ease of difficulty of performing the behaviour.

While TPB was developed to explain individual intention in general, several other intention models have been suggested to explain the impact of intentions on venture creation. In Bird's (1988) model of implementing entrepreneurial ideas (IEI), personal and societal contexts interact with rational and intuitive thinking during the formation of entrepreneurial intentions concerning venture creation or creating new values for existing ventures (Bird, 1988). The social context includes an individual's social, political and economic context, and the personal context includes an individual's history, personality and abilities. Boyd and Vozikis modified the model to include the effects of entrepreneurial self-efficacy, a concept which is similar, but not identical to Ajzen's concept of perceived behavioural control (Boyd and Vozikis, 1994). The IEI model has as yet not been tested empirically.

Another model of entrepreneurial intentions is Shapero and Sokol's (1982) model of the entrepreneurial event (SEE). In this model entrepreneurial intentions are determined by perceptions of desirability and feasibility, and a propensity to act upon opportunities. In this model inertia is assumed to guide human behaviour, until some factor triggers an entrepreneurial action. The triggering mechanism can be negative displacements, either externally imposed (e.g. when mowing from one place to another), job related (e.g. being fired, demoted or promoted), or internal to the entrepreneur (e.g. 'traumatic birthdays'). The state of being out of place or between things can also trigger entrepreneurial action. One is more likely to start a business upon discharge from military service, on completion of studies or upon completion of a project. The last type of triggering mechanism is positive pull, for example the offer of financial support, a contact from a would-be customer, or an offer of partnership from a friend, colleague or customer. Empirical testing has generally supported Shapero and Sokol's model. Perceived feasibility and desirability, and the propensity to act, have been shown to explain more than half of the variance in entrepreneurial intentions (Krueger, 1993; Krueger and Brazeal, 1994).

Self-efficacy

Perceived self-efficacy is a concept that entrepreneurship researchers have linked to intentions (e.g. Boyd and Vozikis, 1994; Chen, Greene and Crick, 1998). According to Bandura (1997, p. 3) 'Perceived self-efficacy refers to beliefs in one's capabilities to organize and execute courses of action required to produce given attainments'. A key point is related to individuals' beliefs that they have the ability, skills and motivation necessary to perform a given task. Generally it is assumed that individuals with stronger perceived self-efficacy in relation to a specific task are more likely to succeed in performing that task. Perceived self-efficacy is changeable and may be influenced by different sources of information. The most important source is mastery experience, followed by modelling (observational learning), social persuasion and judgement of the individual's own physiological states (Bandura, 1997). Unlike general traits, perceived self-efficacy is both task and situation specific (Gist, 1987). This means that a transfer of self-efficacy from one situation to another requires that the situations are related. Likewise, in order to transfer self-efficacy among tasks, there has to be similarity among tasks. As Chen et al. (1998) argued the specificity of self-efficacy might pose challenges with regard to measuring self-efficacy for a general domain such as entrepreneurship. They argued that a possible solution is to identify related tasks within the entrepreneurship domain and to measure self-efficacy for each sub-domain.

For example, do potential entrepreneurs think that they have the ability, skills and motivation necessary to sell their service?

The link between perceived self-efficacy and intentions has been discussed. Bandura (1997) argued that perceived self-efficacy is a major determinant of intentions and claimed that self-efficacy and intentions are conceptually and empirically separable. Moreover, there have been suggestions that perceived self-efficacy and perceived behavioural control (in TPB) are compatible concepts (Ajzen, 1991; Krueger and Brazeal, 1994). However, Bandura (1997) argued that a conceptual distinction can be made since self-efficacy is about perceived capability, whereas perceived behavioural control relates to the perceived ease or difficulty in performing the actions. The concepts also differ with regard to the fact that perceived self-efficacy is concerned with internal cognitive perceptions of control. Perceived control behaviour, on the other hand, relates to more general external factors (Armitage and Conner, 2001).

An example of a study using the psychological perspective

Based on TPB the following hypothesis was tested by Tkachev and Kolvereid: the more favourable the attitude and subjective norm with respect to being self-employed and the greater the perceived behavioural control, the stronger the individual's intention to become self-employed. Their analysis was based on student data collected in St Petersburg, Russia. Their data included 567 students from one medical and two technical universities, including students who were pursuing degrees in medicine, odontology, engineering and economics in their third to sixth year of studies (Tkachev and Kolvereid, 1999).

Their measure of attitude was based on Kolvereid's classification scheme of reasons given for the types of employment opportunities that graduates wished to pursue (Kolvereid, 1996). Some reasons would be linked to preferring self-employment, while others would favour organizational employment. In this classification scheme, the following five reasons were assumed to favour organizational employment: (1) security, (2) leisure, (3) social environment, (4) avoiding responsibility and (5) promotion. Further, the following six reasons were assumed to favour self-employment: (1) economic potential, (2) challenge, (3) independence, (4) authority, (5) self-realization and (6) following work tasks from A to Z. Based on these 11 classes of reasons, a total of 39 items were used to measure employment status attitudes, two to five items representing each of the 11 reasons. Respondents were asked along a seven-point scale to which extent they agreed or disagreed that the item in question was important to consider in their future work career (1 = strongly disagree to 7 = strongly agree). Indexes for each of the 11 employment status choice reasons were created and a score was obtained for each index by averaging the item scores. A measure of self-employment attitude was obtained by adding the index scores of the reasons for becoming self-employed. Similarly, a measure of employment attitude was obtained by adding the index scores of the reasons to become employed. Finally an indicator of employment status choice attitude was calculated as the numerical difference between the self-employment attitude and employment attitude measures.

Tkachev and Kolvereid (1999) measured the subjective norm using three items. The first of these was: 'I believe that my close family thinks that I should not/should pursue a career as self-employed'. The other two items concerned the respondents' belief of 'my close friends' and 'people who are important to me'. All three items were measured along a seven-point scale from $1 =$ should not to $7 =$ should. Motivation to comply was measured by three items referring to each of the belief questions. The first of these questions was: 'To what extent do you care about what your close family thinks when you are to decide whether or not to pursue a career as self-employed?' ($1 = $ I do not care at all to $7 = $ I care very much). The two other items asked the respondents with regard to the opinion of 'my closest friends' and 'people who are important to me'. The belief measures were re-coded into a bipolar scale ($1 = -3$, to $7 = +3$), multiplied with the respective motivation to comply item, and the scores were added in order to obtain an overall measure of the subjective norm.

Perceived behavioural control was measured using the six following seven-point rating scales: (1) 'For me, being self-employed would be ...' ($1 = $ very easy, $7 = $ very difficult); (2) 'If I wanted to, I could easily pursue a career as self-employed ...' ($1 = $ strongly agree, $7 = $ strongly disagree); (3) 'As self-employed, how much control would you have over the situation?' ($1 = $ absolutely no control, $7 = $ complete control); (4) The number of events outside my control which could prevent me from being self-employed are ...' ($1 = $ very few, $7 = $ numerous); (5) 'If I become self-employed, the chances of success would be ...' ($1 = $ very low, $7 = $ very high); (6) 'If I pursue a career as self-employed, the chances of failure would be ...' ($1 = $ very low, $7 = $ very high). Responses to items 1, 2, 4, and 6 were recoded ($1 = 7, 2 = 6$, etc.) and the scores on the six items were averaged in order to obtain an overall measure of perceived behavioural control.

A student's intention to pursue a career as self-employed or to be employed in an organization reflects a choice between these two alternatives. Three items were used to measure employment status choice intentions: (1) 'If you could choose between being self-employed or being employed by someone, what would you prefer?' ($1 = $ would prefer to be self-employed, $7 = $ would preferred to be employed by someone); (2) 'How likely is it that you will choose a career as self-employed?' ($1 = $ unlikely, $7 = $ likely); (3) How likely is it that you will choose a career as employed ($1 = $ unlikely, $7 = $ likely). Items 1 and 3 were re-coded ($1 = 7, 2 = 6, 3 = 5$ etc.), and an index of employment status choice intentions were created by averaging the item scores.

The results showed that the hypotheses were supported with significant regression co-efficients for perceived behavioural control (0.44), subjective norms (0.28) and attitudes (0.11). The model explained 67% of the variation in employment status.

Contributions of the psychological perspective

The entrepreneurial process, including prelaunch, startup and postlaunch activities (Baron, 2007), should be informed by theoretical perspectives on different levels of analysis. Knowledge concerning the individual entrepreneur is of course important. As Baron (2007, p. 25) explained, 'it is clear that individual-level variables play an important role in entrepreneurship and should be included in efforts to develop an accurate and comprehensive model of the entrepreneurial process'. With regard to the individual level of analysis, the psychology of the entrepreneur relates to several interesting research topics providing insights concerning the entrepreneurs' role in the process. According to Baron (2007) there has been greatest attention among researchers directed toward aspects of entrepreneurs' cognition, also including entrepreneurial intentions.

However, there is also a renewed interest in entrepreneurs' personal characteristics as predictors of success (Baum et al., 2007b; Rauch and Frese, 2007). Rauch and Frese (2007, p. 53) argue that 'there are small to moderate relationships between personality traits, business creation, and business success'. They point out that methodological problems (e.g. small sample size), have previously made it difficult to identify 'true' relationships of personality with entrepreneurship. Further, they suggest that broad personality traits such as emotional stability and openness to experience are only indirectly associated with business outcomes. More specific traits such as the need for achievement, risk taking and innovativeness are more strongly associated with specific measures of success that are typically used in entrepreneurship/ small business research. Further, Rauch and Frese argue that there is a need to match independent and dependent variables more appropriately. They give examples and suggest, for example, that a trait such as the need for autonomy may have a stronger association with venture survival than growth. Moreover, Rauch and Frese (2007) suggested mediating approaches to study the effects of personality traits on entrepreneurship. Hence, one could investigate if specific traits influence specific business outcomes through the effect on entrepreneurs' motivation or intentions. Even if the majority of previous research has shown inconclusive results regarding entrepreneurs' traits and entrepreneurship this type of research may very well contribute to entrepreneurship research. More theory-driven research, exploring various links between entrepreneurs' specific traits and concepts such as motivation, intentions and entrepreneurial satisfaction, may indeed provide new insights.

In this chapter, we have limited much of the discussion to the cognitive approach and more specifically to intention models. Therefore, we will offer some arguments relating to why this perspective has the potential to contribute to increased knowledge about entrepreneurship, including both opportunity discovery and exploitation of opportunities. As Krueger argued 'to understand entrepreneurship, then, requires understanding how we learn to see opportunities and decide to pursue them' (Krueger, 2003, p. 306). Intention models may be especially valuable theoretical frameworks helping illuminate the process of opportunity exploitation, for example manifested in a decision to start a business.

With regard to opportunity exploitation, intention models, such as Ajzen's (1991) theory of planned behaviour, highlight individuals' subjective perceptions as key factors in explaining their actions. Presuming voluntary human behaviour, intention is a key concept predicting subsequent actions.

Moreover, if one assumes actions (such as starting a business) to be purposeful or planned the individual's intention is assumed to capture his or her plans and motivation performing the behaviour. Further, as Krueger (2003, p. 115) points out, intention is a cognitive state taking place prior to and immediately proximate to the target action. Hence, if one surveys, for example, individuals' intentions to start a business temporally distal to when the actions actually will take place, intention may be less good at predicting business start-ups. Therefore, when exploring the link between entrepreneurial intention and target behaviour it may be advantageous to survey individuals when they are temporally proximate in taking the decision to start or not start a business. An advantage related to intention models is that they may imply important implications for practitioners. Since the antecedent of intentions, attitudes, social norms and perceived behaviour control are all changeable it is, for example, possible to design policies to improve individuals' perceptions. Further, concerning the theoretical implications, Krueger (2003, p. 119) notes, 'if intentions and its critical antecedents serve as mediating variables, then we can use that knowledge to better assess the impact of other variables (e.g. personality, demographic, situational) on entrepreneurial behavior'. Hence, intention models may very well be appropriate in order to increase the understanding of how various concepts are linked together in the explanation of entrepreneurial behaviour.

Since opportunity discovery is a central element in the entrepreneurial process (Shane, 2003), an important issue is related to those theoretical frameworks that illuminate how individuals discover new opportunities. Perceived self-efficacy may be a promising concept in this regard. Ronstadt (1988) introduced the corridor principle, implying that individuals taking the step of starting their first business will be able to see other and more attractive venture opportunities that they were previously not able to identify. Moreover, the corridor is opened to the entrepreneur because of increased knowledge with regard to the external environment, such as relevant contacts, viable markets or competitive resources (Ronstadt, 1988). A possible complementary explanation could be that these individuals have obtained 'mastery experience' and have therefore strengthened their perceived self-efficacy. Strengthened self-efficacy with regard to opportunity recognition should be related to the fact that these entrepreneurs are more confident and open concerning the discovery of new opportunities. Moreover, Shane (2003, p. 58) points out that 'many observers have argued that those who see opportunities as opposed to risks, in new information, should be more likely to discover entrepreneurial opportunities'. Further, strong self-efficacy may explain why some people see opportunities where others see risks (Shane, 2003).

Critique of the psychological perspective

While clearly the psychology of the entrepreneur has contributed to entrepreneurship research and undoubtedly has the potential to offer new knowledge about entrepreneurship, there are nevertheless challenges. One important challenge relating to research design issues is the possible mismatch between independent and dependent variables (Davidsson and Wiklund, 2001).

With regard to psychological entrepreneurship research this typically implies linking variables at the individual level of analysis (e.g. entrepreneurs' traits) to dependent variables at the firm level of analysis (e.g. business sales, sales growth, and profit). According to Davidsson and Wiklund 'trying to explain venture outcomes solely with individual characteristics is not a wise strategy' (2001, p. 84). One problem associated with this is to relate entrepreneurs' individual level factors to a single business, when it is known that many business founders are involved in several ventures. Another issue is that many businesses are started by teams, which suggests that information should be collected from more than one individual (Davidsson 2007). Davidsson (2007) suggested that an alternative is to utilize an individual level dependent variable and in this regard something approaching 'entrepreneurial career performance'. According to Davidsson (2007, p. 295) 'entrepreneurial career performance' includes the assessment of the quantity and quality of independent and internal ventures the individual has been involved with over a longer period of time. Moreover, Davidsson (2007, p. 294) suggests that there is the opportunity for future research to link individual characteristics to other, not dichotomous, individual level dependent variables. This includes personal financial success, goal achievement, satisfaction and changes in values, motivation and attitudes. While it certainly is important to take into account the possible mismatch between independent and dependent variables, it may nevertheless be advantageous to include individual level factors when exploring new business performance. First, if one assumes that in the business start-up stage the individual and the business are closely linked together, the individual level concepts such as the business founders' intentions, motivations and perceived self-efficacy may be important explanatory variables of new business performance. Second, there is also an issue regarding the inclusion of relevant control variables relating to other levels of analysis (e.g. business and industry levels of analysis).

As discussed above, the trait approach used in entrepreneurship research has been much criticized. Among other aspects, the critique relates to the fact that, according to much previous empirical evidence, individuals' traits seem not be important determinants of specific entrepreneurial actions (e.g. starting a new business). One reason could be that stable personal characteristics are distant (distal) with regard to single events (Davidsson, 2007). Hence, a trait such as external locus of control may therefore not be a very good predictor of entrepreneurial behaviour. Other individual level concepts such as intentions and perceived self-efficacy are closer (proximate) to the action and may consequently be more appropriate with regard to explaining entrepreneurial behaviour. Moreover, many early entrepreneurship studies emphasized discovering traits that distinguished the entrepreneur from other individuals. With reference to a literature review Brockhaus and Horwitz (1986, p. 34) stated 'the research results seem to indicate that there are few psychological characteristics that distinguish the entrepreneur from business managers'. Nevertheless, Rauch and Frese (2007, p. 53) argued, with reference to meta-analyses, that 'business owners as compared to other populations are higher in need for achievement, risk propensity, innovativeness and internal locus of control'. Further, they argued that models of business creation and business success, along with other variables, need to include personality variables as well.

Demographic models (those that link gender, age and parental self-employment to starting a business, for example) have been criticized for several reasons. Katz (1992) argued that role models or tracking models are not widely applicable, and that such models cannot account for situations in which the individual fails to follow in parental footsteps. Robinson et al. (1999) used the following example to illustrate this point. Two individuals born and raised in virtually identical circumstances may have very different conceptions about entrepreneurship. One child may conclude that entrepreneurship is a positive and exciting career option and the other child may conclude that entrepreneurship is for those who cannot hold a regular job. It is the specific reaction to the circumstances, not a given set of demographic characteristics that determines behaviour (Robinson et al., 1999). Demographic models and tracking models treat the individual largely in 'black box' terms. They provide little insight on how family background and social forces shape the individual's decision-making process (Katz, 1992).

Shook, Priem and McGee (2003) reviewed the literature on venture creation that has examined the role of the individual and came out with the following critique and directions for future research on entrepreneurial intentions: empirical research on entrepreneurial intent has relied on student samples and cross-sectional data. As a result, both generalizability and validity remain less than desirable. Future longitudinal research is needed to establish causal order (Shook, Priem and McGee, 2003). Entrepreneurial intent has not been linked to opportunity search or to subsequent venture creation. Since several other models in addition to TPB have been suggested, there is a need to integrate and reduce the number of intention models. Shook, Priem and McGee (2003) also pointed out that some researchers have focused on employment status choice intentions while others have focused on intentions to create a business. They urged future researchers to utilize a consistent definition of entrepreneurial intent.

Several efforts have been made to comply with the suggestions from Shook, Priem and McGee. Kolvereid and Isaksen (2005) used TPB to predict intentions to become self-employed and actual entry into self-employment. They used a longitudinal design whereby 651 new business founders answered a questionnaire shortly after the new business was registered, with follow-up telephone interviews 19 months later. They reported a correlation of 0.63 between intention and behaviour, indicating that intentions alone explain almost 40 per cent of the variation in actual behaviour (Kolvereid and Isaksen, 2006).

Linan and Chen (2009) developed and tested a new measure of attitude, subjective norm, perceived behavioural control and entrepreneurial intentions. Their entrepreneurial intentions questionnaire (EIQ) may become the preferred way of measuring these concepts.

Thompson discussed the concept of entrepreneurial intentions and developed and validated a new measure for them, which also may be useful for future research (Thompson, 2009). Finally, Iakovleva and Kolvereid found that the TPB and the SEE models can be integrated into one model of behavioural intentions, and no longer need to be treated as competing models of entrepreneurial intentions (Iakovleva and Kolvereid, 2009). Bringing to entrepreneurship the methodology to construct tests for such attitudes as entrepreneurial intentions is another achievement of the psychological approach to entrepreneurship. Testing for such constructs as locus of control, and the entrepreneurial intentions are developed through well-documented procedures to ensure validity and reliability. These constructs have been very helpful in understanding the way that more entrepreneurial thinking can influence the performance and behaviour of individuals, and has even been applied to firms.

Future directions

Based on the discussion above there are some additional interesting avenues for future entrepreneurship studies that utilize a psychological approach. As previously noted there is a need to consider carefully the matching of predictor and criterion variables (Hisrich, Langan-Fox and Grant, 2007). Using variables at the same level of analysis may be advantageous. And as Davidsson (2007) noted there are opportunities to select interesting individual level outcome variables such as 'entrepreneurial career performance'. With respect to the trait approach future research could develop a theoretically based model linking traits such as internal locus of control and need for achievement to more proximate concepts and entrepreneurial actions such as motivation, intention and self-efficacy. And as Hisrich et al. (2007, p. 586) suggest, there are research opportunities with regard to clarifying the role of personality in the entrepreneurial process. They suggest using, among other options, longitudinal research, improving operationalization and measurement, and investigating mediating and moderating variables in the personality–entrepreneurship relationship.

Concerning intention models there are clearly opportunities for entrepreneurship research. As Krueger (2003, p. 132) pointed out, 'we know relatively little about how intentions change and even less about intentions about the timing of behavior'. More knowledge is needed with respect to the intention–behaviour relationship.

With regard to perceived self-efficacy there is a need to define key tasks carefully in relation to several phases in the entrepreneurial process. That is, one needs to match relevant self-efficacy variables to the relevant outcomes in question. It is probably unlikely that, for example, self-efficacy with regard to discovering opportunities is a key determinant of business start-ups and business growth. More research is warranted to identify key skills associated with, for example, discovering opportunity, establishing ventures, getting access to key resources and so on. Moreover, as Locke and Baum point out, there is also question of whether perceived self-efficacy could be too high (Locke and Baum, 2007). There is the possibility that overconfidence could relate to the fact that entrepreneurs do not appropriately consider real risks. Hence, it may be worth investigating if there is a curvilinear, rather than a straight linear relationship between perceived self-efficacy and various outcome variables. Moreover, future studies could also investigate interaction effects between perceived self-efficacy and indications of the entrepreneurs' human capital.

For example, are high perceived self-efficacy and high levels of human capital (e.g. education, business ownership experience) associated with entrepreneurial success?

Implications for practitioners

Research on personality traits has few implications for prospective entrepreneurs. However, to the extent that trait models have any explanatory power, they do suggest that prospective entrepreneurs should ask themselves whether or not they possess the traits in question. This can also be done by taking personality tests of different kinds.

Research on role models suggests that their presence in the family and in the media spurs people to think of pursuing an entrepreneurial career. The media is therefore encouraged to present stories about entrepreneurs and their businesses.

Cognitive psychological approaches have important practical implications for prospective entrepreneurs. Among other things, they try to identify how people should think and behave in order to succeed as entrepreneurs. They also try to figure out what type of knowledge and skills entrepreneurs should possess. The theory of planned behaviour suggests that in order to succeed as entrepreneurs people need to have a positive attitude towards entrepreneurship. This theory also postulates that you should take into consideration the opinion of your family and friends, and the extent to which you care about their opinion, when you decide your future career. Finally, TPB suggests that before you pursue an entrepreneurial career you should ask yourself if you will have control over the situation if you become an entrepreneur. All these factors can be learned. For example, Souitaris, Zerbinati and Al-Laham (2006) reported that taking an entrepreneurship training programme positively influenced entrepreneurial intentions and the subjective norm. Research also indicates that graduates from business schools who have taken courses in entrepreneurship are more than twice as likely to start a business and become a business owner/manager, compared to other business school graduates (Garvan and O'Cinneide, 1994a; Garvan and O'Cinneide, 1994b; Kolvereid and Åmo, 2007; Menzies, 2004).

Research on self-efficacy emphasizes experience. This includes experience from being an owner/manager of a business (for example a student business), and from the industry in question. Isaksen studied a large sample of new businesses in Norway and followed them over three years. He found that the similarity between the entrepreneur's previous job and the current business was the single most important predictor of early business performance (Isaksen, 2006). He also found strong support for the positive effect of business ownership experience on early business performance. However, the presence of role models in the family had no effect. Among other factors that had a positive effect on early business performance was the entrepreneur's intention for the business to grow, being successful in obtaining funding and starting the business in a team rather than alone.

Kolvereid asked people whether they preferred to be employed or self-employed, and asked them to state the most important reason for their preference. Two of the most common reasons for preferring employment were security and workload (Kolvereid, 1996). Therefore, in general, governments can promote entrepreneurship by helping to reduce the risk of being self-employed (for example, by reducing the cost of starting a limited liability company, as Sweden did in 2010), and by reducing the workload put on entrepreneurs by the government bureaucracy (for example, by reducing the paperwork for the smallest businesses, as several European countries recently have done).

This chapter has given a broad overview of the different psychological approaches. The trait approach was contrasted with the cognitive approach. The trait approach has been critiqued extensively, yet recent work recognizes its value to studying entrepreneurship. Psychology has given entrepreneurship a method and theory to explain who becomes a successful entrepreneur. It has brought a rigour to its methods. It has brought a way to measure attitudes and concepts and it has shown the importance of intentions as a means to explain entrepreneurial behaviour. The psychological approach has much to commend it and new areas of research are being opened all the time.

Further reading

Baum, J. R., M. Frese and R. A. Baron (eds), *The Psychology of Entrepreneurship* (Mahwah, NJ: Lawrence Erlbaum Associates Inc., Publishers, 2007).
Shane, S., *A General Theory of Entrepreneurship: The Individual-Opportunity Nexus* (Cheltenham, UK: Edward Elgar Publishing, 2003).

Questions for discussion

Can the process of starting new businesses be explained as a planned behaviour or does chance play a crucial role?

Discuss the role of entrepreneurs' heuristics in discovering and exploiting new business opportunities.

What is the role of the individual when explaining performance outcomes in new businesses?

CHAPTER 4

Undertaking Interpretive Work in Entrepreneurship Research

Denise E. Fletcher

Introduction

Today, as I approach my task of refining the final draft of this chapter, I note the date is the 7 December 2009. There are three reasons why I am highlighting this. The first reason is that this was the date of my doctoral viva 12 years ago and it was through my doctoral work that I became interested in interpretive ideas and inquiry. The thesis was an ethnographic study of organizational change in a family business context and I applied interpretive thinking to evaluate the interpretive processes that were being constructed in this setting. The second reason for recalling the date is that I am trying to revive the issues that were troublesome when I began to engage with interpretive ideas. I recall being attracted to the principles of interpretive ethnography (Denzin, 1997) and the idea of 'getting close' to how my respondents 'gave voice', 'constructed meaning' and 'made sense' of things going on around them through interpretive and symbolic interactions. But the actual practice of applying interpretive thinking was more difficult than expected. I also know this is a prevailing issue for doctoral students and those trying to publish interpretive work – whether this be for reasons of language (how one infers or makes claims from interpretive work), or for reasons of volume of field work quotations (how does one show the multiplicity of interpretations in a limited word space). The third reason for drawing attention to the date is that I want the chapter to be written in a way that is appealing for its anticipated audience (students, early career researchers) who are beginning to grapple with some of the issues associated with interpretive inquiry. I am therefore adopting a discursive style of writing that not only engages and relates to the reader but also illustrates how working with interpretive ideas gives prominence to voice, context, reflexivity, interactivity and reduces self–other boundaries.

To open up the discussion, I present an extracted quote from a methodology chapter of one of my PhD students in which he is explaining why he is undertaking qualitative research.

> Generally interpretive analysis will give me the opportunity to make sense of people's interpretations of social issues and thus forming theories of the

data. Field work analysis may be seen as figuring out what to do with the meanings of data comparing the experiences of the respondents of the different areas of study. According to Denzin (1989, p. 11) 'through the use of personal experience stories and thick description of lived experiences, the perspective of clients and workers can be compared and contrasted'. (Yeboah-Korang, 2010, unpublished PhD thesis).

This student is undertaking doctoral work on the informal economy in an African context. He is claiming that he is adopting an interpretive methodology, utilizing regional case studies to incorporate a household survey and interviews with policy makers. Of course, this is only one tiny segment of the full methodology chapter, but I have selected it to present here because it not only tells us why this student wants to use interpretive inquiry but also demonstrates some of the problems students experience when engaging with interpretive ideas. Some of these challenges relate to accounting for how one undertakes interpretive analysis. Others relate to how we bring together the various interpretations that are being negotiated or constructed. In the following chapter, I embark on two tasks:

■ Examine what it means to undertake interpretive work in entrepreneurship. This discussion is opened up by highlighting how a PhD student tries to engage with these ideas in his doctoral work.

■ From this, I outline what characterises interpretive work (and consider how interpretive thinking has been applied to entrepreneurship research).

In order to examine what it means to undertake interpretive work, I will first consider the conventional contrasting of interpretivist with positivist thinking.

What does it mean to undertake interpretive research work?

Defining interpretive work in relation to positivist thinking

Interpretivist philosophies such as pragmatism, phenomenology, hermeneutics, symbolic interactionism and ethnomethodology, followed by social constructionism and post-structuralism), are research traditions concerned with the scientific inquiry of the human/social world. Interpretive philosophies stress that human behaviour/interpretations/social processes and interactions have a significant scientific role to play in the construction of social reality. The significance of an interpretive emphasis was to contrast with positivist thinking about human inquiry. Positivist thinking, with its roots in empiricist philosophy and its rational pursuit of factual truth, advocated the need to strip away questions of meaning and value in order to codify facts or data about phenomena into tidy units which could be verified (Clegg, 2008). The value of stripping out subjective meaning or personal values, from a positivist point of view, is that factual truths or sense data can be revealed, which can then be scientifically verified through the application of repeatable methods. As a result, the philosophical, psychological and sociological schools of thought associated with interpretivism were conventionally juxtaposed with positivism in order to provide socially oriented and context-sensitive scientific methodologies for examining the human/social world. Instead of stripping out the subjective, the value-laden, the ethical, the negotiated and the taken-for-granted, interpretive inquiry privileges the interpretation processes that are central to meaning-making, sense-making, interactivity, reflexivity, storying, language, discourse, narration and social reality construction processes.

Contrasting positivist and interpretivist forms of inquiry is helpful, therefore, for discussing epistemological issues about how we think knowledge and understanding about social phenomena can be realized. When it comes to issues of ontology and making claims about 'how the world is', the juxtaposition is less helpful. This is because, contrary to some claims about the sorts of knowledge positivist inquiry yields, positivist research does not endeavour to make claims about how the resulting findings/statements represent an objective reality (Alvesson and Skoldberg, 2000). 'Positivist science, ... at least in its mainstream variants, never had a goal to represent reality truly, but only aim[s] at filing data into convenient boxes for purposes of prediction leading to successful action' (2000, p. 178). What positivists aim to do through the research process is collect/collate responses to particular issues/ questions with a view to categorizing how people respond (i.e. using quizzes to gather responses about one assesses one's level of entrepreneurial skills/ attributes). The researcher can never fully 'know' whether the responses are an accurate or true representation of whether the person is entrepreneurial, but that is not the positivists researchers' aim. Their aim is to categorise the responses and generalize from these responses/data in order to predict the likelihood of them being an entrepreneur. The positivists' main interest is in how people respond and their stated perspective (rather than why they make such a stated response).

This is an important point, and it matters in our discussion here about interpretivist thinking because it is this (apparent) lack of ability to represent (through scientific methods) an objective reality for which interpretive philosophies are criticized. But, as has just been established, mainstream positivism never had representing reality as its goal. This contrasts with interpretivism, which does make claims about the nature of a socially constructed reality (see below for more discussion on 'an ontology of becoming'). For this reason, the conventional juxtaposing of interpretivist against positivist ideas in doctoral dissertation methodology chapters to discuss issues of ontology is not particularly helpful in explaining what it means to undertake interpretivist work. To address this an alternative and more helpful way of demonstrating the ontological distinctions between realist and interpretivist philosophies is provided in a later section. Before progressing to this, however, it is important to elaborate in more detail why we engage in interpretive research.

Why do we do interpretive research?

Turning back to the extract from the doctoral dissertation above, the student outlined the following reasons for why he wanted to engage in interpretive interests:

to make sense of peoples' interpretations;

to make sense of social issues;

to form theories of the data;

to figure out what to do with meanings of data;

to compare and contrast the experiences/perspectives.

And we might, drawing from the reference to Denzin, add the students' interest in the use of personal experience stories and the use of thick description of lived experiences.

Many of the above are often-cited reasons for engaging with interpretive ideas. Usually, we come to interpretive inquiry because we have an interest in peoples' words, perspectives, experiences or accounts. We strive to understand how they create meaning or make sense of particular activities, or how they draw upon particular ideas or discourses associated with, for example, enterprise culture, small business management, the informal economy or family businesses. We are also keen to locate theory development in the experiences or perspectives of our respondents, which usually means engaging with theory in order to draw out sensitizing concepts or themes that will shape our research questioning rather than superimposing a rigid theoretical framework upon the research setting. In addition, we are concerned with the linguistic, social or contextual aspects of our research material. These aspects are now considered.

Attending to language in interpretive research

Given the interpretivist researcher's interests in meanings, sense-making, experiences and account giving, and so on, it is natural that language and discourse have a central role in interpretive inquiry. This is because it is through language that we construct our experience of ourselves, our thoughts, our identities etc. (Burr, 1995). Also, it is through language (and interaction) that we come to construct subjective statements about objective entities and make objective agreements about subjective experiences/features. When undertaking interpretive work, therefore, there is a long tradition and variety of emphases which underlie interpretive interests. These range from discursive, linguistic, narrative, phenomenological and symbolic interactionist to social constructionist or post structuralist orientations (Berger and Luckmann, 1967; Bruner, 1990; Denzin, 1979, 1989; Gergen, 1999; Gergen and Gergen, 1993; Goffman, 1961; Mead, 1934; Potter and Wetherell, 1987; Ricoeur, 1981; Schutz, 1967; Vygotsky, 1981). Moreover, depending upon their interests, interpretivist inquirers focus on different forms of discourse, talk or mediation. These could be stories, narratives, critical incidents, pieces of autobiography/biography or conversation, multiple speech acts, interpretive repertoires, inter-subjectivity, the notion of selves existing in relation to other-selves, conscious experience, the interpretation of texts, dialogue/exchange, relational processes, life histories or diary notes, whether they are drawn from interviews, participation observation or ethnographic engagement.

In terms of entrepreneurship, more specifically, this field of inquiry has also been the subject of many discursive and linguistic analyses. William Gartner first stressed the multiplicity of meanings, words and vocabulary of entrepreneurship (Gartner, 1990, 1993; Gartner, Carter and Hills, 2003). He identified a cluster of meanings attributed to the term 'entrepreneurship' (such as the entrepreneurial person, value creation, innovation, uniqueness, organization creation and profit) and argued that the words used to talk about entrepreneurship influence our ability to think and make sense of this phenomenon. A number of studies of discourse/language-mediated entrepreneurial identities followed (Down 2002, 2006; Lindgren and Wåhlin, 2001).

A further example of the linguistic emphasis is in Fletcher (2003), where I demonstrate how an enterprising discourse provides business owners with the concepts, language and linguistic resources (Watson, 2002) with which to create meaning and talk about how their organizations came into being. For example, some owner managers draw upon a discourse that relates to personal skills and attributes (such as creativity, leadership, special knowledge, resourcefulness, determination, reward, desire for profit) as they give voice to the emergence of their business. They also interweave verbs or adjectives to describe the activity or 'doing' of entrepreneurship in terms of identifying market opportunities, taking calculated risks, bringing together new combinations of products, services or technologies, utilizing network contacts and acting upon special knowledge. Also, entrepreneurs often speak about forming relationships with others (in partnerships, groups or teams, with customers or international clients, and with peers and senior owner-managers) in order to produce understandings as they realize business development practices. In addition, entrepreneurs also occasionally refer to policies, mechanisms or structures (banks, growth programmes) that have been helpful (or not) in the emergence of their businesses. Thus, the language people use and the concepts upon which they draw (or people to whom they relate) provide a framework of meaning for understanding entrepreneurial activity. Very rarely are direct references to 'entrepreneurship' made. However, discourses and ideas around notions of profitability, growth, innovation, product development, relationships with customers, networks, contacts, luck and trust, are used to frame the processes through which organizational emergence occurs (Fletcher, 2003).

This demonstrates, as Bevir and Rhodes put it in the context of political science, that interpretive analyses are concerned with more than language or linguistic expression. They have a concern with beliefs, ideas and preferences (Bevir and Rhodes, 2002).

Attending to ideas and beliefs in interpretivist inquiry

As we saw in the preceding paragraph, interpretative approaches are well suited to dealing with the realm of ideas (for example ideas about an enterprise

culture). Ideas circulate in the media, through the press and education processes, and through hearing other peoples' experiences that have shaped their
intentions to become self-employed or start a business. We might also say
that that ideas 'travel' across cultural borders, across organizations, across
national boundaries and 'locate' where there is a idle curiosity and/or willing
alertness to engage with new market concepts (Fletcher, 2006, 2007). In this
sense, referring to Giddens, entrepreneurship has a 'stretchiness' whereby
entrepreneurial practices 'stretch away' from the individual producers of the
idea/business to other unrelated people, producing a patterning of entrepreneurial processes that contribute to the social construction of reality (Berger
and Luckmann, 1967; Gergen, 1994, 1999; Giddens, 1979).

Interpretation is important, therefore, because we cannot read people's
preferences from objective facts such as gender, age or ethnicity (Bevir and
Rhodes, 2002). We cannot know why a business idea was located or enacted
without going into the entrepreneur's explanations and reasonings. Thus,
interpretation enables the analysis of ideas and social practices within entrepreneurship and small businesses management. Also, interpretivist thinking
accommodates multiple or contested meanings of events and phenomena.
In addition to opening up opportunities for multi-voicedness it can alert
the inquirer to structural disadvantages imbued by patriarchy, family, ethnicity, gender or social duty/obligation. Ram et al. (2008) stress this point in
relation to resource-rich views of ethnic family social capital. Most inquiries
categorise ethnic minorities as culturally marginalized and structurally disad-
vantaged. Instead, by using interpretive inquiry it is possible to demonstrate,
as is Ram et al.'s intention, how enterprise is constructed through social/
personal resources and the institutional contexts of markets, competition,
state and the regulatory regime. Furthermore, in the context of research in
family business contexts, it is possible, through interpretive inquiry, to consider how small organizations and family businesses are shaped by contradictory and yet complementary discourses of control and nurturing (Ram,
Theodorakopoulos and Jones, 2008). When interviewing family or small business owners, feelings of responsibility and/or obligation are expressed along
with emotional attachments about longevity of the business or the delegation
of tasks. These are often interpreted as controlling behaviours and a lack
of willingness to 'let go'. As such, analysis of the accounts rendered during
interviews are categorised according to themes/concepts related to 'control'.
But equally, nurturing behaviours of discourses can also often be evidenced
in small/family firms, which indicates that discourses are both contradictory
and complementary (Fletcher, 2002).

A further example of how interpretive inquiry can aid the analysis of contested
meanings can be made with further reference to family business research.

Relative merits – family culture and kinship in small firms: A 'classic' study

Part of the brief for this chapter was to show an example of interpretivist
research. Of course, which study to choose is always difficult but there was one

study that inspired me when I was starting my research career. It was a paper published in *Sociology* – the journal of the British Sociological Association – called 'Relative Merits – Family Culture and Kinship in Small Firms' by Monder Ram and Ruth Holliday. This important paper represented a significant achievement and showed how a social construct was used, interpreted and re-interpreted within a small business context.

Ram and Holliday set out to investigate the question: 'What is the actual significance of the family at the level of the workplace?' (Ram and Holliday, 1993, p. 630). Their focus was on the way that family influenced small firm managers both in the processes used within the firm and in recruitment. To answer their question they conducted detailed case studies in six British manufacturing companies within the West Midlands region. They conducted field work in each company for periods of between two and four months and afterwards followed up with weekly visits for a year. These studies were ethnographic because the researchers were 'employed' at least for a time by the companies. They took an 'active member role' as a participant in the firms that they studied. The evidence relied on their fieldwork notes and interviews conducted with the managers and workers in the firms.

Ram and Holliday found that their family firms used family members in critical roles within the factory: for example, as conduits between workers and managers, as the people who set the pay rates for particular jobs or those who marked out the cutting of fabric in the clothing companies. 'Trusted' family members did these critical tasks. Not only was there a family aspect to the business but management was 'gendered', the internal production of the clothing firms was generally organized by women who were 'supervisors' rather than managers and were paid piecework rates. At the same time, family acted as a constraint because family members could be less competent or less diligent than other workers without any fear of being sacked (Ram and Holliday, 1993).

However, Ram and Holliday found a complex system of mutual obligation within their firms. The mutual obligations surrounding the notion of familiness were evident in the recruitment process. Whether the firms had mainly ethnic workforces or mainly white workforces, the recruitment process was always informal. New recruits to the business were usually found from the social contacts of the existing workforce, which gave the existing workforce a stake in the 'familiness' concept (Dick and Morgan, 1987). New recruits had not only to be capable but also to fit with the existing workforce. The paper gave the example of two workers who were recruited by the management outside of the workforce's social contacts and were effectively 'frozen out' and starved of work by the existing workforce. Thus, Ram and Holliday showed that 'familiness' was a complex resource that involved mutual obligations and constraints as well as advantages for the firm's managers.

The role of family in the small firm was not a new contribution. The significance of Ram and Holliday's work lies in showing the nuanced, complex role of mutual obligations within the family firm, rather than previous caricatures of family in business as either: 'happy families' (Ingham, 1970) or family as exerting discipline (Rainnie, 1989). Moreover, they show how through rich case studies and detailed fieldwork we can find out how social constructs like family are not fixed but are negotiated over and contested.

Moreover, this means that, having observed and recorded what people say about their beliefs and preferences, it is important to examine how people act upon their beliefs and preferences. If someone working in a family firm hands in their notice to leave the company because they report that they interpret that family members are more favoured in career terms, they do this not only because they believe in what they are doing but because they are also acting upon what they believe. Interpretation plays a role, therefore, in analysing the ideas, language conventions, rules and customs that underpin social practices (Bevir and Rhodes, 2002). As these authors say, this does not mean that in trying to explain the relationship between beliefs and actions the researcher looks for causal explanations. Instead, action is explained by pointing to the conditional and volitional links between intention and action through some form of 'narrative explanation' (Bevir and Rhodes, 2002). This is now considered.

Interpretivism and narrative explanation

Anyone involved in interviewing entrepreneurs will be drawn into interesting accounts of different disasters, successes or crisis stories about founding or managing a business. This is because when people are recalling events, activities and practices, narrative and storytelling become the main 'vehicles' through which people connect and relate to others.

In terms of entrepreneurship studies, specifically, a narrative explanation might take the form of 'personal autobiographical' narratives, founding/vision stories or generic stories involving conventional procedures such as business planning or marketing strategy (O'Connor, 2002). Vision and founding stories have been well documented (Berglund and Johansson, 2007; Pitt, 1998), also, stories relating to identity (Hamilton, 2006), growth (Johansson, 2004) and the communication of knowledge between business advisers and entrepreneurs (Downing, 2005). Storytelling is reported to recontextualize expert knowledge for the listener to aid the imitation of business action (Johansson, 2004) and so can be an effective alternative to the concise tools and methods of abstract knowledge or logo-scientific knowledge (Bruner, 1990). Storytelling is also a means of business persuasion (Clark and Salaman, 1998; Downing, 2005) and is part of 'storymaking' (Johansson, 2004) about the entrepreneurial process or the relational preparation of a story (with plot) to be enacted (Johansson, 2004; O'Connor, 2002). Let's examine this more closely in relation to the analysis of an account given by an entrepreneur as he recalls the emergence of his business:

In the Marvel Mustang story presented at the start of this special issue, the speaker/entrepreneur (whose name we do not know) constructs meanings and gives expression to how he and a friend (John) began their business. The account given is of the emergence of a business idea and a new business venture. The account is constructed as a story. There is a beginning (the drinks evening) where the idea came about, a middle (the crisis of 'no toys' which escalates deeper and deeper) and an end (solution to the problems encountered). Some characters are introduced and although the speaker places himself at the intersection of the story, other characters and voices are heard. A context is also provided (the speaker's house and dinner party). We hear how the germ of the idea and identification of a gap or opportunity in the market for buying toys at times other than Christmas came about during a social gathering. The listener/reader is informed of how the capital for the business venture is raised from personal savings despite resistance from the spouse and concerns about the dependent needs of his young family. The reader is encouraged to empathise with the protagonists about lack of capital, dependent family and the bad luck in not being able to get toys on consignment. Also embedded in the text are other voices. Although their words are not heard directly, the reader can infer meaning to John, the wives and later, a banker called Bill, through the way in which the speaker of the text is constructing their voices in the narrative. But, then, we are told how the wives are brought into and involved in the venture, the speed with which things start to happen and how their last $ was spent on renting a building. There is also a sense of pace and anticipation, events running ahead of themselves, lack of foresight, planning, market research, a sense of escalating drama and a crisis point. In telling the story in this way, a narrative is constructed and the reader/listener is drawn into the story and tempted to find out what happens next and how the problems are overcome. (Fletcher, 2007)

Narrative is important therefore, because it is the 'basic figuration process that produces human experience of one's own life and actions and the lives and actions of others' (Polkinghorne, 1988, p. 159). Through narrative, understandings and meanings about entrepreneurial activities are produced, reproduced and disseminated. Through narrative we think (Bruner, 1990), talk to ourselves and remember events (O'Connor, 2002), compose meaning out of events (Josselson and Lieblich, 1995) and engage in sense-making (Weick, 1995). It is the means through which events are chronologically connected together in a wider plot and how stories of everyday accounts are transmitted, moral choices evaluated and worries about existential issues are negotiated (Watson, 2002). Also, through narrative, what starts out as fragmented, messy and non-linear – what Boje calls the ante-narrative – becomes connected and integrated (Boje, 2001). In short, our lives are ceaselessly intertwined with narrative and the stories we hear in everyday conversations, see on TV programmes or read in novels and newspapers (Josselson and Lieblich, 1995; Czarniawska, 2003). It is the fundamental way in which people compose meaning, interrelate and connect to each other.

In discussing narrative explanation, this takes us to the third point I want to address in relation to the student extract. In reading the quotation, the student reports an interest in 'making sense of the social issues' of his research. Indeed, a further reason for coming to interpretive inquiry is that we are concerned with the social aspects of our research material which means having an interest in the social situatedness of their activities. This means we want to look at things 'in' (rather than 'out of') context. This is different from other styles of inquiry – that is, positivist – where data is allocated to categories irrespective of context. In using narrative explanations, issues of context are already embedded in the narrative structure of how/why people say/do/act.

If one is not using narrative explanation to demonstrate interpretive processes, however, then the (interpretive) researcher still needs to address context.

Interpretive inquiry and issues of context

In entrepreneurship, there is a long tradition of bringing to the fore the empirical diversity and range of socio-economic contexts in which entrepreneurial activity takes place (Johannisson, 2007). Whether the contexts are industry settings, science parks, industrial districts, family business or intrapreneurial settings, a key concern has been to spotlight the organizing processes that are unique to particular 'local' contexts (Johannisson et al., 1994). In privileging context, research studies have stressed how entrepreneurial phenomena could be differentiated, not just in terms of outcomes, but also in terms of the complexity of action routes that could lead to an entrepreneurial outcome (Johannisson, Ramirez-Pasillas and Karlsson, 2002). This signalling of context was important, therefore, for stimulating a search for contextual differentiation and similarity – efforts which have helped to distinguish between what is, and what is not, the entrepreneurial domain of inquiry. Furthermore, this inclusivity of contexts was important because it stimulated discussion on the social situatedness of entrepreneurial activity (Fletcher, 2006; Jack and Anderson, 2002; Steyaert and Katz, 2004; Zafirovski, 1999). This raises some interesting questions about the role of context in interpretive studies.

Often, in doctoral work, researchers demonstrate context by *framing* their findings with contextual insights, or they 'factor-in' the exogenous variables or contextual factors in order to *validate* the findings. Alternatively, context is seen to be conflated (embedded) in the respondents' words and expressions. Either way, demonstrating context or situatedness in the analysis and research record becomes a major analytical feat because the researcher not only has multiple contexts to consider but also multiple layers of contextualization (Bauman and Briggs, 1990). There is, for example, the *institutional context* of their research programme with the rules and regulations of the funding body or university procedures circumscribing the funding, nature, timing and conventions of the research. There is also the institutional context of the empirical field being investigated (science parks, communities, family businesses). There is also the *individual context* of the researcher and those involved in the field work discussing their lives, identities and orientations (need to publish, prepare a conference paper or acquire a PhD). Then there is the *context of situation* in which issues of gender, ethnicity, social role or status become meaningful. Indeed, other contexts could also be added but what is produced is a seemingly inexhaustible list of contexts. How, then, can we know when all contexts are accounted for? How do we recognize or label (even analytically) the 'social' from the 'cultural' or 'political' contexts? A difficulty arises then because we become concerned with what contexts 'do' or produce for entrepreneurship, rather than what it is, through acting entrepreneurially, that produces contextualization.

When writing up interpretive research findings, therefore, it is the researcher who judges what should be included (Bauman and Briggs, 1990). It is assumed that there can be a known and finite list of contextual factors and the 'knowing' researcher can select from this array of potential contexts to objectify their findings. Also, this implies that all contexts have an equal chance of being selected and just as opportunities are 'discovered on the basis of individual asymmetrical knowledge' (Shane and Venkataraman, 2000), contexts 'sit out' there in the field waiting for the knowing researcher to come along and select them. The researcher then generates understandings from 'context-free propositional content which is then modified or clarified by the context' (Bauman and Briggs, 1990, p. 68). But neither the respondent nor the researcher has full access to a range of contexts. Even when our respondents are drawing attention to particular issues, this does not mean that context and its categories are arbitrarily available for selection (van Dijk, 1999).

This problem can be seen in the thesis extract above. It can be noted that the student puts the main interpretive task upon himself. It is he, the inquiring student, who will 'figure out; 'compare/contrast' and 'make sense'. There is no mention of the respondents' interpretation processes or the context of their situation. Doing interpretation for the student means that he will appropriate the voices/meanings of his respondents in order to demonstrate the relevance of theories about the nature of the informal economy (this issue became more apparent in early drafts of the thesis). Furthermore, there is no referencing of context (beyond a description of the country-regional setting). Although having pictures and descriptions of the local setting where the research took place is an excellent way of 'showing' context, the interpretation processes that shaped what was said, to whom and for what purpose are not discussed. Furthermore, we are given no explanation for the ways in which theories of (in this case) the informal economy are constituted by the very world they seek to describe, known as the 'double hermeneutic' (Giddens, 1987). Beyond the presentation of several 'lay' quotations, the reader is neither provided with an interpretation of the interpretation processes, nor how lay theories have been synthesized back to the academic concepts (and vice versa). This lack of what is called reflexivity takes us to another aspect of interpretive research work.

Thick description and reflexivity in interpretive inquiry

This lack of attention to the reflexive layers of interpretation that go on in all human interaction situations is problematic for two reasons. First, in highlighting the resources, expressions, meaning-making and symbolic interactions that shape discursive processes, there are inevitably asymmetries of information, power and resources. Not everyone has access to an unlimited pool of resources or linguistic devices and while in some situations entrepreneurial discourses provide concepts, words, labels, categories and expressions through which opportunities/new possibilities are realized, for others in some cultures/contexts/situations, entrepreneurial discourses may control and suppress. This has been noted in entrepreneurship inquiry where commentators have been critical of the discriminatory nature of entrepreneurial discourses (Nodoushani and Nodoushani, 1999; Ogbor, 2000). Thus, language and discourse are imbued with power and, along with faithfully re-presenting the sense-making/meaning-making processes that are either reported or observed during fieldwork, an important task of interpretivist inquiry is to explain/examine/theorize these interpretation processes.

This means progressing from providing what Geertz calls 'thin description' (describing what is physically occurring) to 'thick description' (explaining the meaning of what is occurring) (Geertz, 1973). Being concerned with thick description means elaborating forms of communication and how they occur (1) deliberately, (2) to someone in particular, (3) to impart a particular message, (4) according to a socially established code and (5) without cognizance of the rest of the company (Geertz, 1973).

Thick description is important because when undertaking interviews, such as participant observations, the researcher is faced 'with a multiplicity of complex conceptual structures, many of them superimposed upon or knotted into one another, which are at once strange, irregular, and inexplicit, and which he must contrive somehow first to grasp and then to render' (1973, p. 10). Thus, when making interpretations, the researcher is not merely recounting what was said in a mechanical fashion but explaining the situated or contextual understandings that are not apparent in what is being said. This is usually done through participant observation, ethnographic and longitudinal research, and interviews with other people in the setting wherein we get a sense of polyphony (multi-voicedness) and relatedness to others, to past and current situations. As a result, there are several 'layers' of interpretation going on at any one point in the research process which involve the originating practitioner acting/thinking/conversing and giving sense to her experiences/actions (past, present and future) and the participant observer/researcher doing the same in relation to their interaction in the field work setting.

Alvesson and Sköldberg (2000) use the term 'reflexive interpretation' to create awareness of the various interpretive dimensions that occur at several different levels. The word 'reflexive' is added to highlight also the ability of the researcher to handle these layers of interpretation. For Alvesson and Sköldberg, reflexivity is the main activity of interpretive research. By reflexivity they mean 'forms of investigation that help us to reflect critically and appreciatively on our conditions, our traditions, institutions and relationships' (2000, p. 241). They argue for less concentration on collection/processing of data and more on interpretation and reflection in relation both to object of study and researcher (their political, ideological, linguistic context) (p. 241). Practising reflexivity means examining different levels/themes of reflection (where reflective is reflection on one level/specific methodology; but reflexive interpretation is about the movement between different levels of interpretation and indicates open reflection across various levels of interpretation – empirical, hermeneutic, ideologically critical, postmodern).

Other forms of reflexivity, however, highlight the way we construct ourselves socially while constructing others. This view of reflexivity, sometimes labelled as the 'reflexive turn' (follow the 'linguistic turn'), is important for interpretive inquirers because it transforms and challenges the classic realist research text, which sees the subject as separate from the inquirer (Ellis and Bochner, 1996; Denzin, 1989). In realist tales, the inquirer is concerned with mirroring or representing those events uncovered in the field and appropriating the voices of others (England, 1994) to produce representations of a reality which is claimed to be separate from the researcher's experience and interaction with it (van Maanen 1988). However, as Ellis and Bochner (1996) assert when writing our research findings, 'our product can never be an accurate map because the processes of production make transparent representation possible' (1996, p. 19). Field work stories, then, are much more than passive representations of another way of life. As Atkinson argues, the organizational (we should say entrepreneurial) world one enters during research is not a direct experience of that society but a researcher's attempt to interpret and reconstruct the daily organizational life as constructed during interview (Atkinson, 1990). Also, through reflexivity, new forms of reality emerge as tentative interpretations, descriptions and meanings are continuously opened up, examined, debated, synthesized and expanded upon through dialogue and close introspection of critical sub-texts (Alvesson and Skoldberg, 2000; Gergen and Gergen, 1993).

Attending to ontological issues: An ontology of relational becoming

Being concerned with how new forms of reality emerge through multiple interpretations takes us to the final issue for discussion here concerning the reasons why we undertake interpretive inquiry. This is the issue of ontology and how, through interpretivism, one makes claims about the nature of a socially constructed reality. An alternative way of demonstrating the ontological distinctions between realist and interpretivist inquirers is through notions of 'being' and 'becoming' (Chia, 1995) or, as expressed by Dachler, Hosking and Gergen (1995) 'entitative' and 'relational' thinking. The entitative ontology of being assumes that socio-economic reality is constituted by objective 'entities' – atomized objects (individuals, groups, organizations, society, etc.) and discrete states/processes (economic resources, social structures, knowledge, etc.).

In contrast, an ontology of becoming (Chia, 1995) or relational becoming (Dachler, Hosking and Gergen, 1995; Fletcher, 2006, 2007; Steyaert, 2007) gives primacy to the emergent and processual qualities of social phenomena. Rather than privileging an ontological posture of 'being realism' which 'asserts that reality pre-exists independently of observation and as discrete, permanent and identifiable "things", "entities", "events", "generative mechanisms", etc.' (Chia, 1995), a becoming ontology sees meanings, interpretations, sense-making as always in a process of becoming. Furthermore, being sceptical about capacity of a single authority to monopolize meaning, relational becoming emphasizes how things are always an expression of relationship (Gergen, 1999) – to past (and future) actions/conversations (Davies and Harré, 1990), events, experiences, thoughts, ideas, backgrounds and cultures (Fletcher, 2006; Watson, 2002). Activities such as innovation, discovery and entrepreneurship are not, therefore, the product of individual minds, but the result of interaction processes that develop in a highly relational context (Bouwen, 2001) and are continually emergent. The relational context incorporates the personal and family identities or life orientations of people as well as the cultural, social and economic context in which they are located (Fletcher and Watson, 2006). Thus entrepreneurs, the business ideas they enact and the business enterprises that they establish are not seen as having a fixed being. They are always emergent, in a process of becoming – 'coming ever afresh into existence out of an alternation of events that have gone before and will "become" again' (Steyaert, 1998).

Attending to both micro and macro research work through interpretive work

When we carry out interpretive research work, we usually begin at what is referred to as 'the micro level' (the meaning-making processes at the level of individuals and their interactions/relationality as we have been discussing above etc). It should also be noted, however, that when we are interpreting, it is not merely a mind, cognitive or micro activity that is going on. On the contrary, interpretive inquiry is also about relating and seeing social phenomena as expressions of relationships (to our culture, society, the economy and other institutions). This is discussed in more detail in Fletcher (2006) where I refer to social constructionist thinking to demonstrate how the construction of a building project is as much a social, cultural, political and institutional project as it is a tangible, physical and material one.

While it is not my intention in this chapter to have a long discussion on social constructionist thinking, I outline what this thinking means for entrepreneurship inquiry, and I examine how social constructionist work is as much concerned with the 'real' world as a realist study would be. I report on a view from my study window where I watch with a 'birds-eye view' the construction of a two-storey extension on the end of the house. I can see, as Czarniawska-Joerges (1992, p. 33) puts it, physical entities like bricks, mortar, machinery and equipment. There is human labour in the form of bricklayers, labourers and the project manager, etc. And there is architectural design and aesthetic expression as the client-customers enact their house/lifestyle vision in relation to the builder-adviser who is drawing upon his stock of construction knowledge about rural property development. There are also strict building regulations which dictate wall cavities, door openings, foundation depths, roof pitches etc. – all of which have to be adhered to but are open to a small degree of negotiation/interpretation as the physical and material house entity takes shape. As Czarniawska-Joerges (1992, p. 33) comments, these elements or aspects 'are socially constructed and put together by a socially constructed concept of [rural farmhouse] building'. The construction of both the physical features of the building entity and the concept of rural farmhouse building is multi-faceted, multi-dimensional and multi-voiced. Their construction is at the same time real, tangible, physical, material and cultural, social, political, and institutional, shaped not only by the lifestyle requirements of the customers but also social changes in the countryside and legal/political/institutional facts such as property ownership and environmental protection (Czarniawska-Joerges, 1992).

If one was undertaking research work on this project, one might begin at a micro level interviewing the house owners, the architect, the builders, the labourers and the planning officers, but their interpretation processes are multi-faceted, multi-dimensional and multi-voiced. Central to their interpretation processes are issues of gender, masculinity, power, artistic expression, building/environmental regulations, class aspirations, forms of property ownership, environmental protection and labour market issues. In addition, physically present at the interpretation site are material entities such as bricks, mortar, physical structures (buildings), machinery, equipment and land – all of which 'make demands' upon the nature of the social world in which these people are located. For example, the buildings have what is called a size footprint which determines how much new development can be added to the building. The footprint measure is interpreted by the planning authorities and negotiated by the owner of the property when they want to develop or extend. Any additional footprint to the physical entity has implications for council tax banding and the value of the house. Furthermore, the house is built on clay foundations and different levels which imposes physical constraints on what can be built and with what materials.

Interpretive work, therefore, might start at the micro level, involving multiple people/perspectives, but it is much more than that too. It also involves wider meso or macro issues (material entities, negotiations, rules, government regulations, industry conventions, actions, intentions, cultural norms or inter-subjectivities) and analysis can go from the micro to macro and vice versa in order to examine, depending on the research questions, patterns of relationships or structure-agency co-ordinations.

Conclusion: The importance of being relationally responsive in interpretive work

Interpretive work means putting interpretation as central to the research process. This was made explicit in the above student extract. But it also means, as this student went on to do in the final draft of his thesis, being continually 'interpretively responsive' in the inquiry process as research questions are defined, literature is reviewed, methods are evaluated and fieldwork is carried out. Interpretation is not something that just occurs at one moment in the research journey: there are multiple levels of interpretation going on all of the time during the research process. These interpretations occur in the contextualizing relationships between researcher and the originating practitioner (entrepreneur), between entrepreneurs and associates in the field, within the dialogue between students and peer group through supervision, conference presentations, etc., as well as in the reflexive processes of the students' own sense-making process.

The final challenge, then, as interpretive inquirers, is to be relationally responsive ourselves as we move back and forth within our field work settings and account for how the issues, themes, negotiations, material entities, rules, regulations or inter-subjectivities are expressions of a relationship – whether to our society, economy or culture. In so doing, the interpretively sensitive researcher can make judgements relating to the credibility, dependability, confirmability, trustworthiness and 'fitting-ness' of the accounts constructed

(Lincoln and Guba, 1985; Patton, 1990). We should also bear in mind that the activities we label entrepreneurship require immense effort, negotiation and dialogue, and they always 'go on' in relation to something else that has gone before: past conversations, events, experiences, cultures, ideas (Burr 1995; Dachler et al., 1995; Fletcher 2006; Gergen 1999). Thus, in being relationally responsive this means being concerned with contextualizing (and contextualization) processes and moving away from the centrality of individuals in order to theorize social acts or practices and their co-ordination or relationship. It also means being mindful of the 'unfinished discursiveness' of entrepreneurship. I wish I had known this when I was a doctoral student, but better late than never!

Further reading

Down, S., *Narratives of Enterprise: Crafting Self-Identity in a Small Firm* (Cheltenham: Edward Elgar, 2006).

Downing, S., 'The Social Construction of Entrepreneurship', *Entrepreneurship Theory and Practice*, 29 (2005) 185–204.

Fletcher, D. E., 'Social Constructionist Ideas and Entrepreneurship Inquiry', *Entrepreneurship and Regional Development*, 18 (2006) 421–440.

Johansson, A. W. 'Narrating the Entrepreneur', *International Small Business Journal*, 22 (2004) 273–293.

Steyaert, C. '"Entrepreneuring" as a Conceptual Attractor? A Review of Process Theories in 20 Years of Entrepreneurship Studies', *Entrepreneurship and Regional Development*, 19 (2007) 453–477.

Questions for discussion

In what ways are narratives of entrepreneurship helpful to understand entrepreneurship?

What aspects of entrepreneurship are highlighted through conversations and interviews with existing or previous entrepreneurs?

Which is more important, your situation or your beliefs about your situation?

Part II
Macro Perspectives

CHAPTER 5

Feminism, Gender and Entrepreneurship

Susan Marlow

> I myself have never been able to find our precisely what feminism is.
> I only know that people call me a feminist whenever I express senti-
> ments that differentiate me from a doormat.
>
> Attributed to Rebecca West, novelist, in Law (1992)

Introduction

This chapter draws upon a feminist perspective to analyse critically prevailing
perceptions surrounding normative entrepreneurial behaviour. Broadly speak-
ing, the underlying ethos of the feminist critique is founded upon the notion
that a particular group of human beings have been persistently and univer-
sally subordinated merely because they are biologically identified as female
and socially gendered as 'women' (Ahl, 2006; Butler, 1990). Throughout
history, those who have questioned and challenged sex and gender based
subordination have themselves been subject to violence, suspicion, ridicule
and ostracization (Bradley, 2007). So, what is it about feminism and feminist
argument that provokes such strong reactions and denial? Historically, it is
evident that subordination based upon social characterizations such as race,
sex, gender and class was justified on the basis of 'natural' orders which ele-
vated certain groups, generally white heterosexual males, to dominant positions. Thus, those who questioned the social order were, in effect, challenging
prevailing ideologies of power, hence the strenuous rebuttal of the critique
(Rowbotham, 1992).

Yet still within contemporary developed economies, where 'equality', regardless of social characterization, is lauded as a fundamental human right and overt
discrimination is dwindling, criticism of persistent female subordination through
a feminist stance remains subject to overt hostility and ridicule (Bowden and
Mummery, 2009). Indeed, within popular media and broader social commentary, the feminist critique is accused of being outdated given the social, political
and economic enfranchisement of women (Adkins, 2002; McRobbie, 2009).
Moreover, those women who articulate a feminist perspective are popularly
accused of being 'man haters', disruptive and 'unfeminine' (Weldon, 2003);
so, for example, Weldon writing in the *Daily Mail* (which has the highest volume
of female readers in the UK) states that the feminist voice in society has merely

created a 'new generation of women for whom sex is utterly joyless and hollow' (2003, 12–13). Yet even a cursory examination of the contemporary socio-economic ordering within developed economies (and, indeed, more so within developing economies) reveals persistent indicators of female subordination (Bradley, 2007; Butler, 1990, 2004; Cranny-Francis et al., 2003). These range across economic subordination (women are overly represented in low status, low paid work), social/political subordination (women are under-represented in positions of power and influence) and cultural/symbolic/physical subordination (that which is associated with the feminine is linked to weakness, women are still commonly represented as objects to the male subject and are also more likely to suffer domestic violence and sexual assault).

McRobbie (2009) argues that one source of the denial and dismissal of the validity of the feminist voice within contemporary society arises from the growing concentration upon individuality and the emergence of an 'enterprise' culture during the 1980s (Beck, 1992; Giddens, 1991). As such, the contemporary focus upon the agency of the individual within an allegedly meritocratic society to search for and then take advantage of individual opportunities to achieve refutes structurally rooted, collective subordination. Thus, failure becomes individualized and broader explanations for such – feminist theory, for example – are considered outdated and inappropriate. Attacks upon a feminist perspective, however, arise from a more complex foundation than just that of the rise of individualism. Feminism is intimately associated with a challenge to the normative gendered order. Gender is a stereotypical, social construction of masculine and feminine characteristics, which are then mapped onto the biological categories of males and females (Holmes, 2007). Masculinity and femininity are dynamic characterizations but exist within a hierarchical duality that orders social relations between men and women by subordinating that which reflects femininity (Hirdman, 2001). There are no fixed gender identities; rather, gender is a social practice reproduced in performance (Butler, 1990, 2004; Pullen and Simpson, 2009). Doing gender requires the enacting of specific identities through a 'repertoire of practices' (Martin, 2003) that confirm masculine and feminine characteristics that, in turn, make us culturally intelligible as social actors. Indeed, the gendered order and the performances that support and sustain it are taken as natural and normal such that they are largely rendered invisible within daily interaction. Any challenges to this order provoke hostility and confusion – gender trouble (Butler, 1990; Jagose, 1996; Roseneil, 2000) – as the hegemonic assumptions underpinning a presumed natural order are challenged or exposed (Jeanes, 2007). Such 'gender trouble' is evident, for example, in homophobia, where violence and prejudice are invoked when the normative links between gender ascription and sexual preference are defied – when individuals adopt gender identities in conflict with their biological status.

Such is the 'problem' with feminism and why it invokes extreme reactions, since the arguments which inform the perspective are not just about equality, diversity, fairness and individual rights. Rather, they challenge the prevailing social order and threaten embedded ideologies of power and privilege by exposing how gendered assumptions invoke and sustain female subordination

(Ahl, 2002). Hence, the popularized fear and loathing expressed towards feminism. However, gender subordination is dynamic and subject to contextual influence and, in turn, feminism has many explanatory strands and analyses which seek to expose and explain female subordination. To explore the complex field of feminist analyses and the contextual performance of gender, this chapter focuses upon one particular field, that of entrepreneurship.

Given simplistic associations between freedom, self-efficacy and entrepreneurship it might be supposed that women might escape from residual sexism and subordination within contemporary society through the individualism and self expression associated with entrepreneurship. Yet, drawing upon a feminist perspective, it will be argued that female subordination is embedded within the normative socio-economic context and, as such, seamlessly spills over into the entrepreneurial discourse as the 'typical' entrepreneur is consistently reproduced in masculinized form (Ahl, 2002). Moreover, the dominance of this masculinity is assumed as natural and normal, and so endemic sexism remains invisible and, in fact, becomes taken for granted (Marlow, 2002). To explore these arguments further this chapter is arranged thus: the first section offers a brief overview of feminist thought and argument; drawing from this analysis we comment upon the assumptions and philosophy underpinning this perspective. Secondly we explore to what degree a feminist perspective informs our understanding of entrepreneurial activity. Thirdly a 'classic study' by Helene Ahl is described to illustrate these issues (Ahl, 2007). From these arguments we then turn to evaluate critically the contribution of feminism to our understanding of entrepreneurial behaviour and finally consider policy/practitioner implications and future research directions.

The Feminist Critique – a brief overview

Challenges to female subordination – in effect, feminist argument – are evident throughout recorded history, yet the feminist 'movement' or a co-ordinated oppositional voice is largely seen as articulated through two specific eras or waves in modern society (Beesley, 2005). The so-called first wave of feminism occurred during the late nineteenth and early twentieth centuries when women campaigned for political enfranchisement and access to education, work and legal redress (Bowden and Mummery, 2009). As such, there was a move to claim *equality* by allowing women the same economic and social privileges afforded to men, such as the right to vote, the right to a university education, an independent legal identity (so they were no longer the property of fathers and then husbands) and the right to waged work. The movement for universal suffrage was hard fought with women laying down their lives, enduring imprisonment and social ostracization in their quest to be recognized as worthy of what we would now think of basic human rights. Underlying this movement, however, was the assertion that women were the 'equal' of men; thus, the normative model of human behaviour and being was seen to be that of the male subject.

Second-wave feminism emerged as a social movement that resonated with broader protests relating to civil rights, anti-war protests and anti-racism struggles – particularly within the United States. The text, 'The Feminine Mystique' by Freidan critically analysed the influence of subordination, sexism, patriarchy and oppression upon women's lives (Freidan 1963). Moreover, Friedan's work focused attention upon the manner in which a combination of subordinating constraints effectively limited women's potential. While this work was critical in stimulating debate and action – the so called women's liberation movement – it was limited again by a focus upon rights to 'equality' and assumptions that the experiences of white, middle-class housewives effectively reflected the universality of women in general.

However, from this initial exposure of persistent disadvantage, the feminist debate then developed in both complexity and sophistication to recognize intersecting influences such as class, sexuality and race. Such recognition informed the dominating feminist perspectives of the era: socialist feminism (Hartmann, 1983), which situated women as a class and subject to patriarchy arising from the structure of the capitalist system; radical feminism (Rich, 1977), which argued for female separatism on the basis of essential embedded male violence; and black feminism (hooks, 1981), which drew attention to the matrix of discrimination realised through the intersection of sex and race. So, while the notion of female subordination came to the fore in the 1960s and 1970s, distinct strands of feminist thought emerged during this era which engaged with differing and often competing explanations (Beesley, 2005). However, it can be cautiously observed that a common thread underpinning quite radically differing analyses of female subordination related to the notion of structural and institutional patriarchal subordination.

Since the 1980s, a critical evaluation of essentialist (the assertion that there are essential elements of masculinity and femininity which map onto the male and female) and structural analyses of female subordination has emerged through the work of post-structural feminists (Butler, 1990, 2004; Irigaray, 1985; Kristeva, 1982). This complex body of work explores and analyses the dynamic and fluid manner in which female subordination is constructed within and through language. When discussing the relationship between language and meaning, Bowden and Mummery (2009, p. 38) note the tension regarding whether 'individual speakers call up the prior reality of the world and their identities as they speak' or whether it is 'words that call reality into meaningfulness'. So, do we label meanings with linguistic markers, or does language itself ascribe meaning? Those who reflect upon a 'man made language' (Spender, 1980) reveal how those words and metaphors associated with the feminine are consistently represented as weaker, different or subordinate to those of the masculine. Within such theories of language are key notion of dualities that illustrate this argument, so to be caring is not to be aggressive, to be weak is not to be strong, to be a risk taker is not to be risk averse, so to be a woman is not to be a man. So, representations of gender are articulated through oppositional binaries within language itself; these then establish and sustain subordination as that side of the binary associated with femininity.

The work of Foucault is critical to understanding how such linguistic practices can be analysed as a 'discourse' which represents 'a group of claims, ideas and terminologies that are historically and socially specific and create truth effects' (Alvesson and Due Billing, 2002, p. 49). As such, language can be arranged, used and reproduced to represent and privilege specific interpretations and representations (Foucault, 1972). In effect, language is not neutral; it constitutes meaning rather than represents it. Consequently, linguistic discourses generate and critically shape meaning; moreover, they confirm and reproduce power relationships in that they are both exclusionary and inclusionary so they specifically reflect certain characteristics of those who are 'part' of that discourse. There are 'rituals about who can speak, how or when' (Ahl, 2002). So there is a 'discourse of masculinity' that suggests how men can and should act, how they should think, and what are appropriate male attitudes, interests and priorities – subscribing to such a discourse of masculinity privileges males in a myriad of ways as it offers access to power, status and position. However, prevailing discourses also act as gate-keeping devices in that they establish an image or set of characteristics that individuals need to demonstrate to be party to a particular discourse and, of course, it excludes those who do not or cannot subscribe.

To bring this discussion back to the notion of feminism, gendered discourses privilege the male and subordinate the female but are contextual. Thus, discourses reflect dominant power relations but shift over time and space. So, for example, black feminists (Bradley, 2007; Sudbury, 1998) draw attention to the manner in which discourses of race and racism intersperse with those of gender to create a particular context of disadvantage for black women. But even so, there are further divisions within this group relating to class identities, age, disabilities, ethnic identities, etc. Meaning is constituted by language which, in turn, creates, confirms and reproduces prevailing discourses within which specific identities are constructed which themselves reflect context.

Finally, to complete this short section on feminist thought, we consider post feminism (or the feminist 'backlash'). There is an emerging body of thought which suggests that since the 1960s (within developed economies) far reaching social and economic shifts have enabled women to emerge as independent, individual economic actors, protected by regulation to ensure equality (McRobbie, 2009). Accordingly, the feminist movement is outmoded and outdated as women now 'have it all'. The focus of this argument is very much upon the power of individual agency to achieve within an equitable and open society, so free will, ambition and effort fuel achievement. Failure or inadequacy cannot be attributed to collective subordination. The problem here being that this argument fails to recognize that female disadvantage is still deeply embedded within the current socio-economic environment (Bradley, 2007). Such disadvantage is articulated as a persistent pay gap; assumptions around parenting roles, domestic labour or, indeed, with the all-consuming message for contemporary women, epitomized within popular media (see *Sex and The City*, *Bridget Jones's Diary*, etc.) that you might have an income and a career, but you are nothing without a man. In effect, this critique individualizes failure by denying collective and ingrained subordination expressed through discourses that persistently devalue the feminine.

A feminist ontology and epistemology

As can be seen from the debate above, the feminist critique is dynamic, has shifted over time and is context specific. However, there is agreement regarding the notion of subordination and denial that such disadvantage has any basis within an objective reality. In effect, while there remains considerable debate surrounding how best to analyse the roots and persistence of subordination (Bradley, 2007), there is a shared notion that such subordination does not reflect any objective reality. Rather, it arises from a constructed notion of what a woman should be; how she should behave, her position in relation to men, her sexuality and her socio-economic station. As such, there is a constructed ideology which devalues what it is to be 'woman' (De Beauvoir, 1949). As de Beauvoir argues, 'one is not born, but rather becomes, a woman. No biological, psychological or economic fate determines the figure that the human female presents in society; it is civilisation as a whole which produces this creature described as feminine' (1949/1997, p. 249). So, there is no objective set of truths that validate or justify female subordination. Yet, there is a clearly discernible association between epistemology (the production of knowledge) and the perpetuation of female subordination. In general, what questions are asked, how they are asked and why they are asked critically shapes what we know and the value given to such knowledge. So, for example, just over 100 years ago the assumption that women were intellectually inferior to men – taken as a 'scientific fact' – justified the exclusion of women from critical areas of public life (Bowden and Mummery, 2009). Thus, as Code (1998, p. 176) notes, 'epistemologies, in their trickle down effects in the everyday world, play a part in sustaining patriarchal and other hierarchical structures'. Dominant epistemologies also bestow authority upon the 'facts' which are produced in that an assumption of objectivity is accredited to knowledge which is in then legitimated as objective truth (Code, 1998). Put simply, the answers you get depend upon the questions you ask.

Work by Helene Ahl has been particularly useful in exposing epistemological bias in the field of entrepreneurship and how knowledge attains an authoritative legitimacy (Ahl, 2002, 2006, 2007). Drawing upon a wide range of literatures, Ahl demonstrates the gendered nature of the entrepreneurial discourse – in effect, that which is associated with entrepreneurial activity, intentions, traits, behaviours and actions reflects and reproduces masculinity. This assumption in turn affects the presumptions surrounding who and what is an entrepreneur and how the field of entrepreneurship should be investigated. Essentially, the woman business owner becomes the 'other'; this is beautifully illustrated by the very fact of having to qualify the term, 'entrepreneur/business owner/self-employed' with the addition of 'female' or 'women' in this respect. So, there are none who are just 'entrepreneurs'; there are entrepreneurs (i.e. men) and there are female entrepreneurs – not men.

When reviewing what we 'know' about entrepreneurs, it is apparent that until the 1990s mainstream research activities assumed them to be male, and so research instruments reflected this bias and assumption. This is problematic as such presumptions neglect the contribution of women to the field, deny the subjectivity of women and when as Ahl (2002, p. 108) notes, 'when preformulated questions, based on male-centred notions of entrepreneurship are imposed on women entrepreneurs, there will be little chance to capture anything different about women entrepreneurs, only "more" or "less" of what is already imagined'. Analysing the body of evidence relating to female entrepreneurship, what we usually see is that women emerge as having 'less' of the resources and qualities associated with entrepreneurial behaviour (Taylor and Marlow, 2009). The problem then becomes that women are just not men! Thus, attempting to analyse their entrepreneurial activity from an essentially biased stance is problematic as it appears that women just do not 'measure up'. To some extent, this is illustrated with the 'feminist empiricist' approach (the generation of empirical data which compares male and female entrepreneurial activities and experiences) which characterized early analyses of women's business ownership and indeed still prevails; but a rather confusing picture emerges. This comparative approach purports to confirm that women-owned firms – in comparison to their male owned counterparts – are smaller, reluctant to grow, under-capitalized and overly concentrated in services and retail sectors (Carter and Shaw, 2006; Marlow, Henry and Carter, 2009). Such findings underpin the notion that women's businesses underperform. Undoubtedly, seeking out information on growth and profitability does suggest that female entrepreneurs are, once again, not measuring up – particularly in the face of prevailing government policy initiatives to support and encourage growth-oriented businesses.

Yet Ahl argues that despite the epistemological bias in the general entrepreneurial research field there is a more subtle form of subordination emerging within the 'comparative debate'. In effect, a careful reading of the evidence regarding the differences between performance profiles actually suggests a picture of broad similarities, not differences, between male and female owned firms (Ahl, 2002). There are sectoral performance constraints which impact more upon women in that broader socio-economic influences bias them towards retail and lower-order service sector start-ups, which tend to remain small on all parameters; this does create a small 'gender effect'. Yet a closer examination of the performance profiles of the majority of small enterprises within developed economies, whether male, female, family or co-owned, finds that they are small, marginal and their owners have no desire for growth (Marlow, 2009). Yet it is women business owners who are singled out and accused of underperformance, or of not using their full potential or failing to create jobs, or not seeking and using formal finance. Male, family owned and co-owned businesses which remain small and static within their market (the majority of the sector), it seems, are immune from accusations of underperformance based upon owner characteristics. Thus, developing research instruments that reproduce a gendered bias and using them to search for elusive differences rests upon the assumption that women business owners are essentially different from their male counterparts; yet the evidence for this is weak and unconvincing. This does not, however, prevent women from being singled out for particular attention.

In more recent work upon female entrepreneurship there has been a shift from descriptive comparative work, which utilizes the somewhat mythical norm of male achievement as a bench mark for female deficit, to more focused analyses of women's experiences of entrepreneurship (Taylor and Marlow, 2009). So, since the late 1990s, there has been greater recognition of heterogeneity and, moreover, that female entrepreneurs are worthy of study in their own right (Ahl, 2006). But what is noticeable about much of this work is an absence of gender or feminist theory to inform argument

(Mirchandani, 1999; McAdam and Marlow, 2009). Thus the analytical framing for much of this work remains limited and descriptive and so fails to embed research propositions within concepts that attempt to engage with women's lived experiences.

Work that draws upon the post-structural stance has offered a more coherent epistemological critique of the atheoretical nature of knowledge regarding female entrepreneurship. Such work draws upon an interpretist approach which aims to study the realities of women's lives, where private and public spheres blur and overlap, an issue that cannot be captured in closed, economically focused research instruments. As such, much of what informs entrepreneurial activity and mainstream models of 'doing the business' may be seen as irrelevant and excluded. This then leads to the suggestion that wider utilization and increased credibility of qualitative methods (Fletcher, 2011), such as life histories and others with greater sensitivity to feminist methodology, would widen the conceptual net of what entrepreneurship and entrepreneurial behaviour means. This would reveal, analyse and illuminate the meaning of entrepreneurship through women's experiences and so ensure that their activities are afforded greater credibility and legitimacy. In a recent methodology review article, Gartner debates and discusses the need for greater reflexivity in current approaches to entrepreneurial research and makes a case for greater engagement with qualitative approaches, particularly narrative analyses (Gartner, 2010). It is argued that 'In qualitative research there is typically an immersion into the muddled circumstances of an entrepreneurial phenomenon that is cluttered and confusing' (Gartner, 2010, p. 34). However, only by immersion within what Gartner calls the 'critical mess' of entrepreneurship can insight be gained. Thus, there is some agreement within the entrepreneurial field that epistemological challenges are critical to advance debate not only regarding women's experiences of business ownership but also to challenge our understanding of normative assumptions surrounding entrepreneurial activity and behaviour.

To illustrate these arguments, there is now a short review of a classic paper which offers a critical feminist analysis of a teaching case study of entrepreneurial venturing to reveal the fundamentally sexist and subordinating message which informs the narrative.

Sex business in the toy store: A narrative analysis of a teaching case

This paper utilizes a post-structural feminist critique to analyse a teaching case study used to illustrate a 'successful' entrepreneurial journey. As such, this 'journey' is a heroic tale of two people – Terry and John – who, through wit, deceit, charm, cunning, business acumen and a fair share of good luck, manage to create a highly profitable venture. As a teaching case, the story of the business is an exemplar of entrepreneurial opportunity recognition, risk management, market manipulation and profit creation. The narrative relates how, during the 1960s, these two men recognized an opportunity to sell toys on consignment just prior to Christmas. To realize this ambition, the men utilize their savings initially to rent retail space then persuade (not always honestly) a banker to support the venture, struggle to find sufficient stock (a particular toy, 'Marvel Mustang') for the store and experience financial short falls but, they persevere in the face of such adversity. All is nearly lost when their plan to buy up all stocks of the toy from a key competitor – so leaving them as sole market supplier – founders as their competitor then orders a new consignment of Marvel Mustangs.

Happily, however, at the crucial time just prior to Christmas, their competitor's order fails to arrive, so they are left as the major suppliers of the toy and thus 'clean up the market'. On the face it, this narrative is a useful case study as it not only has all the ingredients to illustrate the challenges of the entrepreneurial process but also the rewards to be gained if the protagonists are sufficiently courageous, ambitious and determined. In effect, it enables students to discuss and debate the rewards, triumphs, trials and tribulations of entrepreneurial venturing.

We see all of this illustrated within this case from the account given by one of the founders, Terry Allen. Yet closer reflection also reveals how women are positioned within this story in such a way as to suggest that they are obstacles to entrepreneurial venturing which need to be negotiated, deceived, cajoled and placated in turn. Terry tells how he and his business partner John came up with their idea during a social occasion; their next step is to finance the deal – initially through their household savings, but this required the 'wives' to be cajoled into agreement (the women are never afforded independent identities; they are only know as the 'wife' or the 'wives'). However, even more cash is then needed to support the business – this requires a bank loan which the wives also have to sign, and although there is reluctance to do so again, they are persuaded. When a further loan is required, the objections of the allegedly over-cautious, non-entrepreneurial spouses are bypassed altogether through the simple act of not consulting them. During this early stage of start up, the wives are presented as an obstacle to be negotiated – they do not understand the risk and resort to feminine weaknesses such as crying when the need to borrow more money is discussed. Hence it is quite acceptable to deceive these women by excluding them from such decisions, even though they concern their capital and future security. While the women are presented throughout the story as a rather tiresome obstacle to be managed, particularly when times are tough, the fact that it is the 'wives' who keep the shop going through their unpaid labour during the day, while also running the home and caring for small children, is rather glossed over. This is seen as a natural extension of what wives should do rather than grant them access to any decision-making or risk-taking activities related to the management of the business.

To all intents and purposes, there is a happy ending to this story as Terry and John, through wily behaviour and smart market manipulation, make a considerable profit from the venture. The wives also benefit from their success as Terry tells how he stuffed a stocking full of money and gave it to his wife as her Christmas gift; she is highly delighted with the reward he decides to give for her unpaid labour and trust in his business acumen.

To consider and explore how and why the women in this case are largely ignored or denigrated to a very minor role, Ahl uses a post-structural analysis to deconstruct this case. Her first point of departure is to consider how reality is socially constructed through the use of language which forms the building blocks of narrative accounts. As noted above, language is not a neutral tool; rather, it constitutes meaning rather than merely representing it, but such meaning has to be shared otherwise, as social actors we could not make sense of our world. Thus through linguistic interchange we exchange, reproduce, challenge and reconstitute dominant and legitimated versions of reality. However, such narrative exchanges are not freely exchanged but, rather, align as discourses, which in turn embody power and legitimacy (Ogbor, 2000). As Ahl (2007, p. 679) notes, 'not every one has the same freedom to reconstruct social reality, however. The power to shape discourses is unevenly distributed in society' so some have greater influence to shape social meaning and, thus, reality. In her critical reading of this case, Ahl analyses how the assumptions underpinning this 'normative' tale of everyday entrepreneurship seamlessly reproduces the message of a male-dominated sphere of activity where women are peripheral. As Bruni et al. note, 'gender and entrepreneurship are performed by constantly shuttling between different and dichotomous symbolic spaces' (2005, 423). In this case, being female effectively excludes these wives from any opportunity or invitation to assume an entrepreneurial identity (Bruni, Gherardi and Poggio, 2005). Indeed, within the case women are deceived, bullied and denied any subject identity – they only exist as the 'wife' or 'wives', even though they make a considerable contribution to the success of the venture. This exclusionary and discriminatory approach is neither recognized nor acknowledged within the case. As the business was a success, the wives are then rewarded for their contribution but, again, on terms decided by their husbands. Indeed, throughout this tale, despite the contribution of these women to running the shop (both men had other full-time jobs) they are only represented as extensions of their husbands' will – so initially they have to be persuaded to part with saving; it is then acceptable to deceive them; their labour can be seamlessly co-opted as required; then they can be rewarded as the men see fit – and all of this without ever being given subject identity. As 'the wives' they remain object to the male subject. It is also some what sobering, as Ahl notes in her discussion of the case (2007, p. 688), that there is no embarrassment or reluctance to tell such a story openly, 'How is it then possible that Allen can tell such a story which positions women in this way? And how can the audience accept it?' Of course it is possible and the audience do accept it as such presumptions reflect the normative gendered social ordering in society which seamlessly reproduces female subordination with little question or concern.

Contribution, implications and critique

This case analysis makes an important contribution to challenging normative representations of the entrepreneurial discourse. Through the deconstruction of the assumptions and actions which surround the entrepreneurial journey taken by Terry and John, we see how it is presented as entirely unproblematic, indeed positively normal, to describe and present women as secondary and subordinated. As such, the contribution of this paper lies in the manner in which it challenges normative accounts of entrepreneurial venturing that reinforce the essence of a masculinized discourse while uncritically reproducing female subordination. Rather than being carried along with the merits of the case – which certainly do offer interesting examples of the entrepreneurial process – the subordinating sub text is exposed, analysed and critically evaluated. Thus, the subtleties of how a masculinized discourse, which underpins normative entrepreneurial behaviour, is effortlessly reproduced are clearly illustrated.

There are a number of implications which arise from this particular narrative. In broader terms, there are normative, unquestioned representations of masculinity and femininity. Gendered characterizations are effortlessly reproduced with the key protagonists, Terry and John, represented as competitive, market-savvy risk-takers; these men saw an opportunity and aggressively pursued it. The (anonymous) wives, however, are cautious, conservative and risk averse – they are defined by domesticity, weakness and anonymity. At no point are there any reflections upon the fact that during this 'entrepreneurial journey', Terry and John lie to their bankers, lie to the owner of the retail outlet and indeed belittle and lie to the women whose savings, home and security are put in jeopardy. Moreover, these anonymous women are expected unquestionably to provide unpaid labour and blind faith in a high risk venture, but this is not seen as either unreasonable or, indeed, foolhardy. The women themselves are described as 'conservative' and 'cautious' when they express concerns regarding the use of family savings to fund a new venture in which neither of the owners can work full time (having other employment), where they have no prior knowledge of the retail sector or previous experience as entrepreneurs. From the details of the case, it would appear that the venture succeeds through pure serendipity as the main rivals experience problems with the delivery of a new consignment of 'Marvel Mustangs'. Had such a delay not occurred, regardless of their optimism, Terry and John – and their wives and children – would have lost everything. This would have made for a very different 'Toy Story' with a rather unhappy ending.

Finally, Ahl makes a further thoughtful comment upon the very merits of this narrative as a 'teaching case'. What does it teach students about being an entrepreneur? This story tells us that adopting an entrepreneurial identity makes it perfectly acceptable to lie, cheat and deceive bankers, business colleagues and family members, as all of these activities are feted within the case. Moreover, the epistemological approach here is founded upon an acceptance of gendered subordination – the 'knowledge' this case illustrates is profoundly gendered and suggests that it is normal and natural to reduce women to anonymous objects in relation to the male subject. As such, is this the kind of classical teaching case which should be used to illustrate successful normative entrepreneurial behaviour? What message does this give to women studying entrepreneurial behaviour? Positive role models of women business owners are rare both within research papers, teaching cases and as examples of entrepreneurial actors and educators (Ahl, 2007; Jones, 2009). The continued celebration of stories which reproduce women within normative gendered roles where they appear as subordinated, secondary actors merely camouflages the perpetuation of gendered orders both within entrepreneurship and the wider socio-economic context. Moreover, such assumptions reinforce the subtext that women are not entrepreneurs; rather, their place within the entrepreneurial discourse is as passive observers or directed actors.

In terms of critiquing this case analysis, there are two crucial issues that might be considered further: the dated aspect of the case and the value and credibility of post-structural analyses and argument. In respect of the first point, the activities described within this case occurred during the 1960s; while this was at the height of second-wave feminism it might be argued that entrenched values regarding the position of women in society were merely reflected within this case. As such, the representation of the gendered relationships and expectations were in keeping with contemporary norms and expectations; as such, it would not happen now. Yet, as Ahl notes, we might hope that this story is 'Not Valid Here and Not Valid Now' (2007, p. 689) but this hope is rather undermined by the fact that this case features within a textbook published in 2001. Consequently, despite two distinct waves of feminist action, post-war regulation regarding equal opportunities, fairness and equity and the alleged elevation of women's primary identity as independent economic actors within the twenty-first century, it is still absolutely fine casually to represent women as anonymized objects subordinated to the male entrepreneurial subject. Moreover, given the persistence of an entrepreneurial discourse that is defined by assumptions of white, male heterosexuality (Marlow, 2002; Ogbor, 2000; Taylor and Marlow, 2009) the underlying message regarding a 'woman's place' would seem to have shifted little within the entrepreneurial field. Of course, there has been some change – gender relations are dynamic – so within contemporary literature there is a greater engagement with, and a sensitivity to, the experiences of women business owners. However, the assumption that any analysis of female entrepreneurship has to be qualified (with the label of 'female' or 'women'), the persistence of comparative work which takes what men do as the norm and so relegates women's activity as the 'other', and the casual attachments of labels such as 'underperforming' to women's businesses (one could go on here but the point is made) are strong indicators that while things have changed, the shift is glacial. Thus, the sentiments underpinning this 1960s case study are of relevance today.

The second point of critique here relates to the theoretical framework that informs the analysis of the case study. The post-structuralist stance has been critical within feminist debate to challenging the notion of female essentialism and assumptions of shared subordination arising from a homogeneous biological identity and socio-economic positioning. As such, the notion of gender as constructed, fluid and performed is emphasized. This has enabled a greater focus upon difference and context; as Bradley (2007, p. 71) notes a critical contribution of this stance, 'has been to expand the knowledge of how gender is experienced and to gain a deeper and more detailed understanding of different shades of relations, not only between men and women, but among women themselves'. Yet the focus upon differentiated experience also prompts criticism. Hartsock, for example, argues that the focus upon language, specificity and difference denies common experiences of subordination and so challenges collective movements to address inequality and discrimination (Hartsock, 1990). As Soper argues, 'theoretically, the logic of difference tends to subvert the concept of a feminine political community of women' (1990, p. 96). The tendency increasingly to deconstruct experience and embed it within linguistic constructions and ever smaller local narratives must inexorably lead to hyper-reflexivity; the consequence of such being the denial of any possibility for collective mobilization as there can never be any basis for such (Soper, 1990).

In terms of this case study it could therefore be argued that this story merely reflects a specific representation of gender relationships within a particular context. When exploring accusations of hyper-individualism, Bradley notes that while gender may be 'performed' as a series of individual acts (Butler, 1990), it is done so as a routinized repetition such that an impression of a stable, gendered self is produced and reproduced (Bradley, 2007). As such, gendered characterizations and subordination become institutionalized, stereotypical and normalized within prevailing discourses. So, it is possible to remain sensitive to the micro-constructed nature of gender identity while acknowledging how this coagulates into collective subordinating assumptions. Consequently, this critical analysis of gendered representations within 'Toy Story' might be dismissed as an account of a 'local narrative' that has little relevance or bearing beyond its specific context. However, drawing upon wider considerations refutes this argument; the case is an illustration of how constructed discourses uncritically represent and reproduce gendered relations that persistently subordinate women. Thus, while sensitive to critiques of post-structuralism, this theoretical framing illuminates how prevailing discourses effortlessly reproduce normative assumptions that underpin female subordination.

Future directions

As has been argued above, the literature exploring 'female entrepreneurship' has developed in scope and sophistication over recent years and, since the mid-1990s, the female entrepreneurship project has gained credibility and respect such that it is accepted as a critical element within current debate (Marlow et al., 2009). Unlike some other perspectives in entrepreneurship, such as interpretism (see Chapter 4) or psychological approaches (see Chapter 3), feminism is an emancipatory perspective (Grix, 2004). The aim is to expose and challenge female subordination; however, in pursing this project there is not a common foundation in terms of methods and views of the world (ontology) as in the case of interpretism or rational choice theory, for example. There remains a lack of theoretical focus and development within the debate, particularly around the concept of feminism and gendered theory. Indeed, links between existing feminist literatures within the fields of sociology, economics and politics, for example, are still rarely drawn upon to create explanatory theories by which to analyse women's experiences of entrepreneurship. Moreover, the tendency to analyse women in relation to, and in comparison with, male entrepreneurs persists. The charge here is that of essentialism; accordingly, to what extent are there essential differences between the genders, as suggested by women's studies and women's entrepreneurship, rather than gendered entrepreneurship? Despite such weaknesses, it is fair to suggest that female entrepreneurship is now firmly on the enterprise 'map' in terms of respect and attention from the academic, policy making and practitioner community.

Thus, in terms of future directions, greater attention must be paid to creating theoretical links between entrepreneurial behaviours, gender theory and feminist analyses. This would enable the development of stronger critiques of the female entrepreneur 'underperformance thesis' and greater suspicion of the suggestion that if only women behaved more like men, their entrepreneurial challenges (and so many more problems) would be easily addressed. Regarding other substantive areas which are recognized as critical, more work is required upon the definition and measurement of women's enterprise which has historically been populated by descriptive local studies (Carter and Shaw, 2006). Initiatives such as the Global Enterprise Monitor (GEM) study, which publishes a standardized comparison of women's entrepreneurship (Minitti, Arenius and Langowitz, 2005), offers scope to develop international analyses that supplement existing data sources. Recent work has also drawn attention to the potential pitfalls of using the United States as the international benchmark for women's enterprise, cautioning against casual comparisons of numbers and trends without regard to socio-economic and welfare policies (Marlow, Carter and Shaw, 2008). Thus work that explores institutional influences upon the context of female entrepreneurship is critical; this theme constitutes only a small proportion of research output at present. Such studies are essential to build upon our understanding of how labour markets, welfare systems and family structures overlap to position female entrepreneurship as a subordinated activity. Moreover, such studies will also illuminate the complexity surrounding the accrual of entrepreneurial capital and how gender shapes this process (Shaw et al., 2009).

Consequently, using an interdisciplinary approach to explore the impact of gender upon women's business ownership will confirm that entrepreneurship cannot be adequately analysed from a gender neutral perspective. So, as Ahl (2006, p. 595) notes, prevailing research practices inadvertently contribute to the social construction of women entrepreneurs by recreating 'the idea of women as being secondary to men and of women's businesses being of less significance'. The provision of research responses and extensions to this perspective are critical. Finally, drawing upon a feminist perspective to analyse the extant and future body of entrepreneurial research is crucial to illustrate how gender is performed within this field; it is not sufficient to see feminist analyses and gender issues as corralled within the realms of 'women's business ownership'. This is to miss the point; as this chapter has argued, the assumptions that inform the masculinized entrepreneurial discourse per se have to be exposed in order to reveal their pervasiveness in terms of how they shape what is taken to be normal, natural and common sense. Thus, the greatest challenge for future research is to argue that a feminist perspective should not only be applied to 'women's business ownership' but the field of entrepreneurship more broadly.

Practitioner implications

It may seem that a theoretical feminist analysis has little relevance to small business practitioners; however, arguments regarding how women are represented within the entrepreneurial domain are critical. As greater attention was afforded to female entrepreneurship in the 1990s, a raft of policy and support initiatives were generated, which aim not only to encourage more women to begin new firms but also to draw attention to gender related challenges. While this is broadly positive, not all of these policies have been helpful to women and have attracted criticism from a feminist stance as many merely aimed to encourage women to adopt an honorary man persona. Other initiatives, such as the 2003 DTI strategy (SBS, 2003), while helpful in focusing attention upon women's entrepreneurship, based arguments upon spurious US comparisons to support the idea of some kind of missing 'economic potential' represented by women's under-representation as business owners. Such approaches are not helpful as they do not recognize context, rarely address issues of inequality or challenge hegemonic normative masculinity within the entrepreneurial field; however, the general focus upon women's enterprise has stimulated recognition of the gendered nature of small business ownership. As such, it can be seen that broader debates within and among policymakers, practitioner representatives and support agencies do now recognize that gender is an issue and does have an impact. If current and future research does draw more upon feminist theory and critically engage with differing analytical frames such as post-structuralism, these arguments will filter through to influence understanding of practitioner activities and, in turn, perhaps shape policy and support initiatives which inform such behaviour. So, while theoretically rooted, this perspective can challenge and critically engage with the normative assumptions which surround entrepreneurial behaviour. And in so doing, such arguments become crucial to drawing attention to the effortless production and reproduction of women as subordinate entrepreneurial actors, as is so eloquently demonstrated within the case study which illustrates this chapter.

Further reading

Ahl, H., 'Why Research on Women Entrepreneurs Needs New Directions', *Entrepreneurship Theory and Practice*, 30(5) (2006) 595–621.

Bruni, A., S. Gherardi and B. Poggio, *Gender and Entrepreneurship: An Ethnographical Approach* (London: Routledge,2005).

Brush, C., A. de Bruin and F. Welter, 'A Gender Aware Framework for Women's Entrepreneurship', *International Journal of Gender and Entrepreneurship*, 1(1) (2009) 8–24.

Butler, J., *Gender Trouble* (London: Routledge, 1990).

Holmes, M., *What is Gender?* (London: Sage, 2007).

Lewis, P., 'The Quest for Invisibility: Female Entrepreneurs and their Masculine Norm of Entrepreneurship', *Gender, Work and Organization*, 13(5) (2006) 453–469.

Marlow, S. and D. Patton 'All Credit to Men? Entrepreneurship, Finance and Gender', *Entrepreneurship, Theory and Practice*, 29 (2005) 717–735.

Marlow, S., 'Self-employed Women: A Part of or Apart from Feminist Theory?' *Entrepreneurship and Innovation*, 2(2) (2002) 23–37.

Ogbor, J., 'Mythicizing and Reification in Entrepreneurial Discourse: Ideology-Critique of Entrepreneurship Studies', *Journal of Management Studies*, 37(5) (2000) 605–635.

Taylor, S. and S. Marlow, *Engendering Entrepreneurship: Why can't a Woman be More Like a Man?* Paper to the 26th EURAM Conference, Liverpool, 4–6 May 2009.

Questions for discussion

Critically evaluate to what extent the case study described in this chapter reflects assumptions and attitudes pertaining to contemporary entrepreneurial behaviour.

Critically discuss to what extent specific government policy initiatives and support and advice agencies should focus specifically upon 'female' entrepreneurship.

If most small enterprises within the contemporary economy have limited growth options and remain marginal performers within their sectors, critically evaluate why women-owned firms are singled out as 'underperforming'?

CHAPTER 6

An Introduction to Network Approaches and Embeddedness

Sarah Drakopoulos Dodd

The network approach to studying entrepreneurship is founded on the recognition that economic interactions between people also, de facto, contain social elements. People live out their lives within a spider's web of human relationships: with family, old school friends, former and current business colleagues, competitors, suppliers, customers and neighbours. We also belong to a whole range of formal and informal social groupings, such as religious bodies, ethnic societies, sporting clubs, business associations, local charities, the pub and professional bodies. Our interactions within these relational networks, within which we are 'set' – embedded – shape a whole range of economic transactions, including those specific to the entrepreneur. I will argue that these social ties shape what information entrepreneurs can discover, what new technological developments they find out about (and when), which resources they can access, who will buy and sell from them, and on what terms, how legitimate they are perceived to be within the 'market', and so on.

The people we meet through social interactions, both in the workplace and outside, play a very important role in shaping entrepreneurship. Networking has long been a subject of considerable interest to the disciplines of organizational behaviour and management studies. This is particularly true since the widespread acceptance of Granovetter's observation that 'economic action is embedded in ongoing networks of personal relationships rather than carried out by autonomous actors' (Granovetter, 1973 cited in Gatley, Lessem and Altman, 1996, p. 78). Granovetter means that because all activities take place in interaction with other people, the nature of our relationships with these people affects how we carry out a range of actions. This is as true for economic activities as for any other, and it holds particularly for the entrepreneurial firm, where the business and the person of the owner-manager are tightly interrelated.

Entrepreneurial networks can be defined as the sum total of relationships in which an entrepreneur participates and which, at least some of the time, are utilized to further his or her business. These relationships may be articulated through the mechanism of membership in formal organizations, through the links an entrepreneur develops with suppliers, distributors and customers, or through the utilization of social contacts, including acquaintances, friends, family and kin. As Johannisson and Mønsted (1997) write, 'Entrepreneurial networks provide a framework for processes aiming at organizing resources according to opportunities'.

How well positioned someone is, socially, will determine the extent to which they can spot opportunities, secure resources, gain information and advice, find customers and suppliers. 'Good' social positioning is about more than class, gender or race, although in many societies these remain important.

While it is somewhat arbitrary to mark a definite and specific point at which networking became recognized as highly relevant to understanding entrepreneurship, nevertheless from the mid-1980s there is evidence of a notable trend taking off. Sue Birley's (1985) article in the *Journal of Business Venturing* established that informal social networks appear to be more often enacted by start-up ventures than more formal industrial support bodies. Aldrich and Zimmer's 1986 book chapter similarly sets out clearly the critical role of networks to the entrepreneurial process. Among other important early developments was the series of linked international studies centred around Howard Aldrich, which continued the process of highlighting the significance of networking to nascent entrepreneurs and small business owner-managers.

The developing body of work on entrepreneurial networks has since benefitted from a series of periodic reviews, which as well as presenting extant literature also address the 'networking metaphor' as a broad conceptual perspective (Drakopoulou Dodd, Jack and Anderson, 2006; Hoang and Antoncic, 2003; O'Donnell et al., 2001; Johannisson and Mønsted, 1997; Slotte-Kock and Coviello, 2010; Szarka, 1990). Many of these reviews consider the related topics of network structure, content, process and governance. Of increasing relevance is a fifth topic, that of contingency.

> Structural issues address questions such as who do entrepreneurs relate to, who are the members of their network and to whom are they, in turn, connected?
>
> Content research focuses on what is transferred through the network; for example, information, financial resources, advice, knowledge and so forth.
>
> Process mechanisms relate to how these transfers are made, structures built and maintained and relationships developed. What do actors actually do and say?
>
> Governance topics tackle the co-ordinating mechanisms that underpin and facilitate network exchang including trust, power, contracts and influence.
>
> Contingencies act so as to make networks, and the actors which comprise them, different from each other. Such contingencies include national, regional and sectoral cultures, as well as entrepreneurs' gender, class and ethnicity. As an example of finer-grained research which explores such contingency, a range of studies examining international similarities and differences in entrepreneurial networks will be presented below.

Networking studies are furthermore useful as a conceptual linking mechanism, between economic and sociological approaches, between micro and macro levels of analysis, joining quantitative and qualitative methodologies, and bridging universalist and relativist approaches to entrepreneurship (Johannisson and Mønsted, 1997, p. 109).

As a model of scholarly elegance and pragmatism combined, and an example of a 'mainstream' organizational studies approach to considering entrepreneurial networks, I have selected Brian Uzzi's work on embeddedness. Before moving on to present this overview of a classic study, however, I will discuss in more detail the characteristics and critiques of entrepreneurial networking scholarship.

The contribution of the perspective for entrepreneurship

Entrepreneurship research which adopts a networking and embeddedness perspective has made a substantial contribution to our understanding of how the social environment of the entrepreneur shapes, supports and perhaps also inhibits their new venture. Major advances have been made in terms of appreciating the benefits and drawbacks offered by embedded networks, in differentiating between the correlates of strong and weak ties in specifying key network characteristics susceptible to study and exploring these empirically, in mapping the inter-relationship between networking and venture growth over time, and in considering entrepreneurial networks at the level of regional cluster or industrial district. Each of these contributions will now be briefly presented, before the perspective's gaps and limitations are discussed.

Entrepreneurial network functions, benefits and drawbacks

Curran and colleagues have argued that 'networks are best seen as primarily cultural phenomena, that is as sets of meanings, norms and expectations usually linked with behavioural correlates of various kinds' (Curran et al., 1995). What benefits do these sets of culturally conditioned relationships offer the entrepreneur? In fact, entrepreneurial networks potentially provide the entrepreneur with a great deal of help, as Uzzi's study has illustrated. Indeed, it is difficult to see how venture creation is possible without access to an effective set of network relationships, see especially Szarka (1990). What is it that networks bring to the entrepreneurial firm to facilitate their development?

As Table 6.1 shows, there is strong evidence that the benefits of networks are multiple: knowledge (of themselves, opportunities and the environment); and the contrasting benefits of strong and weak ties.

Contrasting strong and weak ties

Brian Uzzi's study, presented below, is typical in differentiating, both empirically and conceptually, between two types of tie, based on their intensity. Uzzi's work highlights how important both types of tie are within a productive network structure. The best known of the typologies which contrast types of tie is that set out by sociologist Mark Granovetter (1973), who divided network relationships into two groups, of strong and weak ties. According to

Table 6.1 Entrepreneurial network functions, benefits and drawbacks

Network Function	Benefit / Drawback	Study
Transmission of private, specific, timely commercial information	Offers opportunities and acts as an 'early-warning system' in the face of strategic threats	Burt (1992); de Koning (1999); Hills, Lumpkin and Singh (1997); Uzzi (1997)
Support and advice provision	Helps to offset the managerial isolation of the entrepreneur	Johannisson (1998, 1996)
Provision of resources on speedy and amicable terms, including financing	Eases the path of the nascent or growing business, saves time, reduces 'governance' costs	Ostgaard and Birley (1994); Uzzi and Gillespie (2002, p. 613); Shane and Cable (2002, p. 377); Brüderl and Preisendörfer (1998)
Sharing of knowledge and expertise	Develops the human capital, and potentially the competitive advantage, of the firms involved	Uzzi (1997)
Bridging structural holes by providing links to 'friends of friends'	Widens network structure and provision, enhances diversity of available resources (including informational and knowledge resources)	Burt (1992); Jack (2005)
'Personal and business reputations are maintained, extended and enforced'	Generates legitimation for the entrepreneur, helps to overcome the inherent liabilities of small new firms	Jack (2005); Shane and Cable (2002)
Helping to find suitable and trustworthy employees	Increased employee 'fit' and performance	Jack (2005)
Provides implicit, relational governance structure for doing business	Guides, facilitates and 'manages' interactions in a rapid and efficient manner towards positive-sum outcomes	Uzzi (1997)
Innovation systems	Co-enactment of opportunities, clustered knowledge interactions, shared learning	De Propis (2000)
Many strong ties in a very dense network may create sterile and overly social ties	Limits resource access, opportunity perception, creates social tensions, reduces efficiency	Jack (2005); Ram (1994); Uzzi (1997)

Granovetter, relationships can be classified as being weak or strong ties on the basis of their quality and strength. The person whose network we are studying is called the **ego**, and those with whom he has relations are called **alters**. (Within entrepreneurship, the ego on whom we focus tends to be, unsurprisingly, an entrepreneur!)

It is usually argued that an effective entrepreneurial network will combine a few strong-tie alters with many weak-tie alters. Weak ties may be especially helpful in bridging the gap between the entrepreneur and other networks he needs to access. Our strong ties are most likely to circulate in our own social arena, sharing the same information as us, and, like us, do not pay much attention to the separate networks which weak ties inhabit. Similarly, our weak ties, even though they are linked to us, spend most of their socio-economic life interacting, learning, exchanging within their own social arena, not focusing on what is going on in our adjacent network system. The two systems are connected by our relationships with a weak-tie alter, but, for all practical purposes, neither is attending to the information and resources of the other: there is a *structural hole* separating them. Burt (1992, p. 208) likens these structural holes to 'buffers, like an insulator in an electrical circuit'. Because the information either side of the structural hole is separate, fundamentally different, from that on the other side, it adds new, vaulable knowledge to those who can use their weak ties to bridge the structural hole (Burt, 1992).

Uzzi, as we shall see, points out that under- and over-embedded networks (with too few or too many strong ties) each offer dangers to the entrepreneur and his firm. However, there is ever more evidence that strong ties offer special benefits to the entrepreneur and that many ties in any case have a tendency to strengthen over time. The two types of tie are differentiated in the following ways (see Table 6.2).

The study of entrepreneurial networks demands that we find ways of analysing their structure. The balance between types of tie is an important structural component, as we have already seen, and is often studied in terms of the strong-tie/weak-tie composition: what is the proportion of strong and weak ties in the network? Other concepts for analysing network structure include centrality, density, diversity, size, formality and reachability.

Network characteristics: Elements and international empirics

To make sense of entrepreneurial networks, it is essential to develop a toolbox of characteristics which can be used to compare, contrast and analyse these important socio-economic phenomena. This section will introduce some of the most important network characteristics before illustrating their application in a series of international studies.

Network centrality is the degree to which a specific ego can be seen to be central to the wider network, to be acting as a network hub. Centrality, if it exists, is considered a good thing, because the entrepreneur can to some extent direct the network from a central position. Mønsted has argued, however, that it might be more realistic to visualize the network as 'a pattern of contacts,

Table 6.2 Contrasting strong and weak ties

Differentiator	Strong Ties	Weak Ties
The amount of time spent on the relationship	Interacted with at least twice a week	Less than twice a week but more than once a year
The emotional intensity and intimacy of the relationship	Will probably be considered as friends, or close friends	Will probably be considered as acquaintances
The level of reciprocal services	Will do a lot for us, and we for them. The services may be social or professional (advice, information, services)	Will carry out fewer services for us, and we for them
The number of each type of relationship	Most people have a fairly small network of strong ties	Weak-tie networks will contain many more people, at least potentially
The benefits of each type of tie	Trust, loyalty, openness, reliability, altruism	Diversity of information and resources
The disadvantages of each type of tie	May be sterile, and too homogeneous	May lack the necessary trust and loyalty to deliver resources when needed
The cost of the services	Usually a mutually fair price, often very good value, may even be free, in monetary terms	More costly, in money terms, than strong

the socio-centred network: a spider's web' (Mønsted 1995). This also allows more scope for the study of network changes, or dynamism.

Density is another important structural facet: How many people in the entrepreneur's network also know each other? If the network is dense, and most alters are also known to each other, information will pass quickly through the network (Aldrich, Rosen and Woodward, 1987; Staber and Aldrich, 1995). This is an advantage. However, dense networks may well be composed of similar kinds of people, and so be somewhat homogenous and sterile. Also, the more links there are between alters within the network, the less chance for the entrepreneur/ego to occupy a central, or hub, position.

Also of great significance when considering network structure is the issue of diversity. How diverse or heterogeneous is the network? Does it offer access to a wide range of different people, and hence to a variety of advice, information and other resources? The more heterogeneous a network, the greater the chance of the entrepreneur picking up on new opportunities. However, humans in general have a very strong tendency towards homophily: we group together with people who are like us, and are more likely to befriend similar people. It seems that the stronger the ties within a network, the more likely that homophily will be found, and, with it, a reduction in network diversity.

Size does indeed matter: how large is the actual number of contacts in the entrepreneur's contacts, compared with those potentially available? This is, of course, very difficult to measure, because it involves taking some kind of decision as to which potential contacts might be available within the locality, the industry, the customer base, etc. In general, entrepreneurs are found to have comparatively small networks, which may be related to the scant time they have available (Curran et al., 1995).

Turning to formality, it is important to ask if the network is primarily structured through membership of formal organizations, or is it informal and ad hoc? Formal organizations can include chambers of commerce, university-led technology networks, exporters groups, trade associations and so forth. Note that some social organizations are also formal in this sense, like sports clubs, political parties or churches. Informal organizations are not officially structured, and may be groups of friends or professional acquaintances. Birley (1985) argues that both formal and informal are likely to be important. Formal structures are likely to be more professional, but may be too bureaucratic to appeal to the entrepreneur.

Finally, network structure can be analysed to consider reachability: is the entrepreneur's network structured so that they can reach lots of potentially useful people? This is very hard to measure, of course, but should not be confused with simple strong-tie network size. Even one well-connected strong tie can potentially provide very extensive reachability (Mønsted, 1995).

International studies into the structure and process of entrepreneurial networking have revealed a 'general picture of a degree of broad international homogeneity in networking, offset by specific areas of national idiosyncrasy' (Drakopoulou Dodd, Jack and Anderson, 2002). Aldrich et al. (1989) examined the differences and similarities between samples of entrepreneurs from the United States and Italy. Matched studies were carried out in Sweden (Johannisson and Nilsson, 1989), Northern Ireland (Birley, Cromie and Myers, 1991), Japan (Aldrich and Sakano, 1995), Canada (Staber and Aldrich, 1995), Norway (Greve, 1995) Greece (Drakopoulou Dodd and Patra, 2002) and Scotland (Drakopoulou Dodd et al., 2002). Because these studies were international, they also indicated that networking is important and relevant for all entrepreneurs, wherever they are from. It seems clear that 'at least some aspects of business networking are generic' (Staber and Aldrich, 1995, p. 443).

For each of the variables studied, one of the nine countries (at least) was found to be substantially divergent, whereas the majority often clustered tightly around specific universal norms. Note, however, that the core questionnaire utilized throughout the study varied to some degree over time, as did the sampling frames and techniques utilized. Thus results indicate broad trends, rather than completely robust statistically valid findings.

As Table 6.3 shows, the mean number of contacts per month varies between ten (USA) and 17 (Greece), with the exception of Japan, where just 3.5 contacts per month were reported. For most countries business ties account for between 55 per cent and 65 per cent of all strong ties, but for Canada this is just 14 per cent of total reported strong ties. The proportion of family

Table 6.3 Networking characteristics across countries

	Canada	Greece	Japan	Ireland	Italy	Scotland	Sweden	USA
Mean contacts per month	16	17	3.5	11	15	13	15	10

Types of Tie (Percentage)

	Canada	Greece	Japan	Ireland	Italy	Scotland	Sweden	USA
Family	18	31	13	13	24	24	23	14
Friends	45	35	45	22	28	15	32	50
Business Ties	14	55	70	55	54	61	54	65
Other	n/a	0	4	0	2	n/a	22	6
Total %	77	100	122	100	108	100	131	135

Respondents for Japan, Italy, Sweden and USA were allowed multiple responses for their ties, hence totals add up to more than 100%. The Greek, Irish and Scottish samples selected the most important tie type for each alter. It seems likely that the 'Business Tie' grouping is somewhat larger for those countries where respondents have reported this additional dimension to a family and/or friendship tie.

	Canada	Greece	Japan	Ireland	Italy	Scotland	Sweden	USA
Percent Strangers	42	24	–	41	45	17	42	43
Average hours per week on network Maintenance & Development		44	8	29	24	24	–	11.4

Note that the Scottish, Northern Irish and Greek samples were asked to differentiate between customers and other contacts for these questions.

is much lower than the proportion of friends for Canada, Japan, Ireland, Sweden and the United States. Friends and family ties are an evenly balanced proportion for Greece and Italy (perhaps indicating a Mediterranean trend). The Scottish sample, however, was unique in reporting far more kin-based strong ties within its network, than friends. Network density, measured as the percentage of strangers within the entrepreneurial personal contact network, is very tightly clustered at between 41 per cent and 45 per cent for all countries studied, except Greece and Scotland, where networks are much denser. Time allocated to networking activity shows a European cluster of between 24 and 30 hours, with much higher time expenditure for the Greeks (44 hours), and much less time reported for respondents from the United States and Japan.

Development of networks through the entrepreneurial process

Given the networking functions and characteristics presented thus far, what have entrepreneurship scholars found out about network dynamics over time? How can we 'read' the entrepreneurial process as a networking phenomenon? How do network structure and process adapt as an entrepreneur moves from pre-start-up activities, on through venture establishment and then (in the ideal scenario, at least) on to substantial venture growth?

Networks and regional development

As well as specific entrepreneurs, and their respective network alters, networks themselves have been studied, as environments that can stimulate, shape, inhibit and influence entrepreneurial development at the local, regional or sectoral level. When the effects of venture growth described above are multiplied throughout the network, it is perhaps no surprise that at the meso level, entrepreneurial networks clustered into industrial districts or milieux have been argued to facilitate regional-level new wealth creation and innovation:

> The actual rate of entrepreneurship creates a network externality that, by favoring the concentration of a significant quantity of economic activity and by encouraging alertness, also promotes growth ... entrepreneurship possesses a self-reinforcing property, then its effect on the aggregate level of activity exceeds the value of each entrepreneurial action, and the contribution of the entrepreneurial sector to economic growth is more than proportional to the relative size of the sector itself. (Bygrave and Minitti, 2000, p. 25)

The parallels between industrial district/industrial milieu (Camagni, 1991) literature and the network literature are ever clearer (Pihkala, Varamäki and Vesalainen, 1999), with community-based trust acting perceived in both as an essential ingredient in the development of regionally dispersed, but potentially available, competencies. This is perhaps not surprising: the ego-centric networks of entrepreneurs have often been shown to be embedded in wider 'socio-centric' networks, from which they draw, and to which they contribute, in a 'dynamic interplay' (see Lechner and Dowling, 2003, p. 4). The recursive nature of these interactions is also increasingly well recognized (Boisot and Cohen, 2000): the network is enacted by its actors, who are in turn shaped by the network's influences, opportunities and constraints.

One of the major themes pulling the network and industrial district literature together is the recognition of the importance of collective learning and knowledge creation within networked clusters (Camagni, 1991; Pages and Garmise, 2003), mediated through trust-based informal social relationships and exploiting intangible, un-traded interdependencies (DePropris, 2000; Johannisson and Mønsted, 1997; Storper, 1995). Learning is, after all, a social process, so it should come as no great surprise that it is often 'located in the

Table 6.4 Development of networks through the entrepreneurial process

	Stage 1: Pre-start-up	Stage 2: Establishment	Stage 3: Growth
Larson and Starr (1993)	Identifying key contacts to secure resources Significant time expended tapping existing social contacts – family, friends and business contacts Building new instrumental (quid pro quo) contacts	Relationships become multiplex: instrumental become social Social ties take on added economic dimensions Governance moves to trust and reputation-maintenance	Relationships become still more complex More and higher quality information exchange Continued interaction becomes routinized
Lechner and Dowling (2003)	New firms initially use their social networks to build a foundation for their ventures	Increase sales substantially by developing marketing networks Leverage their technological base by co-opetition networks	Some co-opetition networks extended into full technological partnering Relational limits are reached
Anderson, Jack & Drakopoulou Dodd series	Family members are often especially important and promote entrepreneurship, identify opportunities, offer practical assistance, provide specialized advice and act as sounding blocks Former colleagues and customers offer a mid-level entry point for the new venture	Recognizing the need to shift the level, managerial position and status of contacts to a higher plane Gathering a very wide pool of potential strong-tie contacts, pre-tested for affective affinity and pre-assessed for position, resources and knowledge	Internalizing high-level strong ties through the mechanism of board directorates Building strong ties – often through a brokered connection – to explore specific new product, service and market development Innovating products and services in line with the articulated needs of these new strong ties

(continued)

Table 6.4 Continued

	Stage 1: Pre-start-up	Stage 2: Establishment	Stage 3: Growth
Greve and Salaff (2003)	Most time spent on developing and maintaining key contacts	More time spent on network expansion, building new ties	New ties being fully 'exploited' as growth drivers
Additional evidence	Early *social* ties, often drawn from an immediate circle of family and friends, may be essential to launch the business (Pages and Garmise, 2003; Ram, 2001)	Tendency for relationships to become multiplex (Johannisson, 1996)	Entrepreneurs can be held back by over reliance on family and friends ties (Johannisson and Mønsted, 1997)

relations among actors' (Uzzi and Lancaster, 2003, p. 398). Participation in formal networks has been shown to increase the knowledge of SMEs, not only with regard to their industrial sector, but also their own organizational capabilities, in an environment where learning is not accompanied by the hard knocks administered by the market's lessons (Human and Provan, 1996). As well as direct learning through network contacts, network transitivity also facilitates learning by one embedded network member, through the knowledge held by a second member, about a third, as shown in Uzzi and Gillespie's (2002) study.

Innovation is increasingly seen to derive from these dynamic environments where firms both contribute to and benefit from 'an adaptive system of collective learning' (DePropris, 2000). Zeleny goes still further, and posits that networks-as-living-organizations exist through information input: 'knowledge is process itself' (2001, p. 201). Similarly, Boisot and Cohen (2000, p. 130) argue that any structured organization, including, presumably, entrepreneurial networks, is 'an embodiment of knowledge'. Without innovation, whether radical or incremental, the entrepreneurial firm cannot grow (Hanna and Walsh, 2002, p. 201). Recent studies have shown that inter-firm collaboration substantially improves the likelihood of innovation occurring (DePropris, 2000, p. 85), although the type of innovation (radical or incremental) may vary, depending on the nature of the tie, and the direction of knowledge flows (Biggiero, 2001; Romijn and Albu, 2002).

The relationship between network dynamics, environmental turbulence and industrial context has been postulated to be a significant determinant of enterprise growth. By facilitating innovation, acting as the embodiment of knowledge and mechanism for collective learning, and by progressively moving to the selection norms and mindsets which promote environmental fit, clustered networks are a critical ingredient in the development of local populations of growing entrepreneurial firms.

Social structure and competition in interfirm networks

Brian Uzzi's doctoral study into interfirm networks and embeddedness provides the basis for his (1997) article in *Administrative Science Quarterly* (discussed here), as well as his related (1996) *American Sociological Review* paper. As well as continuing to influence work in the field, Uzzi's study has also been very extensively cited, and been awarded several prestigious prizes. This recognition is well-deserved, and explains the choice of Uzzi's study as an exemplar of entrepreneurial networking studies, even though the term 'entrepreneurship' per se is barely mentioned in his writing. Uzzi's sample of mostly small businesses, in a sector dominated by family firms or entrepreneur-managed ventures has been adopted by entrepreneurship scholars as providing a shining example not just of method, but of very precise findings about what is actually happening within networks, between embedded ties. Like all Uzzi's work, this paper contains an exceptionally well-specified ethnographic methodology, a clarity of written style which renders even his most complex propositions accessible and a generous, rich presentation of the 'voice' of his respondents, through quotations and vignettes.

Uzzi begins by reiterating the fundamental principle upon which the embeddedness approach rests: that social ties shape economic action in ways that can have negative as well as positive effects. Uzzi notes the relevance of this approach for both sociologists and economists, while recognizing that the extant theory was not well able to account for embeddedness. Regarding economics, Uzzi argues that economic theory cannot fully account for key phenomena within networking processes and structure. Neo-classical economic theory presupposes calculating rationality, inherent self-interestedness and a concern for only price-related information. Even 'revisionist' economic approaches – such as transaction cost theory, agency theory and game theory – also struggle to accommodate, for example, the multiple roles held by network actors (as both agents and principals), the lack of explicit network control mechanisms, network dynamics which extend beyond the dyad and the tendency towards altruism often found within networks.

Uzzi's goal, then, was to provide a coherent socio-economic theoretical appreciation of embeddedness, addressing some of these conceptual gaps. He selected a very 'conservative' research environment, the 'women's better-dress firms in the New York City apparel industry, a model competitive market with intense international competition, thousands of local shops, and low barriers to entry, start-up costs, and search costs'. His rationale was that if embeddedness and related social phenomena could be found to be important in such an environment, then they must indeed be seen to be significant. Most (16) of the firms studied had fewer than 50 employees, and Uzzi interviewed the Chief Executive Officers of these small and medium enterprises. He carried out extensive ethnographic research within 23 such firms, which included interviews with CEOs and staff, extensive field observations, and analysis of financial and other data. He built a framework based on the literature, and then moved between this frame and the themes, insights and interpretations emerging from his data analysis. The results that this interplay of data and theory generated were then validated by conferral with leading industry players.

One of Uzzi's major findings was that his respondents differentiated strongly, clearly and consistently between arm's-length ties and special relationships. His study indicates that:

> (a) arm's-length ties may be greater in frequency but of lesser significance than close ties in terms of company success and overall business volume and that
>
> (b) stringent assumptions about individuals being either innately self-interested or cooperative are too simplistic, because the same individuals simultaneously acted 'selfishly' and cooperatively with different actors in their network – an orientation that was shown to be an emergent property of the quality of the social tie and the structure of the network in which the actors were embedded. (1997, p. 42)

With regard to the special relationships, or embedded ties, Uzzi identified three critical regulating components: 'trust, fine-grained information transfer, and joint problem-solving arrangements' (1997, p. 42).

Uzzi finds that trust is essentially heuristic, a shared assumption that embedded ties will not seek their own advantage, and that it emerges from a shared history of doing more than is demanded for each other in an un-negotiated, un-enforced reciprocation of favours. It is not calculative in nature, and it is not associated with arm's-length ties. If repeatedly infringed it can also be withdrawn, but this mutual care for each other's interests is clearly valued by Uzzi's respondents. As one of them states:

> With people you trust, you know that if they have a problem with a fabric they're just not going to say, 'I won't pay' or 'take it back'. If they did then we would have to pay for the loss. This way maybe the manufacturer will say, 'OK so I'll make a dress out of it or I can cut it and make a short jacket instead of a long jacket'. (1997, p. 43)

The second embedded tie process Uzzi identified was the transfer of fine-grained information which went far beyond simple price data, but instead comprised 'chunks' of sometimes tacit expert knowledge specific to the industry, such as 'style'. Uzzi demonstrates very clearly the richness, privacy and specificity of this fine-grained information, which he illustrates with the following quotation from a respondent:

> A designer explained how these factors improve a firm's ability to bring products to market quickly and to reduce errors: 'If we have a factory that is used to making our stuff, they know how it's supposed to look. They know a particular style. It is not always easy to make a garment just from the pattern. Especially if we rushed the pattern. But a factory that we have a relationship with will see the problem when the garment starts to go together. They will know how to work the fabric to make it look the way we intended. A factory that is new will just go ahead and make it. They won't know any better.' (1997, p. 46)

The third element identified by Uzzi was joint problem solving, where strong understanding of each other's business, and a sense of ownership of mutual success, promoted alters into taking responsibility for fixing problems that arose with their work for each other. By stimulating innovation and learning, the overall network is enriched through this process, of which Uzzi provides a graphic illustration:

> a contractor showed me a dress that he had to cut to different sizes depending on the dye color used because the dye color affected the fabric's stretching. The manufacturer who put in the order didn't know that the dress sizes had to be cut differently to compensate for the dyeing. If the contractor had not taken the initiative to research the fabric's qualities, he would have cut all the dresses the same way – a costly mistake for the manufacturer and one for which the contractor could not be held responsible. Both the manufacturer and the contractor reported that this type of integration existed only in their embedded ties, because their work routines facilitated troubleshooting and their 'business friendship' motivated expectations of doing more than the letter of a 'contract'. (1997, p. 47)

Uzzi also found that the more dense a network becomes, the greater the embedded nature of ties, and the less like an atomistic market the network becomes. In terms of benefits emerging from this type of structurated process, he argues for economies of time due to greater speed in decision making and problem solving, whose speediness also improves allocation within the market and reduces waste of resources. Uzzi proposes that search processes will be deeper in networks characterized by a high number of embedded ties, and wider in networks with more arm's-length relationships. Problems within special relationships are not solved in a zero-sum fashion, but in an integrative, positive-sum way that aims to enhance the benefits to all involved. Equally, risk is managed differently in a network characterized by embeddedness, because matching of investors with new projects, new technologies, new ventures and new fashions is underwritten by the network norms and the social capital of the entrepreneurs. The multiplex nature of embedded ties – where relationships have many layers, many roles – promotes such brokerage of investing within the network. These networks are also more adaptable and flexible than those run along strictly 'rational', self-interested economic lines, due to their speed, their deep problem solving, their enhanced risk sharing and opportunity-pursuit collaborations, their potential to pool resources and their reluctance to exit alliances.

In spite of all these benefits to the embedded network structure, Uzzi also reminds us of potential dangers, which include the unexpected exit of a core network player, institutional forces pushing towards rational atomistic decision making and over-embeddedness stifling the economic element in the network to an untoward degree. He concludes that it is very helpful to be connected to an interfirm network primarily through strong, special embedded ties (for all the reasons discussed above), but that the network itself is optimally comprised of a mixture of arm's length and embedded ties, so as to avoid the dangers of over-embeddedness (like sterility and heightened exposure to exogenous shocks).

The various components which come together to make Uzzi's study such a classic include the sound empirical foundation upon which he builds, his clear appreciation of the theoretical implications of his analysis within the broad sweep of related scholarship and the detailed and precise description of the processes that he has identified between embedded ties. Many of these traits can also be found in other studies of entrepreneurial networks, and perhaps explain the contribution which this approach continues to make, as it bridges the gap between economics and sociology.

Contributions in summary

To reiterate, a substantial contribution of scholarship addressing entrepreneurial networking has been its recognition of the variation that a range of factors can generate upon otherwise similar structures, processes and practices. Research into entrepreneurial networks has shown a capacity to address areas of broadly universal process and practice, while also recognizing specific contingencies that shape variations on this theme. Gender, ethnicity, rurality and – as we examined in more detail above – national differences, as well as stage in the entrepreneurial process, have all been shown to impact entrepreneurial networking.

A further benefit of networking approaches is in that they have been adapted, adopted and applied in a variety of ways by entrepreneurship scholars associated with diverse perspectives. This chapter commenced with the observation that networking approaches bridge a potential gap between sociological and economic theories of entrepreneurship, and we have also discussed overlaps with industrial district scholarship. However, the potential usefulness and reach of networking theory as a bridging concept goes much further than this. Most obvious, perhaps, is its role in explaining how micro-decisions impact upon meso-level structures and processes. Also relevant is the connection between network theory and other perspectives from management and the social sciences. For example, the early work on entrepreneurial networks emphasized the importance of these structures as mechanisms for identifying, securing and organizing a unique set of resources for the new venture. Such approaches have much in common with resource-based theories of the firm, as Johannisson and Mønsted (1997) have pointed out.

Social psychologists recognize the importance of socio-economic context and embedded experiences in shaping cognitive schemata and heuristics. We perceive the world, analyse it, interact with it and enact it as social beings, using mental frameworks which are largely learnt. The social desirability of entrepreneurship within a specific milieu, for example, will have a substantial impact upon the quantity, quality and nature of individual entrepreneurial intentions within that networked setting.

A further advantage of networking scholarship is that it has shown itself amenable to a number of methodological tools. Survey instruments have been used to gather quantitative data about, for example, network structure. Ethnographic studies, like Uzzi's, have provided rich insights. Indeed, it is worth reminding ourselves that a second phase in Uzzi's (doctoral) study involved administering and analysing a structured quantitative survey.

Overall, then, it is clear that 'social networks, in diverse ways, provide entrepreneurs with a wide range of valuable resources not already in their possession and help them achieve their goals' (Klyver and Hindle, 2007, p. 22).

Critique and future directions

In spite of the substantial contributions made in the past two decades by scholars of entrepreneurial networking, gaps, limitations and weaknesses of course remain. For example, several of the various sampling frames used in the series of international studies have been criticized for reflecting interests in specific groups, or for being opportunistic in nature (Klyver and Hindle, 2007).

Other weaknesses with studies of entrepreneurship networks have also been identified. Paramount among these is a call for longitudinal studies, which engage in field work over a substantial period of time, so as to capture more fully the subtleties of network development and dynamics over time. Thus far, only a handful of studies in the field have adopted a longitudinal methodology, so that opportunities for deeper understanding of networking processes over time certainly exist.

A further issue is related to the lack of multi-level work. Studies have tended to focus either at the level of the network itself, or at the level of individual entrepreneurs. Not enough as yet have succeeded in a simultaneous examination of the individual and their network. Similarly, while entrepreneurial egos have been interviewed, and surveyed, in great numbers about their networking practices, it has proved hard to gather complementary insights from their alters, or ties.

As Slotte Kock and Covielle (2010) have recently pointed out, an over-reliance on teleological and lifecycle process approaches to studying entrepreneurial networks has meant perhaps a lack of a more dialectic approach. As a corollary to this, topics of potential importance, such as power, control and exploitation within the network, have barely been touched upon.

Perhaps most significantly, it has also been argued that the recent popularity of networking studies overestimates the significance of such approaches to all groups of entrepreneurs. Essentially, it is suggested that economic, commercial and financial aspects of entrepreneurial decision making may be neglected in the face of a dominant socio-cultural networking approach. Bates (1994), for example, has argued that Asian immigrant entrepreneurs in the United States are *less* likely to succeed if they rely on social networks and strong ties to support their ventures. His empirical study rather indicates that strong investment of human and financial capital in a new venture is the key to success. His wider point – that entrepreneurial networks can become introspective, sterile, local circles of ever-smaller conservative businesses serving ever-fewer customers – is certainly worth taking cognizance of. It must be noted, for example, that not all networks (or clusters) are growth-generating. Indeed, as successful networks become established, it can be very hard indeed for them to continue to act in an innovative and creative fashion. As 'norms and behaviours become entrenched, so that change and innovation are severely restricted' (Drakopoulou Dodd et al., 2006), a 'transformative Schumpeterian model of entrepreneurship' is precluded (Venkataraman, 2004). Ram (1994) has suggested this inhibiting factor of the network may be especially relevant for ethnic minority entrepreneurs, where more rational economic decision making is supplanted by the socio-cultural demands of the ethnic community.

Although much has been learned about entrepreneurial networks, and their importance is now well established, much remains to be done. More longitudinal work, more rigorous and comparable sampling frames, stronger attempts to work across levels of analysis and a deeper appreciation of dialectic issues are all areas where more work would be beneficial.

The message for entrepreneurs

The first and most important message for entrepreneurs to emerge from this research perspective is that networks matter very much indeed. Strong ties, in particular, deliver a rich, timely, specific and relevant stream of resources to the entrepreneur. Spending time on building friendships, on socializing with people, on earning their trust by going the extra mile for them, can be seen as a substantial investment in one's venture. This is not to recommend a calculative, rational, rather cold-hearted approach to hunting down suitable contacts and courting them. Rather, an open and even altruistic willingness to embed oneself in a network of mutually supporting relationships, and to live up to one's commitments to network partners is a key element in the entrepreneurial process. Becoming embedded in a strong and innovative network potentially provides a wealth of benefits to the entrepreneur, including speedy and accurate information, high-quality resources on favourable terms, personal legitimation and a social mechanism which inhibits malfeasance.

The dangers of over-embeddedness should also be recalled, nevertheless, as well as the importance of some weaker ties to act as structural bridges enhancing diversity of informational and other resources at the entrepreneur's disposal. Too many strong ties, and too insular a network, can lead to sterility of information and norms, to entrepreneurial ossification.

Further reading

Anderson, A. S., Drakopoulou-Dodd and S. Jack, Network Practices and Entrepreneurial Growth, *Scandinavian Journal of Management*, 26(2) (2010) 121–133.

Burt, R. S., *Structural Holes* (Cambridge, MA: Harvard University Press, 1992).

Granovetter, M., 'The Strength of Weak Ties', *American Journal of Sociology*, 78(6) (1973) 1360–1380.

Jack, S. L., 'Approaches to Studying Networks: Implications and Outcomes', *Journal of Business Venturing*, 25, no. 1 (2010) 120–137.

Hoang, P. and B. Antoncic, 'Network-Based Research in Entrepreneurship: A Critical Review', *Journal of Business Venturing*, 18(2) (2003) 165–187.

Larson, A., 'Network Dyads in Entrepreneurial Settings: A Study of the Governance of Exchange Relationships', *Administrative Science Quarterly*, 37 (1992) 76–104.

Lechner, C. and M. Dowling, 'Firm Networks: External Relationships as Sources for the Growth and Competitiveness of Entrepreneurial Firms', *Entrepreneurship and Regional Development*, 15(1) (2003) 1–26.

Uzzi, B., 'Social Structure and Competition in Interfirm Networks', *Administrative Science Quarterly*, 42:1 (1997) 37–70.

Questions for discussion

How much homogeneity and heterogeneity do you judge there to be across entrepreneurial networks? Can you identify any underlying causal themes which might explain the nature of differences in the structures and processes of entrepreneurial
networking?

There has been much debate about whether strong or weak ties are the most helpful
network relationships for entrepreneurs. Given the dynamic nature of entrepreneurship over time and (social) space, which do you believe to be the most important
type of tie?

Consider an entrepreneurial story (of success or failure) with which you are very familiar.
Map key concepts from the networking literature onto this story, and critically assess
the insights which your networking analysis reveals to you.

CHAPTER 7

Entrepreneurship and Neo-Institutional Theory

Paul Tracey

Introduction

A cursory analysis of the contents of the major management and organizational journals would reveal that entrepreneurship has become a significant focus of inquiry in these outlets. It would also reveal that institutional analysis has become one of the most prominent, perhaps the most prominent, theoretical approach adopted in these journals. It is perhaps surprising, then, that relatively few researchers have sought to bring the two together, and to draw on neo-institutional theory to study entrepreneurship. However, although the literature is relatively limited in size, I see the contribution of neo-institutional theory to entrepreneurship research as being very significant indeed – it provides a novel set of insights with profound implications for the entrepreneurial process; insights that are not provided by any other theoretical perspective included in this volume.

Neo-institutional theory: An overview

A sensible starting point for a chapter on the relevance of neo-institutional theory for the study of entrepreneurship is to consider the foundational concept in institutional analysis, namely institutions. You might suppose that this would be a relatively simple task. After all, neo-institutional theory is more than 30 years old; surely researchers must agree on some kind of definition by now? If only it was so simple! There are many definitions and no agreement as to precisely what the concept means. Lawrence and Suddaby's description of institutions as 'enduring elements in social life ... that have a profound effect on the thoughts, feelings and behaviour of individual and collective actors' (2006, p. 216) has the advantage of clarity and parsimony, unlike many of the more commonly used definitions, and is the one I use here. In the context of entrepreneurship we can think of business planning, formal accounting controls, the banking system and venture capital as institutions that each have profound effects on the thoughts, feelings and behaviour of entrepreneurs.

The neo-institutional view of institutions is essentially a cognitive one in which the behaviour of actors is not simply considered to be influenced by the social context in which they operate but is actually 'constructed in and by it' (Meyer, 2008, p. 794). This constructivist perspective on institutions is rooted in a phenomenological ontology and represents a clear departure from the realist conception of institutions that underpins much institutional thinking in economics and political science. The emphasis is on systems of meaning that guide action, with the role of symbols and language featuring particularly prominently. From this perspective, 'actorhood is a role or identity, as in a theatrical world' (Meyer, 2008, p. 794), with actors working from a series of institutionalized scripts or logics[1] that shape their responses to particular situations. Interestingly, despite their phenomenological underpinnings, both qualitative and quantitative methodological approaches are deemed legitimate ways of studying institutional dynamics within neo-institutional theory, although there has been a shift in emphasis from quantitative to qualitative research as neo-institutionalism has become increasingly concerned with agency and change.

While institutional approaches to the study of organizations can be traced to the middle part of the twentieth century (Selznick, 1949), the theoretical building blocks of what is now known as neo-institutional theory (and sometimes as new institutional theory or as organizational institutionalism) is much more recent, dating back to a series of seminal papers in the late 1970s and early 1980s (DiMaggio and Powell, 1983; Meyer and Rowan, 1977; Tolbert and Zucker, 1983; Zucker, 1977). These papers continue to form the basis of much work in institutional theory although, as noted below, there have also been significant developments in neo-institutional thinking since these papers first appeared in print.

This early work had a profound impact on the study of organizations. As Greenwood et al. (2008) note, they were published at a time when organization theory assumed that managers made rational or boundedly rational decisions on the basis of maximizing organizational efficiency and effectiveness. Meyer and Rowan's (1977) seminal insight that many formal practices in organizations are rational myths that reflect socially legitimate behaviour rather than technical efficiency or enhanced co-ordination challenged these assumptions. Thus organizations are managed in particular ways not because they are 'optimal' or maximize value creation, but because they are considered appropriate behaviour in a particular context and because conformity is a prerequisite for legitimacy[2] – and hence survival – in a given industry or sector. However, because legitimate practices are not necessarily the most efficient, organizations may adopt practices that adversely affect their performance. Because organizations in a given industry or sector of the economy face similar legitimacy pressures, early work in neo-institutional theory emphasized that they may become isomorphic (i.e. more similar) to one another over time. Indeed, the notion of *isomorphism* constituted the main focus of neo-institutional analysis at this time.

By the late 1980s and early 1990s, however, a number of problems with neo-institutional theory had become apparent; particularly with respect to its conceptualization of isomorphism. Greenwood et al. (2008) point out that isomorphism was originally intended to explain the relationship between organizations and the institutional contexts in which they are embedded, but quickly came to be (mis)understood as a process whereby organizations respond in identical fashions to their institutional contexts. This caricature of the concept of isomorphism – which twisted subtly the assumptions underpinning Meyer and Rowan (1977) – undermined neo-institutional scholarship and raised a number of inconsistencies in some neo-institutional thinking (Greenwood et al., 2008).

First, the idea that isomorphism has such pervasive effects is inconsistent with the empirical observation that a range of different organizational forms and practices co-exist in particular industries and sectors; it is clear that organizations respond to their institutional contexts in different ways. It is also clear that institutional contexts and the rational myths that characterize them are interpreted in different ways by actors in different organizations, in part because these rational myths are often ambiguous and contradictory and in part because different organizations experience their environment in different ways. Second, the spread of a particular practice across a population of organizations need not necessarily be indicative of the forces of legitimacy; firms may well adopt a new practice because it appears to have beneficial effects for competitive advantage and because failing to do so would undermine their market position. The assumption that organizations' motivation for the adoption of particular practices is rooted in their leaders' desire to be considered legitimate rather than 'rational' considerations based on market conditions encapsulated the weaknesses of institutional theory at this time: it denied actors agency and the capacity to behave in ways that are inconsistent with prevailing institutional conditions. Third, and perhaps most significantly, how could a theory based around the notion of conformity explain organizational behaviour in a world that was increasingly concerned with innovation? Indeed, early neo-institutional theory did not contain within it a satisfactory explanation for institutional change (the idea that change was rooted in environmental jolts or exogenous shocks, the orthodoxy at this point in the theory's development, again denied a role for agency or strategic action).

At this juncture the implications of neo-institutional theory for entrepreneurship research was limited to the idea that entrepreneurs needed to be legitimate in order to be viable, and that to be legitimate entrepreneurs need to imitate other firms in the same industry. It is perhaps unsurprising, then, that few entrepreneurship scholars chose to adopt a neo-institutional perspective during the 1980s and early 1990s. Over the past 15–20 years, however, and partly in response to the concerns outlined above, institutional theorists have become increasingly interested in understanding processes of institutional change and the role of agency in this process. Greenwood and Hinings' (1996) paper in the *Academy of Management Review*, which sought to combine 'the old and the new institutionalism' through an examination of the processes through which 'individual organizations retain, adopt, and discard templates for organizing' (1996, p. 1022), represents an especially significant contribution, and was a critical moment in neo-institutional theory's development. A special issue of the Academy of Management Journal on institutional change (Dacin, Goodstein and Scott 2002) provided important empirical evidence that augmented neo-institutional theory's agentic turn. Around this time the notion of institutional entrepreneurship, first proposed by DiMaggio (1988), in which organized actors 'leverage resources to create new institutions or transform existing ones' (Maguire, Hardy and Lawrence, 2004, p. 657), became a key concept in institutional theory. In another important development Lawrence and Suddaby (2006) proposed the notion of institutional work – 'the purposive action of individuals and organizations aimed at creating, maintaining and disrupting institutions' (2006, p. 215). In doing so they extended institutional theory's capacity to explain the role of agency in institutional change by categorizing the different types of strategies that actors employ when seeking to manipulate their environment.

Neo-institutional theory's recent focus on agency and change has provided new opportunities to connect entrepreneurship and neo-institutional theory. The result has been a gradual increase in scholarship in the leading management journals studying entrepreneurship through the lens of neo-institutional theory. Specifically, this emerging stream of research has shown the variety of ways in which entrepreneurs seek to build legitimacy for their ventures, with a particular focus on discursive and symbolic action. It has also highlighted the role of social movements and institutional change in the creation of opportunities for entrepreneurs. Finally, it has shown that entrepreneurs engaged in radical innovation often need to act as institutional entrepreneurs and perform particular kinds of institutional work in order to legitimate and acquire resources for their ventures. More broadly, neo-institutional theory highlights that entrepreneurship is a multi-level process in which social and institutional pressures should be considered alongside individual and organizational ones. I expand on these points in the next section in which I outline in more detail the contribution of neo-institutional theory to entrepreneurship research. It is notable, however, that much of the work on entrepreneurship and institutions has been conducted by institutional theorists who have used entrepreneurship as a context to extend neo-institutional theory. Entrepreneurship scholars have been less keen to draw on neo-institutional insights: the economic view of institutions (North 1990) continues to be the dominant one in entrepreneurship research.

The contribution of neo-institutional theory to entrepreneurship research

Given the relatively small number of researchers who study entrepreneurship from a neo-institutional perspective, it could be argued that neo-institutional theory's contribution to entrepreneurship research has been marginal. However, some of the insights provided by these researchers are very significant indeed and shed new light on the entrepreneurial process. In this section I outline what I see as the three main contributions of neo-institutional theory to the study of entrepreneurship: (1) the role of symbolism and culture in the legitimation of new ventures; (2) the relationship between the environment in which entrepreneurs operate and entrepreneurial opportunity; and (3) the role of institutional entrepreneurship (strategic institutional change on the part of entrepreneurs) in some kinds of entrepreneurship.

Probably the main focus of researchers studying entrepreneurship from a neo-institutional perspective concerns the relationship between legitimacy and new venture creation, with a particular focus on the use of language and other symbols for building credibility among a range of actors, thereby overcoming firms' liability of newness (Cornelissen and Clarke, 2010; Lounsbury and Glynn, 2001; Zilber, 2006; Zott and Huy, 2007). The key insight from these papers is that, because new ventures do not have a proven track record, entrepreneurs need to explain, contextualize and promote them in order to garner resources from resource providers.

Within this body of research Lounsbury and Glynn's (2001) article has had an especially strong impact. It is a conceptual piece in which the authors build a compelling set of theoretical arguments about the role that storytelling plays in the creation of a distinct identity for new ventures. This identity acts as a conduit through which investors, competitors and consumers confer legitimacy on the organization, which gives entrepreneurs access to resources of various kinds. This allows them to build competitive advantage through two types of entrepreneurial capital, namely firm-specific resource capital and industry-level institutional capital. A particularly impressive feature of the paper is the way the authors integrate insights from institutional theory with the literatures on culture, organizational identity and strategic management. Zott and Huy (2007), described in detail in the following section, build directly on Lounsbury and Glynn's work to explore empirically the relationship between symbolic action designed to build legitimacy and resource acquisition, finding a strong positive relationship between them.

A second contribution of neo-institutional theory to entrepreneurship research is to highlight the role of changing social and institutional arrangements in the creation of entrepreneurial opportunities (Hiatt, Sine and Tolbert, 2009; Sine and David, 2003; Sine, David and Mitsuhashi, 2007; Sine and Lee, 2009). This work shows that opportunities are context dependent and are not rooted solely in the skills of the individual entrepreneur. In a particularly interesting contribution, Hiatt et al. (2009) draw on institutional and social movement theory to examine the effects, both intended an unintended, of the Women's Christian Temperance Union (WCTU) on two different groups of organizations in the United States between 1870 and 1920: breweries and soft drink manufacturers. The authors show that as the WCTU gained in strength (from a small, locally based organization to one of the most powerful political actors at both state and federal levels) it not only had a major disruptive effect on breweries through its campaign against alcoholic beverages, it also had a major effect on the soft drinks industry. Specifically, by changing the norms surrounding alcohol consumption and successfully lobbying for changes in the laws governing the sale of alcohol, the WCTU inadvertently sparked new opportunities for entrepreneurs to manufacture and sell soft drinks. Some of these entrepreneurs deliberately aligned themselves with the temperance movement.

A third contribution of institutional theory to entrepreneurship research concerns the relationship between entrepreneurship and strategic institutional change (Aldrich and Fiol, 1994; Hargadon and Douglas, 2001; Tracey et al., 2011). In particular, this work highlights that in order to create and grow their ventures, entrepreneurs sometimes need to engage in institutional entrepreneurship and to engender change in the institutional environment. In other words, they need to act as institutional entrepreneurs as well as entrepreneurs. This situation is most likely to arise when entrepreneurs are involved in developing some kind of radical innovation, one which cannot be supported by existing institutional arrangements. Hargadon and Douglas (2001, p. 478) noted that '[t]he concrete details of an innovation evoke interpretations among potential adopters that are based on adoptors' past understandings and experience'. This presents entrepreneurs with a dilemma: they must demonstrate the novelty of an idea and show its value to potential adopters, but at the same time locate their idea within a set of existing institutional understandings which they must ultimately alter if their innovation is to become widely adopted.

Tracey et al. (2011) explored this dilemma through a case study of a UK social enterprise named Aspire. The two entrepreneurs who created the venture – Paul Harrod and Mark Richardson – came up with the idea of a for-profit retail business, which, in addition to generating surpluses for investors, would also employ and support the homeless. In institutional theory terms, the entrepreneurs combined the logic of for-profit retail with the logic of homeless support to create a new organizational form underpinned by a new, hybrid logic. It therefore incorporated aspects of a for-profit retail business and a non-profit charity designed to support homeless people. However, because this was the first organization of this type it lacked the legitimacy it needed from key actors, including customers, investors and the homeless community. The entrepreneurs therefore spent considerable time and effort working to alter strategically their institutional context so that Aspire was accepted as a legitimate business venture *and* as a legitimate approach to tackling homelessness. Interestingly, the authors found that while the entrepreneurs were able to legitimate their venture in both the for-profit and non-profit sectors (i.e. they were successful institutional entrepreneurs), they were unable to make the venture work commercially (i.e. they were unsuccessful entrepreneurs). Indeed, Aspire collapsed just six years after it was founded. However, the organizational form they created survived as other entrepreneurs picked up on and developed the template Harrod and Richardson had 'invented'. This suggests that the skills and capabilities required to be an entrepreneur may be quite different from those required to be an institutional entrepreneur.

Entrepreneurship and legitimacy: A 'classic' study

Part of the brief I was given in writing this chapter was to describe a 'classic' study which examined entrepreneurship through the lens of neo-institutional theory. Deciding which study to choose was not an easy task even though, as noted above, the number of potential papers to select from is relatively small. In the end I decided to focus on a study by two scholars – Christoph Zott and Quy Huy – who might not describe themselves as institutional theorists, but in their 2007 *Administrative Science Quarterly* paper entitled 'How entrepreneurs use symbolic management to acquire resources' draw heavily on neo-institutional ideas to develop their arguments and in doing so make a major contribution to the literature. I should say that I am a little uncomfortable describing a paper published in 2007 as a 'classic'. I do feel, however, that this is an extremely important paper that (at the time of writing this chapter) represents the most significant attempt to examine empirically the role of institutional forces in shaping entrepreneurial behaviour and the performance of new ventures.

Zott and Huy set out to examine the following question: 'How can … [entrepreneurs] establish legitimacy to attract enough resources to build and sell their first products' (2007, p. 74). Their particular focus was on the symbolic actions that entrepreneurs use to build legitimacy and the effects of these actions on resource acquisition. To answer their question they conducted an inductive study involving 26 UK-based entrepreneurs and their 'resource providers' over a two-year period. The interviews were semi-structured. Interviews with the entrepreneurs focused on the key resources acquired, how they were acquired, and how the entrepreneurs presented themselves to resource holders. Interviews with resource holders focused on the resources provided, the reasons they were provided, the nature of the interactions between the entrepreneurs and the resource holders, and what the resource holder liked/disliked about their interactions with the entrepreneurs.

Using the case replication method (Eisenhardt, 1989) and focusing on 7 of the 26 cases (which they labelled 'extreme' cases), Zott and Huy found that entrepreneurs were more likely to attain the requisite resources for their ventures if they performed particular symbolic actions; 'actions in which the actor displays or tries to draw other people's attention to the meaning of an object or action that goes beyond the object's or action's intrinsic content or functional use' (2007, p. 70). More specifically, the authors delineate four types of symbolic action which help entrepreneurs to acquire resources: (1) action which conveys or emphasizes the personal credibility of the entrepreneur, (2) action which conveys or emphasizes the quality of the venture's structures and processes, (3) action which conveys or emphasizes the past achievements of the entrepreneur and his/her venture and (4) action which conveys or emphasizes the quality of the entrepreneur's relationships with key stakeholders. Zott and Huy were able to show that entrepreneurs who are skilled in performing these types of action and do so frequently are more successful in obtaining resources for their ventures than those who do not perform such actions or who are not skilled in performing them.

Interestingly, the authors also identified three moderating factors that have a bearing on the relationship between symbolic action and resource acquisition. The first moderating factor was *structural similarity*. This refers to the similarity between the entrepreneur and the resource holder with respect to norms, expectations and status. Zott and Huy found that the more similar the entrepreneur and the resource holder, the less necessary it was for the entrepreneur to engage in symbolic management – resource holders familiar with the entrepreneur and/or the context may need relatively little persuasion before giving their support. The second moderating factor was *intrinsic quality*. This refers to the track record and achievements of the entrepreneur. Perhaps unsurprisingly, the greater the intrinsic quality of the entrepreneur and his/her venture, the less necessary it was for the entrepreneur to engage in symbolic management. For example, entrepreneurs who are able quickly to develop a solid base of customers, suppliers, employees and investors send a powerful signal to resource providers regarding the viability of the venture. The third moderating factor was *uncertainty* about the value of an entrepreneur's offering in the marketplace. High levels of competition and low barriers to entry were deemed especially significant in this regard. Where the uncertainty surrounding a particular venture was high, entrepreneurs needed to work harder with respect to symbolic management in order to legitimate their venture and attain the necessary resources.

The notion that entrepreneurs require legitimacy to establish their ventures successfully was established long before Zott and Huy's paper. The significance of this piece of work lies in the fact that it provides empirical evidence about how entrepreneurs go about building that legitimacy as well the effects of varying levels of legitimacy on new venture survival and performance. The authors emphasize that the legitimation of a new venture is ultimately a symbolic and discursive process in which meaning is created and communicated in different ways to different actors. In doing so, Zott and Huy illustrate the value of a neo-institutional perspective on entrepreneurship and have helped to move neo-institutional theory from the margins of entrepreneurship research.

Criticisms levelled against neo-institutional theory

In general we can say that two basic criticisms have been levelled against neo-institutional theory. The first concerns the balance between structure and agency within institutional analysis. I discussed this issue earlier in the chapter so will not focus in detail on this point. As noted, much of the early work in neo-institutional theory was concerned with processes of isomorphism and conformity. A core assumption was that to be legitimate and acquire resources from stakeholders in a given institutional environment, organizations needed to adopt widely accepted practices. However, the validity of these assumptions came under increasing scrutiny as the dominant discourse in organization studies became one of innovation and change. How could neo-institutional theory hope to explain contemporary organizational life when it did not contain the theoretical tools to conceptualize these issues? In response to this critique institutional theorists developed the concepts of institutional entrepreneurship (DiMaggio, 1988) and institutional work (Lawrence and Suddaby, 2006), both of which are designed to help explain the role of agency and strategic action in institutional change.

Interestingly, however, this new wave of neo-institutional scholarship has been criticized for neglecting social structure and exaggerating the capacity of actors to manipulate their institutional environment. Lawrence et al. (2009), for example, suggested that both the early focus on isomorphism and the recent focus on institutional entrepreneurship represent 'somewhat stylized interpretations of the relationships among actors, agency and institutions' (2009, p. 3) and berated some recent neo-institutional research for endowing actors with heroic qualities. Thus it seems that in addressing early criticisms with respect to isomorphism and conformity, neo-institutional theorists have over-compensated, the result being that questions concerning the relationship between individual agency and institutional structure remain unresolved.

The second main criticism against institutional theory pertains to levels of analysis. Specifically, neo-institutional theory has become focused overwhelmingly at the societal or organizational field[3] levels and has paid scant attention to the effects of institutions *inside* organizations, that is, the micro and meso levels. Barley (2008) noted that the neglect of the micro-level aspects of institutions is particularly disappointing because the seminal early work that characterised neo-institutionalism was firmly rooted in micro-sociology. For example, Zucker (1977) and Meyer and Rowan (1977) drew heavily on ideas from constructivism (Berger and Luckmann, 1967) and ethnomethodology (Garfinkel, 1967) to develop their arguments. Barley implores institutional theorists to return to the 'coalface' of institutions, by which he means the way that individual actors experience institutions in everyday life: 'For over 30 years, the coalface has lain largely idle while institutionalists have sought their fortunes in the cities of macro-social theory. As a result, there is plenty of coal left to mine. What we need are more miners' (2008, p. 510).

In a similar vein Powell and Colyvas (2008) suggest that we need a micro-level theory of institutionalization. They too stress that institutions are rooted in the everyday actions of individual actors. There has been too much focus, they argue, on momentous events, exogenous shocks, and heroic change agents, and too little attention paid to less powerful actors and their relationship to broader institutional configurations. Powell and Colyvas suggest linking important concepts from micro-organization studies (e.g. identity, sense-making, schemas) with processes of institutionalization at a macro level. Indeed for these authors it is the linkage between the micro and macro levels of analysis that 'holds promise to better explain institutional dynamics' (2008, p. 278) and should form the focus of neo-institutional inquiry.

These pleas for a better understanding of the microprocesses underpinning institutions have not gone unnoticed. Most notably, in 2007 the *Academy of Management Journal* issued a Special Research Forum call for papers entitled 'Organizations and their institutional environments: Bringing meaning, culture, and values back in', the aim of which was to 'reconnect institutional research with processes that occur inside the organization' (Suddaby et al., 2007, p. 468). The issue has not yet been published, but it will be interesting to see how the constituent papers conceptualize the micro aspects of institutions and the extent to which they address the criticisms of Barley (2008) and Powell and Colyvas (2008), outlined above. More recently, there was also a call for papers for a sub-theme at the European Group of Organization Studies Conference (the main European conference for organization theorists) on the 'microfoundations of institutions', which exhorted neo-institutional theorists to 'make the microfoundations of institutional theory more explicit' (Battilana, Lok and Powell, 2009, p. 1).

The upshot is that neo-institutional theory remains vulnerable to the criticism that it is essentially a macro-level theory in which the microdynamics underpinning institutions have been marginalized, but there is a growing group of neo-institutional researchers who are seeking to respond to this critique. This increasing focus on the microfoundations of institutions offers particular opportunities for entrepreneurship researchers to consider both the micro and macro dimensions of the entrepreneurial process. Entrepreneurship researchers could therefore take advantage of neo-institutional theory's renewed interest in micro-level phenomena to build a multi-level understanding of entrepreneurial behaviour. Some of the suggestions outlined in the following section on future directions for research in entrepreneurship and neo-institutional theory are concerned with precisely this connection.

Entrepreneurship and neo-institutional theory: Future directions

Despite the criticisms outlined in the previous section, it seems clear that neo-institutional theory has taken major strides forward in its short history and continues to develop new and important insights for the relationship between organizations and the contexts in which they operate. I believe these developments hold considerable promise for entrepreneurship researchers who have tended to focus on entrepreneurs and their ventures at the expense of broader social processes. At the same time, entrepreneurship offers an intriguing context for institutional researchers; the creation of new ventures can be a powerful driver of social change, and institutional theorists could improve their understanding of institutional processes through a stronger focus on entrepreneurship research.

In the introductory chapter of the *Handbook of Organizational Institutionalism*, Greenwood et al. (2008) outline eight directions for future research in neo-institutional theory. In this section, I take five of these eight points and connect them with key issues in entrepreneurship research. In doing so, I seek to provide concrete suggestions both for entrepreneurship researchers interested in neo-institutional theory, and for neo-institutional theorists interested in new venture creation.

Greenwood et al.'s (2008) first suggestion is for research that better explains the processes that underpin, and the motivations for, mimetic (i.e. imitative) behaviour in organizations – while we know that organizational actors in a given field tend to adopt similar sets of norms and practices, we know much less about *why* they do so. In the context of entrepreneurship research, it would interesting to examine why entrepreneurs in established industries and/or regions tend adopt similar strategies and templates for organizing. It would also interesting to examine why some entrepreneurs appear to 'break free' from these mimetic processes, and to create highly innovative business models based on fundamentally different norms and practices.

A second suggestion is to engage meaningfully with issues of power and politics, which have tended to be absent from institutional analysis. Greenwood et al. note that while there has been some conceptual development in this area (Hargrave and Van de Ven 2006), there is notable shortage of empirical work. Indeed, the relationship between power, conflict, control and broader institutional processes remains weak despite 'clarion calls for giving attention to the systematic structures of power and domination that define institutions and that privilege their ruling elites' (Greenwood et al., 2008, p. 25). Interestingly, the role of power and politics also remains relatively marginal to entrepreneurship research, in part because these concepts are not easily accommodated within the dominant economic approaches that characterize the discipline. One important exception is Perren and Jennings, who examine what they term 'a colonizing discourse of subjugation' (2005, p. 173). It is interesting to note that the notion of legitimating discourses forms a central strand of their article, but they do not use neo-institutional theory to inform their understanding of legitimacy. Doing so would arguably have strengthened their arguments further.

A third suggestion is a greater focus on understanding the stages of institutionalization and their effects on organizational behaviour. There is a particular need, Greenwood et al. (2008) argue, to understand the process of institutional entropy and deinstitutionalization. This raises some especially intriguing issues in the context of entrepreneurship. Specifically, what are the effects on entrepreneurs when highly institutionalized practices or technologies decline? For example, in a fascinating study Ahmadjian and Robinson (2001) examined the de-institutionalization of the institution of life-long employment in Japan. It would be interesting to explore the effects of this change on Japanese entrepreneurship. More broadly, the decay of institutions can have important effects on entrepreneurial opportunity and behaviour, which may form the basis of an interesting set of research questions for entrepreneurship scholars.

A fourth suggestion for future research is for cross-national studies. Neo-institutional theory would seem ideally suited to cross-national research, yet (until recently at least) there have been relatively few studies outside the confines of North America, and even fewer that compare institutional processes between countries. This has led to neo-institutional theory being criticized for its ethnocentrism. Similar criticisms have been levelled against entrepreneurship research, but it is interesting to note that entrepreneurship researchers appear to have gone much farther in incorporating an international dimension into their theoretical and empirical work. This is perhaps best exemplified by the growing body of scholarship on entrepreneurship in emerging markets, which has become one of the 'hottest' areas of entrepreneurship research. My view is that neo-institutional theory offers an especially useful theoretical frame for international and cross-national entrepreneurship research, particularly research that examines the effects of social and cultural processes on entrepreneurial behaviour and performance. While a small number researchers have begun to use insights from institutional theory to understand and explain entrepreneurship in emerging markets (Ahlstrom and Bruton, 2006), much remains to be done with respect to a neo-institutional perspective on international entrepreneurship.

Finally, I noted above that institutional analysis has been conducted mainly at the level of the organizational field (i.e. the environment in which firms operate), and that it is relatively uncommon for organizational researchers to use the organization as their level of analysis. This has led to calls for studies that consider how institutional processes manifest themselves within organizations or even how an organization itself 'might be treated as an institutional context for understanding *intra*organizational behaviour' (Greenwood et al., 2008, p. 29). In addition, Greenwood et al. explicitly call for neo-institutional theory to be combined with micro level theories in order to develop a more complete picture of organizational behaviour. I believe that integrating a micro perspective into institutional theory offers considerable potential for entrepreneurship researchers – the entrepreneurship literature can also be criticized for focusing on a single level of analysis (i.e. the entrepreneur), and so a multi-level approach of the sort being proposed here offers considerable potential for improved theory building. For example, the psychological view of entrepreneurship outlined in Chapter 3 of this volume could usefully be augmented by incorporating insights from institutional theory.

Implications for entrepreneurs

In the main entrepreneurship journals such as *Journal of Business Venturing* and *Entrepreneurship Theory and Practice*, it is standard practice for authors to devote a significant amount of space outlining the practical implications of the arguments presented. In organization theory, such sections are less common. This is unfortunate, because neo-institutional theory offers important practical insights that researchers often fail to tease out. In this section I briefly outline what I see as the main practical implications that a neo-institutional perspective on entrepreneurship offers prospective entrepreneurs. I do so by re-visiting the three contributions that I consider neo-institutional theory to have made to entrepreneurship research, outlined above.

First and foremost, neo-institutional theory highlights the central importance of legitimacy for entrepreneurs. A given entrepreneur may have identified a high quality opportunity but unless he or she is able to convince a range of different actors that he or she is credible and the venture viable in a given market, he or she will not be able to acquire the necessary resources to build the business. Under these circumstances the venture is liable either to fail to get off the ground, or if it does manage begin trading, to quickly wither and die. Moreover, neo-institutional theory has shown that entrepreneurs need to tailor their interactions (i.e. develop different narratives) to appeal to different stakeholders. In other words employees, customers, suppliers and investors will each be looking for different types of signal to convince them that it is 'safe' to commit resources (broadly defined) to a given new venture. Thus being an effective entrepreneur requires effective discursive and symbolic management capabilities as well as effective business planning and commercial knowledge.

Second, neo-institutional theory highlights that social change may be a source of entrepreneurial opportunities. While some entrepreneurs find ways to create value in mature or stable industries, for many prospective entrepreneurs the uncertainty resulting from changing institutional conditions opens up the potential for entrepreneurship. Often these institutional changes and their associated opportunities are driven by social movements, which, when successful, often have both intended and unintended consequences for entrepreneurs. For example, the environmental movement has created a range of entrepreneurial opportunities in areas such as renewable energy. This suggests that entrepreneurs who are able to identify changing social trends and their likely implications quickly and accurately may be in a strong position to exploit opportunities for value creation.

Third, neo-institutional theory highlights that entrepreneurs seeking to exploit radical innovation are likely to need to develop institutional strategies and engage in institutional work in order to legitimate their innovations. As Aldrich and Fiol noted, for innovation to succeed and new industries to become established, a 'new vocabulary must be coined, new labels manufactured, and beliefs engineered' (1994, p. 657). But entrepreneurs must develop these new vocabularies, labels and beliefs in ways that resonate with actors current understandings. This is an extremely challenging endeavour that requires a different set of skills from those required to create a new venture whose products or services are consistent with existing institutional arrangements.

Further reading

Batttilana, J., B. Leca and E. Boxembaum, 'How Actors Change Institutions: Towards a Theory of Institutional Entrepreneurship', *Academy of Management Annals*, 3 (2009) 65–107.

Greenwood, R., C. Oliver, K. Sahlin and R. Suddaby (eds), *The SAGE Handbook of Organizational Institutionalism* (London: Sage, 2008).

Hwang, H. and W. W. Powell, 'Institutions and Entrepreneurship', in S. A. Alvarez, R. Agarwal and O. Sorenson (eds), *Handbook of Entrepreneurship Research* (Dordrecht: Kluwer, 2005) 179–210.

Phillips, N. and P. Tracey, 'Opportunity Recognition, Entrepreneurial Capabilities and Bricolage: Connecting Institutional Theory and Entrepreneurship in Strategic Organization', *Strategic Organization*, 8 (2007) 313–320.

Questions for discussion

What role does legitimacy play in the creation of new ventures?

What are the limitations of neo-institutional theory as an approach to the study of entrepreneurship?

How might neo-institutional theory be combined with other theoretical perspectives to further our understanding of entrepreneurship? Which of the perspectives covered in this book hold the most promise in this respect? What about other perspectives?

Notes

1. The concept of institutional logics – sets of 'material practices and symbolic constructions' that constitute the organizing principles of society (Friedland and Alford, 1991, p. 248) and which guide the behaviour of actors within a particular context by providing context-specific practices and symbol systems (Thornton 2004) – has become one of the most important conceptual tools that neo-institutional theorists use to explain how institutions influence behaviour. For a detailed discussed of this important concept see Thornton and Ocasio (2008).

2. Legitimacy lies at the heart of neo-institutional theory. Summarizing the literature on legitimacy, Haveman and David (2008, p. 579) note that organizations are legitimate 'when they are comprehensible and taken for granted as the natural way to achieve some collective goal ... when they are justified and explained on the basis of prevailing values, role models, and cultural accounts ... when they are sanctioned or mandated by authorized actors ... and when those involved cannot conceive of alternatives'. Organizations that are legitimate do not need to expend effort actively justifying their existence; their right to exist and mode of operating is taken for granted by other institutional actors. High levels of legitimacy also increase an organization's

access to resources: investors, customers and employees are all more likely to want to be associated with an organization whose goals and rationale are not questioned.

3. An organizational field is 'a community of organizations that partakes of a common meaning system and whose participants interact more frequently and fatefully with one another outside of the field' (Scott, 1995, p. 56). It comprises 'all of the actors that have an influence on a particular organization, and often includes government, investors, competitors, customers, professional bodies and trade associations'. It is the principle level of analysis in institutional theory. For a detailed discussed of this important concept see Wooten and Hoffman (2008).

CHAPTER 8

Evolution and Entrepreneurship

Dermot Breslin

> From so simple a beginning endless forms most beautiful and most wonderful have been, and are being, evolved.
>
> (Darwin, 1859, p. 490)

An introduction to the evolutionary perspective

In the closing lines of Darwin's *Origin of the Species* he wonders at the force of evolution in biology, while at the same time putting forward the tantalizing possibility that evolutionary forces might be at work in other domains of study. Since the publication of *Origin of the Species* (Darwin, 1859), researchers in domains of study at times far removed from biology have expanded the key principles of Darwinian change to disciplines such as language, psychology, economics, behaviour and culture (Aldrich and Ruef, 2006; Dennett, 1995; Durham, 1991; Nelson and Winter, 1982; Plotkin, 1994; Richerson and Boyd, 2005; Tooby and Cosmides, 1992). While there are differences in approach among these diverse strands of research, a perspective has emerged which has been labelled the Universal or Generalized Darwinist approach (Dawkins, 1983; Hodgson and Knudsen, 2010; Stoelhorst, 2008). Generalized Darwinists argue that at a sufficiently general level of abstraction a core set of general Darwinian principles of variation, selection and retention can be used to describe evolution within a variety of domains (Campbell, 1965; Hodgson and Knudsen, 2004), including biology, psychology, culture and economics. In this way the words of Darwin quoted above might even describe the evolution of different forms of organizations and industries from the simple beginnings of an entrepreneurial start-up in a Schumpeterian style industry birth.

In the biological world evolution occurs over time through the key Darwinian mechanisms of variation (of genotypes), selection (of the consequent phenotype) and retention (of the underlying genotype), where the genotype is defined as the information inherited by an individual from its parents (i.e. genes), which has the potential to be transmitted to future generations. The phenotype on the other hand is the developmental expression of the genotype in a particular environment, as manifest through the physical characteristics of the organism. In Generalized Darwinism the concepts of 'replicator' and 'interactor' are substituted for the genotype and phenotype in biological evolution (Dawkins, 1976; Hull, 1988), where the replicator is defined as anything in the universe of which copies are made such as genes in the biological world. In *The Selfish Gene*, Dawkins (1976) introduced the idea of memes as replicators, where a meme is defined as a self-replicating element of culture, passed on by imitation, such as behaviours or skills, like 'brainstorming'. Interactors are defined as entities that interact as a cohesive whole with their environment in a way that causes differential replication of these elements (Hull, 1988). In this way, Hull might argue that while an individual uses certain skills or behaviours, it is the individual who interacts with the environment and not these replicators. This interaction will in turn lead to some behaviours being continued and some being dropped based on feedback from the environment. So the evolution of replicating units such as skills and behaviours over time occurs through the interaction of the individual with the world outside, as skills and behaviours are expressed through the actions of that individual. In this manner, while the details of socio-economic evolution may be different from biological evolution, the concept of Generalized Darwinism can nonetheless be used as a starting point for the development of theory in both (Breslin, 2011). These concepts of replicators and interactors are critical to explanations at different levels in Generalized Darwinism. For example, at the organization level organization forms are replicated, such as wine companies or newspapers or brewers (Delacroix and Carroll, 1983). To build theory to describe changing behaviour within organizations, scholars have taken concepts from the routines, learning and behavioural literature. In this way, Generalized Darwinism involves processes of variation, selection and retention. The next section examines how these processes of variation, selection and retention operate at two levels of analysis.

When studying organizations and entrepreneurship, evolutionary research can be broadly categorized in terms of the level of analysis. Those who study the interaction of organizations are known as population ecologists. Population ecologists study the evolution of organizational forms, where a finite amount of resources within the population determines the changing frequency, birth and death rates and distribution of types over the various niches within the population space (Aldrich and Ruef, 2006; Brittain and Freeman, 1980; Hannan and Freeman, 1977). The mechanisms of variation, selection and replication can be used to describe this evolutionary system (Aldrich and Ruef, 2006).

Variation: Population ecologists assume that firms are structurally inert and cannot change at the same rate as environmental change occurs (Hannan and Freeman, 1977). As a result variations are introduced via new foundings, and selection drives population level change. Population ecologists examine the dynamics of founding and disbanding rates of organizations within populations, studying key influencing factors such as population density, and their effect on legitimacy, knowledge, networks, learning and competition (Aldrich and Ruef, 2006). Ecologists also classify organizations into types such as generalists and specialists (Hannan and Freeman, 1977), where generalists serve the mass market and specialists serve niche markets. In terms of the resources devoted to new ventures there are r- and K-strategists (Brittain and Freeman, 1980), where r-strategists devote few resources to many new ventures and K-strategists devote large resources to a carefully selected venture.

The suitability of these organizational 'types' in different environmental conditions and population niches is then discussed and assessed.

Selection: Population ecologists therefore give primacy to the environment (Breslin, 2008), with new foundings facing considerable selection forces when starting up (Aldrich and Martinez, 2001; Delmar and Shane, 2004), including liability of newness (Stinchcombe, 1965), low credibility (Birley, 1996), a lack of both cognitive and socio-political legitimacy (Aldrich and Ruef, 2006) and a lack of well-established routines and competences (Delmar and Shane, 2004; Nelson and Winter, 1982; Schumpeter, 1934b). In light of these forces most nascent entrepreneurs start small reproducer organizations in established populations, such as online retail outlets, learning vicariously from early successful foundings. However, a minority of innovator foundings deliberately depart from established organizational forms and can thus transform an existing population or create a new one (Schumpeter, 1934b; Tushman and Anderson, 1986). Lack of legitimacy is even more pronounced for these innovator start-ups when the founding is attempting to create a new population.

Retention: Retention and replication therefore occur through the spread of routines and competences, as nascent entrepreneurs learn vicariously and copy other prior successful foundings (Delacroix and Rao, 1994).

While the population ecology perspective sheds light on the dynamics of competition and changes in founding and disbanding rates of types of organization at the population level, it largely ignores the dynamics of the entrepreneurial process at the level of the founding entrepreneur (Aldrich and Ruef, 2006; Breslin, 2008). Using the variation, selection and retention mechanisms other researchers have focused more on the organization and the entrepreneur as a level of analysis, and, drawing on related concepts from the routines, learning and behavioural literature, have described the social, political and behavioural aspects of change within organizations (Aldrich and Ruef, 2006; Burgelman, 1991; Murmann, 2003; Nelson and Winter, 1982). While population ecologists define the organizational form as the replicator, micro-level evolutionary scholars have put forward the routine (Aldrich and Ruef, 2006; Hodgson and Knudsen, 2004). Though there are many competing definitions for the routine (Becker, 2005), most authors agree that they are collective phenomena and involve multiple actors (Becker, 2004). Routines depend on the interactions between individuals (Pentland and Feldman, 2005) as they learn their parts within these patterns of behaviour (Cohen and Bacdayan, 1994), and establish coalitions or truces between those giving and those executing the orders (Cyert and March, 1963; Nelson and Winter, 1982). As a result, the routine allows for greater co-ordination between individuals (Becker, 2005), as one individual can form an expectation of the behaviour of others, which can result in decisions being made which have a greater mutual fit. While past definitions of the routine have focused on the collective knowledge of groups, less consideration has been given to intentionality and choice at the level of the individual (Felin and Foss, 2009). Felin and Foss (2009) argue that organizational activities originate in the intentions and choices of individuals, and stress the need to build these micro-foundations of routines, which are rooted in individual action and interaction. This becomes even more apparent when studying the entrepreneurial process of new venture creation. To meet this gap, the habit has been put forward to represent the replicator at the level of the individual (Breslin, 2008; Hodgson and Knudsen, 2004).

Scholars have also used the Generalized Darwinist mechanisms of variation, selection and retention to describe the entrepreneurial process at the level of the organization.

Variation: During the entrepreneurial process founders continually adapt to changes in the external world by varying both habits and routines. In some instances this might result in new heuristics or means–ends relationships being created in response to a changing world or indeed in anticipation of a changing world (Gartner, 1988; Kirzner, 1997; Shane and Venkataraman, 2000). By continually varying the firm's replicators the entrepreneur generates more options for selection, and in so doing increases the chances of finding an effective strategy in a changing business environment.

Selection: While the environment will ultimately select the organization based on its offering of products and services, at a micro level the entrepreneur selects particular habits and routines when completing key entrepreneurial activities. The enactment of these activities then results in products and services which are presented to the external world. However choices made by the entrepreneur during the selection of habits and routines are complicated by a number of factors, including the misinterpretation of environmental feedback as a result of cognitive bias, where positive outcomes are attributed to the actions of the entrepreneur and negative outcomes to external factors beyond their control (Baron, 1998; Busenitz and Barney, 1997).

Retention: The entrepreneur retains chosen habits or routines over time based on the interpretation of environmental feedback. This retention or 'routinization' of knowledge, through the establishment of habits, allows the entrepreneur to free up scarce cognitive resources for generating new heuristics and habits needed to meet the demands of a changing world (Becker, 2005; Loasby, 2007). In this way, as the firm grows the individual habits of the entrepreneur must be transformed into collective routines. Indeed, it could be argued that an entrepreneur's failure to establish a library of replicators overloads these scarce cognitive resources. As Loasby (2007) argues, 'entrepreneurship defies routine; but it requires routine and results in routine' (Loasby, 2007, p. 1104), and a failure to achieve a balance between routinization and creativity is a major difficulty which few entrepreneurial ventures overcome.

While both macro and micro level evolutionary scholars use the variation, selection and retention mechanisms as their starting point, the eventual conceptual, epistemological and empirical approach adopted will depend on the development of the theory, including choices made regarding the level of analysis and unit of selection. Population ecologists who give primacy to the environment and assume that organizational foundings are average types within that environment largely adopt survey techniques in their research. On the other hand, micro level scholars who focus on the multi-level, path-dependant and context-specific nature of changing habits, routines and heuristics have adopted a variety of methodological approaches including ethnographic studies and experimental methods. However, two key epistemological approaches have more recently gained support not only in the application of evolutionary approaches to study entrepreneurship, but organizational studies research in general.

Campbell (1974) put forward an 'evolutionary epistemology' of organizational science research, reflecting a critical realist stance, as scientists search for the 'ultimate truth' of a 'real world'. These 'Realist Evolutionary Epistemologists' argue that there is an objective reality 'out there', and that researchers should aim to generate accurate descriptions and understandings of that reality. Over time these explanations become more truthful as the idiosyncratic interpretations of individual researchers are socially cross-validated into more coherent, collective views held by scientific communities (Baum and Rowley, 2002). Campbell argued that these socially constructed theories are tested against 'real-world' phenomena, with 'less accurate' interpretations and social constructions being winnowed out through an evolutionary process (Campbell, 1974). Drawing on Popper, Campbell (1974) thus describes an evolutionary process in which socially constructed theories evolve through variation, and selective retention through rigorous scientific enquiry and experimentation. At a macro-level Campbell (1974) even conceptualized the evolution of scientific discoveries competing to fill unexploited niches in the population spaces of scientific knowledge.

While realists assume there is a reality 'out there', other 'Interpretivist Evolutionary Epistemologists' argue that in organization studies the subjects of analysis are the socially constructed habits, routines and heuristics used by individuals and groups. In this way individuals actively perceive, construct and make these 'realities', which are strongly influenced by socio-political factors. Collective, socially constructed paradigms develop within different research groups, and define the rules and standards for scientific practice within that particular tradition. In this way different paradigms restrict the phenomenological field open to investigation at any given time (Kuhn, 1996), making dialogue between competing paradigms impossible as sides disagree on how they view and approach phenomena. In this manner different theories reflect different languages, which are unique to the historical, context-specific nature of the groups that adopt them. Therefore the mechanisms of variation, selection and retention, and the concepts of replicator and interactor merely represent a linguistic tool used to present one interpretative view of changing entrepreneurial behaviour in a kind of language game (Wittgenstein, 1953). Like Campbell, Kuhn also used the metaphor of biological evolution to describe the evolution of these competing paradigms as they struggle to gain favour among groups of researchers. 'Selection by conflict' results in paradigms, which are perceived to be more successful in solving particular research problems, surviving over time (Kuhn, 1996).

While both epistemological approaches agree that theoretical perspectives or paradigms are socially constructed and evolve through variation (through the generation of new hypotheses), selection (by the scientific community) and retention (within that scientific community), key differences exist in the details of the selection mechanism. These differences can be explained by key ontological differences between the two epistemologies. Realist Evolutionary Epistemologists argue that selection is based on the 'truthfulness' and 'accuracy' of these theories in terms of their ability to explain the 'real world', and that over time only more 'truthful' theories will be able to explain these 'realities'. Interpretivist Evolutionary Epistemologists, on the other hand, argue that this 'reality' is socially constructed and cannot exist outside the context-specific, historical and socio-political interpretations of the group. Selection then becomes a process whereby paradigms which are perceived to offer better solutions to the particular research problems under investigation at that time are selected by the group.

As outlined above both macro- and micro-level approaches have been taken in the application of the evolutionary approach to studying entrepreneurship (Breslin, 2008), and consequently examples of a 'classic' study could be chosen from either field. Population ecologists have used the variation, selection and retention framework to study the evolution of founding and disbanding rates in various industries including the wine, newspaper, brewing, music recording, book publishing and microprocessor industries (Carroll and Swaminathan, 1992; Delacroix and Carroll, 1983). As noted above other studies have used the variation, selection and retention framework to study the evolution of knowledge components within organizations, though disagreement exists within this group regarding the appropriate unit of analysis or replicator. However one classic study can be used to illustrate the approach when studying the process of entrepreneurship or, in this case, corporate entrepreneurial behaviour. In this study Burgelman (1991) used the mechanisms of variation, selection and retention to interpret longitudinal empirical findings of Intel during its transition from a memory to a micro-processor company in the 1970s and 1980s. He conceptualized the changes that occurred at Intel during this period as a struggle for survival between competing strategic initiatives within the organization. In this manner, different strategic initiatives are varied by individuals, selected by managers and retained over time through learning and the development of distinctive competences within the organization. The replicator or unit of analysis in this study is the strategic initiative and not the individuals through which the evolution of these entities are mediated.

Using the mechanisms of variation, selection and retention Burgelman (1991) described the evolution of strategic initiatives through two key strategic processes, which he terms the induced and autonomous:

Induced: In this process the evolution of initiatives fits largely within the scope of the company's existing strategy and learning. As a result the mechanism of variation is constrained by the existing perceptions of managers, as initiatives are made to fit with the existing way of doing things and expectations regarding what initiatives would be acceptable and supported. Burgelman (1991) argues that Intel's top management established administrative and cultural mechanisms in order to control the internal selection mechanism at all hierarchical levels within the organization, including control systems, resource allocation rules and behavioural norms. These internal selection mechanisms in turn constrained the choices made by managers, as initiatives were chosen to fit within existing structural and cultural constraints.

Autonomous: This process describes the evolution of initiatives which fall outside the organization's existing strategic scope. Managers on the frontline of technological development or changes in the marketplace attempt to vary initiatives as they try to get the organization to move outside existing strategies. These variations ultimately result in the creation of new competences within the organization. At Intel these initiatives were internally evaluated, selected and driven by champions, alongside initiatives developed under the induced strategic process. In some cases viable autonomous initiatives were adopted and integrated into the induced strategic process, as new competences were developed and retained within Intel.

While the induced strategic process put forward by Burgelman describes the evolution of initiatives based on existing organizational knowledge, competences and worldviews, the autonomous strategic process can result in a radical departure from prevailing norms and worldviews (Kirzner, 1997) creatively disrupting the prevailing equilibrium (Schumpeter, 1934b). Balancing both processes allowed Intel on the one hand to develop existing competences within the induced strategic process, while at the same time allowing new competences to be developed outside existing practices. While the former process allows distinctive competences to develop within the organization and overcome liabilities of newness, the latter acted to resist consequent inertial effects which became established. Both processes together allowed the internal selection mechanism to follow changes in the external selection environment. Ultimately organizations need both to exploit existing competences and explore new ones (March, 1991) in order to align themselves with changes in the marketplace, and in light of this Burgelman's (1991) evolutionary view of organizational change at Intel has some interesting implications. If attention is focused on an evolving population of strategic initiatives, the involvement of individuals and managers is then viewed in terms of the structural and cultural context that both constrains and drives this evolutionary system. This in turn comes down to the management of this evolutionary process through the mechanisms of variation, selection and retention, directed at reducing and increasing variation through the induced and autonomous strategic processes respectively, to ensure that the organization follows changes in the external selection environment.

The contribution of the evolutionary approach to entrepreneurship research

Some approaches to studying entrepreneurship have studied the phenomenon at the macro level, examining how the entrepreneur establishes a new venture in face of extreme environmental selection or institutional forces (Aldrich and Ruef, 2006). For example, while the institutional approach focuses on macro-level institutional forces that constrain the behaviour of entrepreneurs and organisations, research has tended to ignore aspects of agency, change and, as a consequence, entrepreneurial behaviour at lower levels of analysis within the organization (Tracey, 2011). Other research in entrepreneurship has increasingly focused on micro-level considerations, looking at behavioural and cognitive processes used by the entrepreneur in launching a new business (Baron, 1998; Busenitz and Barney, 1997; Davidsson and Wiklund, 2001; Shane and Venkataraman, 2000), and examining the way entrepreneurs think and use heuristics to make decisions (Forbes, 1999).

While entrepreneurship research has focused both on macro-level environmental and institutional forces, and micro-level behavioural and cognitive processes, fewer approaches have examined the multi-level, interactive, co-evolution of habits, routines and heuristics in nascent and growing small businesses. As noted above the evolutionary approach has been used to study entrepreneurship at both the macro and micro levels of analysis, and as argued by Aldrich and Fiol (1994) it offers the possibility of simultaneous multi-level analyses of the new venture creation process, giving a broader understanding of the overall process than an analysis at one level only. In this way, the evolution of habits at the level of the individual is nested within the evolution of routines in groups and organizational routines within the firm (Breslin, 2008; Hodgson and Knudsen, 2004), and some scholars have explored this multi-level co-evolution both conceptually and empirically (Baum and Singh, 1994; Murmann 2003; Rosenkopf and Nerkar, 1999). This advantage becomes even more apparent in the study of small firm growth. Indeed Penrose (1959) used the 'evolutionary' metaphor of the caterpillar changing into the butterfly to describe the changing character of the firm as it grows. The evolutionary approach offers researchers the opportunity to develop an integrative theory capable of reflecting the idiosyncratic, path-dependant nature of small firm growth (Breslin, 2010; Dobbs and Hamilton, 2007). From stages of growth models, which have been critiqued for being linear, sequential, deterministic (Phelps, Adams and Bessant, 2007), to behavioural and learning approaches, there is still a relative lack of research that focuses on the process of evolving management behaviour (Phelps et al., 2007). In the evolutionary approach, growth is not assumed to follow some pre-given trajectory as with the stages of growth models (Churchill and Lewis, 1983; Greiner, 1998; Scott and Bruce, 1987); rather the evolution of competences within the firm is idiosyncratic, path-dependent and context-specific, as knowledge is acquired and utilized to overcome certain crises in a firm's development (Phelps et al., 2007; Macpherson and Holt, 2007). The evolutionary approach can thus shed light on the difficulties surrounding the integration of arriving managers (Penrose, 1959) and establishing collective practices as the firm struggles for survival (Breslin, 2010).

As noted above the evolutionary approach and Generalized Darwinism has been used to develop theory to research fields of study as diverse as language, psychology, economics, behaviour and culture (Aldrich and Ruef, 2006; Dennett, 1995; Durham, 1991; Nelson and Winter, 1982; Plotkin, 1994; Richerson and Boyd, 2005; Tooby and Cosmides, 1992). This broad application across such a wide variety of domains presents an opportunity for the cross-fertilization of ideas and new insights across disciplines. This universal appeal therefore represents a key advantage in adopting the approach to study socio-cultural change, cutting across a range of disciplines.

Criticisms of the evolutionary approach

Despite developments made in using the evolutionary approach to study entrepreneurship at both a macro and micro level of analysis, a number of critics have argued against the approach and particularly against the use of the Generalized Darwinist mechanisms of variation, selection and retention, and the concepts of the replicator and interactor (Buenstorf, 2006; Cordes, 2006; Nooteboom, 2006; Witt, 2004). Many of these criticisms are directed at the use of biological analogies in social science, despite the insistence of proponents of the approach that such analogies are erroneous (Aldrich et al., 2008; Breslin, 2011). For example, Witt (2004) argues that using Generalized Darwinism in the study of socio-economic change excludes the possibility of intentionality, cognition and learning. Cordes (2006) likewise argues that the Generalized Darwinism cannot capture motivation, creativity, imagination and deliberate adaptations within organizations. In essence these scholars assume that when an evolutionary approach is used to study organizational behaviour, entrepreneurs and the organizations they create are helpless in the face of the forces of environmental selection. In this restricted view, organizations are analogous to biological organisms unable to change their genetic structure during their lifetime, and whose fate lies in the hands of the environment.

While population ecologists might agree with aspects of this critique in terms of structural inertia and environmental determinism, no such assumptions are made when the approach is used to study the evolution of knowledge and competences within firms. By shifting the units of analysis from the organization to components of knowledge within organizations, individuals become the mediators through which the mechanisms of variation, selection and retention are played out. In this manner habits and routines are varied, chosen for enactment and retained by individuals who express their intentions, creativity, cognition and imagination. Using the Generalized Darwinian mechanisms as a starting point for the development of theory to explain this evolutionary process does not entail a commitment to a full analogy with genetic evolution in biology. In this manner critics argue against an evolutionary approach, with Witt (2004) arguing that the cognitive processes at play during the creation of a new business venture are unlike genetic selection processes, and Nooteboom (2006) arguing that the replication of genes and the replication of knowledge differ in fundamental ways. Nooteboom (2006) argues that the replication of knowledge involves intentionality, as individuals choose to replicate knowledge, or even parts of a bundle of replicators, that they perceive as being 'successful'. In addition he argues that the replication of knowledge involves an element of variation, through distortion, copying errors, extensions and so forth. Clearly such processes do not occur in the replication of genes. A commitment to using generalized principles as a starting point for the development of theory does not entail a commitment to a wholesale analogous transfer of theory developed using these principles in another domain of study (namely biology). Whether Darwinism (in the original sense of natural selection of biological creatures) includes the possibility of intentionality is not relevant to the question of using Generalized Darwinism to study the evolution of competences within a nascent or growing small business (Breslin, 2011).

Other scholars have argued against using the mechanisms of variation, selection and retention as the starting point for the development of theory to study entrepreneurship. Cordes argues that in transferring these meta-theoretical principles between domains of study the concepts become vacuous, void of content and lose their 'logical coherence and explanatory power' (2006, p. 534). Cordes in essence argues against using the abstracted concepts of variation, selection and retention as a starting point for the development of theory to describe changing organizational behaviour. However, such approaches have been taken in numerous other fields of study, including Darwin himself, who abstracted ideas from the economist Malthus's work on population growth (Malthus, 1798) in the development of his theory of natural selection. Others maintain that when the mechanisms of variation, selection and retention are used in the context of organizational behaviour there is a great deal of overlap between them (Nooteboom, 2006). In this manner the process of creating and retaining variants is not entirely independent of the process that selects them (Murmann, 2003), as individuals use cognitive frameworks to anticipate environmental selection. Similarly the transmission of routines between individuals involves an element of variation (Sperber, 1996). Indeed it can be argued that all three mechanisms are strongly intertwined in changing organizational behaviour and indeed intertwined with the evolution of entities at multiple levels, in a way that biological evolution is not (Breslin, 2011). However, this criticism still does not prohibit the possibility of using the abstracted mechanisms of variation, selection and retention to describe the changing behaviour of individuals, groups and organizations, but may necessitate a shift in understanding the evolutionary process in terms of simple, sequential patterns of variation, selection and retention that might appeal to the mental framework of a mathematical modeller. Instead it might be more helpful to view the process as a rich, complex, multi-layered pattern of interacting entities, where the three mechanisms are overlapping, intertwined and part of the same overall process.

The evolutionary approach and entrepreneurship: Future directions

As discussed above the use of the evolutionary approach has adopted both a macro and micro level perspective. What is apparent from both this research and criticisms of the approach in general is that consensus regarding the development of theory has yet to be reached. Indeed many of the key criticisms outlined above are directed at a theoretical explanation of the detailed mechanisms of evolution in organizations which as yet do not exist. Therefore the conceptual development of the approach to describe the entrepreneurial process represents a key area for further development. Disagreements between proponents of the approach centre on both the detailed mechanisms of variation, selection and retention, and the definitions of the replicator-interactor or unit of analysis.

While population ecologists analyse organizations and organizational forms, when the approach has been used at the micro level disagreement exists regarding the unit of analysis. Some have drawn much more directly on biological and genetic analogies in their conceptualization of the unit of analysis (McKelvey, 1982). In this manner McKelvey (1982) argues that the 'comp' should be the focus of attention, which is defined as an irreducible element of organizational competence, including operations and management competences. McKelvey (1982) views these comps as being combined together within organizations in much the same way as genes are combined in biological organisms. However, by selectively drawing on analogies on the one hand, while using abstracted mechanisms of variation, selection and retention on the other, this research runs the risk of leading to misunderstandings as to what Generalized Darwinism means within the wider management community (Breslin, 2011). Other researchers have avoided drawing on such analogies in their conceptualization of the replicator, with 'knowledge' being identified as the focus of analysis (Fleck, 2000; Mokyr, 2000; Murmann, 2003). In this regard differentiation has been made between replicators at different levels of analysis, with the habit at the level of the individual (Hodgson and Knudsen, 2004) and the routine at the level of the collective (Aldrich and Ruef, 2006; Hodgson and Knudsen, 2004; Nelson and Winter, 1982). Indeed the routine has achieved broader consensus within the evolutionary school as a unit of analysis, as it has in the resource-based view (Barney, 1991). Key differences in definitions of both this concept and others put forward at different levels of analysis remain to be resolved, and this represents a key area of future research. Indeed while some have conceptualized the changing behaviour in small and growing organizations (Aldrich and Ruef, 2006; Breslin, 2010), much work remains in terms of the elaboration of evolutionary descriptions for multi-level systems including the individual, group, organization, industry and wider society. A key element in this development will involve drawing from related literature in entrepreneurship and wider organization science.

In addition to differences in the conceptualization of the approach, different empirical approaches have been taken in studying concepts such as routines and habits. Given the interactive, multi-level nature of routines within small businesses it is important that empirical studies capture the process and context in which they develop, including the interaction between the founder and individuals within the group and beyond (Breslin, 2011). Routines are collective phenomena and involve multiple actors (Becker, 2004), and the resultant behaviour depends on the connections or stitching together of multiple participants resulting in a pattern of actions (Pentland and Feldman, 2005). In order to capture the degree to which collective routines act to constrain and police the behaviours of individuals within the group, they must be studied in the actual circumstances in which they occur, with no constraints on internal or external influences, other than those imposed by the development of the group itself (Breslin, 2011). While some have adopted experimental methods, it can be argued that the a priori identification, manipulation and controlling of influences can diminish the possibility of identifying the extent to which collective routines themselves can resist these same influences. While the most common approach in studying routines uses survey techniques (Pentland and Feldman, 2005), routines are treated like 'black boxes' and such an approach can lack the richness of information needed to understand the dynamics of changing behaviour. Ethnographic approaches on the other hand capture the particular setting in which collective routines develop, including the process and context in which routines develop, and the interaction between the founder and individuals within the small business.

Implications for entrepreneurs

If changing behaviour with small and growing businesses is conceptualized as a multi-level struggle for survival among competing habits, routines and heuristics, this might have some interesting implications for the way in which entrepreneurs behave and make decisions. In this perspective the entrepreneur must manage the evolution of habits, routines and heuristics through the evolutionary processes of variation, selection and retention. In this sense, the entrepreneur must firstly create an environment in which habits, routines and heuristics are continually varied, as these variants become the raw material for future competences, as noted above in Burgelman's Intel study. The entrepreneurial team must then correctly select habits, routines and heuristics for enactment over time. The alignment between this internal selection mechanism and the external selection of the company's products and services becomes critical to the firm's longer-term survival. In this sense the entrepreneur must strive to improve the 'accuracy' of his/her understanding of the marketplace, and the interpretation of feedback from that environment. Finally the entrepreneur must ensure that 'successful' competences are retained and collectivized within the team. As the small business grows, this evolutionary process becomes further complicated with the broadening of the management team, and the involvement of more individuals in key operational and strategic decision-making (Breslin, 2011). In this way, the evolutionary entrepreneur acts to innovate and experiment with different practices, by changing habits and routines used by the team. Crucially the entrepreneur strives to understand clearly and interpret feedback from the marketplace based on the enactment of these habits and routines, and select those which lead to desired performances. Finally the evolutionary entrepreneur acts to retain those successful habits and routines. In this manner the entrepreneur acts as an artificial breeder, continually varying, selecting and retaining desired knowledge within the organization to meet the changing needs of the marketplace in much the same manner as Darwin's pigeon fanciers vary, select and retain desired characteristics in their prize pigeons. Interpreting survival and growth in these terms might have some interesting implications for the eventual evolution of businesses.

A number of researchers have viewed the evolutionary approach as a useful tool or language when informing entrepreneurial management practices. In this way Burgelman (1991) developed the variation, selection and retention framework to guide and inform the development of strategic management practice within Intel, as the organization adapted to meet the changing needs of their external environment. Likewise Murmann (2003) saw an evolutionary approach influencing managerial practice in organizations, as managers establish and maintain internal selection criteria guiding the actions of individuals and groups to meet the challenges of the external world. Indeed Murmann (2003) argued that the organization's CEO might be viewed as the Chief Evolutionary Officer! The continued conceptual and empirical development of the approach offers the future prospect of using an evolutionary language as a constructive tool for practicing entrepreneurs, as they re-interpret their understanding of the evolution of their business.

Further reading

Aldrich, H. E. and M. Ruef, *Organizations Evolving*, 2nd edn (London: Sage Publishing, 2006).

Hodgson, G. M. and T. Knudsen, *Darwin's Conjecture: The Search for General Principles of Social and Economic Evolution* (Chicago: University of Chicago Press, 2010).

Murmann, J. P., *Knowledge and Competitive Advantage: The Co-evolution of Firms, Technology and National Institutions*. (New York: Cambridge University Press, 2003).

Questions for discussion

When used to study the entrepreneurial process within organizations, how does an evolutionary approach compare and contrast with other perspectives, such as the institutional approach or resource-based view?

What are the key advantages and criticisms of the evolutionary approach when used to study entrepreneurship and socio-economic behaviour?

A key element in using the evolutionary approach to study entrepreneurship relates to the identification of what is evolving or the unit of analysis. In what ways might this influence the study and practice of entrepreneurship using this perspective?

CHAPTER 9

Entrepreneurship in the Context of the Resource-Based View of the Firm

Nicolai J. Foss

This chapter discusses entrepreneurship in the context of the resource-based view (the RBV). What does the RBV have to say that the study of entrepreneurship may usefully draw on? And, conversely, how can entrepreneurship research further the RBV? I begin by sketching the RBV. I then discuss the relation between the RBV and entrepreneurship research, before I characterize a new research stream that has emerged over the last decade or so in the intersection of the RBV and entrepreneurship research, namely 'strategic entrepreneurship'.

Introduction

Strategic management is ultimately about how to best deploying input factors to serve markets in ways that result in high levels of value creation from the interaction between the firm and its customers, and simultaneously making sure that the firm actually appropriates a substantial share of the created value. If a firm has the potential to do this better than the competition and on a long-term basis, it is said to possess a 'sustained competitive advantage'? But where do such advantages come from? Who creates them, and how? What is the context for their emergence?

While competitive advantage has traditionally been addressed by strategic management research (and industrial economics), the latter questions are more in focus in entrepreneurship (and the economics of entrepreneurship), where they are linked to the notion of pursuing opportunities. In turn, according to entrepreneurship scholars this pursuit will often involve forming a new firm. Entrepreneurs are people who believe that they are better informed than other people and exploit their supposed informational advantage in the pursuit of opportunities for profit.

Though complementary, the two fields have their own research traditions, speak to different audiences, pose different questions, and so on. In this chapter, I discuss the relation between strategic management, specifically the resource-based view, and entrepreneurship. What are their relationships? What has been done to integrate the two fields? What can be done? How will practising managers benefit from a closer integration? I take a basic knowledge of entrepreneurship theory as a given and relate this theory to the RBV.

The RBV is the dominant view in strategic management (Acedo, Barroso and Galan, 2006; Newbert, 2007). Moreover, it has influenced a number of other fields in management research, such as international management, technology management, HR management and organization theory. There is little doubt that it has had significant effect on managerial practice, if perhaps mainly through related ideas on core competencies, capabilities and so on. The RBV encompasses a broad set of ideas. Thus some use the term in a narrow sense for a set of ideas based on mainstream economics about what are the conditions that must obtain for firms to enjoy sustained competitive advantage. Others use it more broadly for all approaches that somehow trace firm performance to firm 'resources', broadly conceived. This includes ideas on 'dynamic capabilities', 'core competencies' and 'capabilities' that draw on more heterodox ideas in economics, cognitive science insights and sociology.

The origins of the RBV are often claimed to be in the work of Edith Penrose (1959). Penrose explained how firms may diversify in a related manner based on excess firm-specific resources, argued that different firms would learn to extract different services from the same kind of resources and emphasized that what are 'productive opportunities' to a firm lie in the eyes of the top management team (Kor and Mahoney, 2000). Another precursor of the RBV is economist Harold Demsetz (1973, 1982), whose work in industrial economics stressed, among other things, how firm-specific advantages could simultaneously drive a tendency towards increasing industrial concentration and high returns. This implies that concentration does not cause high returns, as claimed by traditional industrial organization economics. Demsetz also explained how such advantages may derive from superior information.

Note how Penrose and Demsetz put forward ideas that are close to the phenomenon of entrepreneurship: both trace (superior) performance to unique insights that are not necessarily easily imitated. Specifically, Demsetz attributes superior performance to the 'combination of great uncertainty plus luck or atypical insight by the management of a firm' (1973, p. 3). Similarly, entrepreneurship research in economics and management sees entrepreneurs as people who believe that they have lower information costs than other people (Casson and Wadeson, 2007) and/or privileged information about, for example, the future preferences of consumers (Knight, 1921, Mises, 1949, Rumelt, 1987). Entrepreneurship consists in using such privileged information to exercise decisions over the use of resources in servicing markets and so seize opportunities. The latter are defined as hitherto unrecognized possibilities of realizing a profit. Thus there are quite striking overlaps between entrepreneurship and the RBV, and one would therefore expect their relation to be a very close one. However, this is hardly the case; specifically, at least until recently, the two research streams have developed rather independently.

In the following, entrepreneurship is considered in the context of the RBV. What does the RBV have to say that the study of entrepreneurship may usefully draw on? And, conversely, how can entrepreneurship research further the RBV? I begin by sketching the RBV. I then discuss the relation between the RBV and entrepreneurship research, before I characterize a new research stream that has emerged over the last decade or so in the intersection of the RBV and entrepreneurship research, namely 'strategic entrepreneurship.'

The resource-based view of strategy: Content and foundational assumptions

Strategic management and economics

Ultimately, strategic management is about creating and maintaining 'sustained competitive advantage' (SCA). Strategies may be defined as plans for creating SCA. SCA is thus the central thing that strategic management scholars seek to explain, or, if you like, the central dependent variable in strategy research. It may be defined as a firm's ability to create and appropriate more value than the competition on a sustained basis. In other words, SCA is usually interpreted as a firm-level phenomenon; that is, as something that somehow emerges from the interaction of members of the coalition of input owners (owners of financial, physical and financial capital) and is jointly held by this coalition. Note that possessing a SCA does not necessarily translate into superior financial performance; SCA is rather a *potential* for such performance. It may or it may not be realized.

Almost since its inception in the late 1960s, strategic management has been heavily indebted to economics, particularly the mainstream economics of intermediate micro-economics textbooks (i.e., 'Marshallian price theory'), industrial organization economics and financial economics. This is hardly surprising: central, arguably *the* central, constructs of strategic management – namely, value creation, value appropriation and sustained competitive advantage – lend themselves directly to an economic interpretation. The notion that all of strategic management ultimately boils down to creating and appropriating more value than the competition (Peteraf and Barney, 2003) can be usefully addressed in terms of very basic economics. The tools of industrial organization theory, game theory and bargaining theory can be applied to refine the analysis (Makadok, 2010).

In fact, at its core most modern strategic management theory – whether the RBV or the positioning approach of Porter (1980) – is based on a logic of 'competitive imperfection'. This means that, ultimately, *some* deviation from the ideal of the perfectly competitive model of economics explains the central phenomenon that strategy is concerned with, namely sustained competitive advantage. In the Porter (1980) approach these imperfections stem from barriers to entry at the level of industries or strategic groups within industries. Such barriers mean that firms are protected, enabling them to gain market power, raising prices and giving rise to profits.

The resource-based view

In its modern version, the RBV was developed in a string of important contributions by Lippman and Rumelt (1982), Rumelt (1984), Wernerfelt (1984) and Barney (1986). In actuality, later contributions have added rather little to the fundamental insights of these papers.

The RBV is often presented as a 'theory of the firm.' However, it would be more correct to say that the RBV is first and foremost a theory of SCA. To repeat, SCA refers to the potential of a firm to create and appropriate more value than its competition. This raises the issue of what may be meant by 'competition'. If this is taken to include all other firms, only one firm in an industry can hold SCA. However, in some formulations, SCA is defined relative to the marginal firm, that is, the firm that exactly breaks even (Peteraf and Barney, 2003). An additional issue is what is meant by 'creating and appropriating value'. Briefly, a firm creates value when it creates producers' and/or consumers' surplus (i.e., $P - C > 0$ and/or $P -$ reservation prices > 0). It appropriates value when it can capture parts of these surpluses. The better the firm is at capturing such surpluses, the higher its financial performance.

The RBV is characterized by tracing the potential to create and appropriate more value than the competition to the resource endowments of firms, and the characteristics of these resources. The crowning achievement of the high church RBV has been the formulation of criteria that must be jointly met for resources to give rise to sustained competitive advantage (Barney, 1991; Peteraf and Barney, 2003; Peteraf, 1993). The seminal contribution in this regard is Jay B. Barney's 1991 article, 'Firm resources and sustained competitive advantage', one of the most influential of all strategic management texts. Barney (1991, p. 102) explains that:

> A firm is said to have a competitive advantage when it is implementing a value creating strategy not simultaneously being implemented by any current or potential competitors. A firm is said to have a sustained competitive advantage when it is implementing a value creating strategy not simultaneously being implemented by any current or potential competitors and when these other firms are unable to duplicate the benefits of this strategy.

(Note how economics underlies the analysis: SCA is defined in terms of situations in which all attempts by competitor firms at imitating or substituting a successful firm have ceased, that is, when the familiar situation of Nash equilibrium obtains.) SCA can be enjoyed, Barney explains, by firms that control resources that are *valuable*, *rare* and *costly to imitate* and *substitute*. These conditions make up what has become known as the 'VRIN framework', or, adding the organizational ('O') embeddedness of resources, the 'VRIO framework.'

Barney (1991) is not entirely forthcoming about the precise meaning of these criteria (Foss and Knudsen, 2003). He talks about 'value' in terms of being able to exploit an opportunity or neutralize a threat in the environment (i.e., the SWOT framework). He also hints that 'environmental analysis' (e.g., Michael Porter's 5-forces framework) may be useful for understanding the criterion of value. Somehow, of course, value is a matter of driving a wedge between the reservation prices (i.e. the maximum willingness to pay of the customers) of the products made possible by the relevant resource and the costs of production of those products. However, he does not discuss how exactly that wedge arises. Implicitly, value creation is seen as something that is covered in other approaches.

A firm that possesses valuable resources may deploy them to execute a strategy 'not simultaneously being implemented by any current or potential competitor'; that is, it has competitive advantage. Whether that competitive advantage is sustainable depends on the three other criteria (RIN or RIO). The criterion of 'rareness' should be understood in a simple counting sense (implying that not 'too many' other firms can implement the same strategy(ies) as the firm enjoying a sustained competitive advantage), and the two remaining criteria refer to the costliness of imitating or substituting the resource or bundle of resources that give rise to the competitive advantage.

Earlier work by Barney (1986) established the necessary condition for sustained competitive advantage that the relevant underlying resources or the services thereof be acquired or rented at a price that is lower than their net present value. Otherwise, any competitive advantages will be offset by supply prices on 'strategic factor markets.' This is explicitly included in Peteraf's (1993) closely related contribution, which introduces a condition of relative immobility of resources: essential but highly mobile resources can appropriate most or all of the value they contribute to the firm. Peteraf also includes resource heterogeneity of resources (this is captured by the 'valuable' and 'rare' conditions in the Barney framework), 'ex ante limits to competition' (this is Barney's (1986) condition that resources must be purchased at a p < NPT to be of strategic value) and 'ex post limits to competition' (this is Barney's (1991) condition of costly imitability and substitutability).

Extensions of the basic RBV model

Much subsequent work on the RBV has consisted in elaborating, refining, extending and testing the core ideas of the RBV as well as refining the more specific criteria for sustained competitive advantage.

Resource accumulation: A central question in the RBV is what factors make resources hard to imitate. The seminal contribution here is the resource accumulation model advanced by Dierickx and Cool (1989). They argue that competitive advantages stem from firm-specific resource stocks that need to be accumulated internally. Strategists are mainly concerned with the building of valuable stocks of resources (like brand reputation, manufacturing capabilities, technological expertise) by making appropriate choices about strategic investments flows. The imitability and sustainability of competitive positions result from the characteristics of the mapping of investment flows onto resource stocks. Dierickx and Cool argue that *time compression diseconomies* explain early-mover advantages, since higher investment outlays over a shorter period of time by a follower are required to catch up with an early-mover. *Asset mass efficiencies* confer an advantage to a firm that has already accumulated a critical mass of a resource, cf. Cohen and Levinthal (1990). However, in the presence of *asset erosion* (i.e. assets decay in terms of their potential to add value), Knott et al. (2003) argue and show empirically that time compression diseconomies and asset mass efficiencies are not sufficient to gain sustainable competitive advantages.

Rather, the *interconnectedness of asset stocks* and *causal ambiguity* appear to be necessary to explain long-term differences in resource stocks (Lippman and Rumelt, 1982, Barney, 1991). The value of an asset stock depends on the presence of complementary resources, sharply increasing the investment costs for an imitator (e.g., a firm may benefit for having a marketing department and an R&D department that happen to 'click'). Causal ambiguity obfuscates the link between resources and firm performance. It points to the tacitness, complexity and specificity of the resource base (Reed and Defillippi, 1990). Recent work has particularly highlighted the complexity of a firm's resource base as an effective barrier to imitation (Winter, 2000, Rivkin, 2000). Many scholars argue that knowledge-based assets such as firm-specific capabilities are particularly likely to meet these criteria, because these have emerged through complex and path-dependent historical processes and embody a great deal of knowledge that is costly to articulate (Barney, 1991; Winter, 2000).

These characteristics also impact the ease with which resources can be traded. Thus, while generic resources may be acquired in factor markets, the firm-specific and idiosyncratic resources underpinning competitive advantages result from internal accumulation processes. Lippman and Rumelt (2003, p. 1082) succinctly summarize RBV's insistence on the primacy of internal resource accumulation:

The resource-based view predicts that firms will focus their energies on the development of complex 'home-grown' resources, taking time and care to develop knowledge, know-how, social capital, and other socially complex, difficult-to-transfer resources.

However, Makadok (2001a, 2001b) argues that resource development may not constitute the only causal mechanism for explaining competitive advantages. Firms may also be better than others at picking undervalued resources in the market for resources. They are more alert – more entrepreneurial, if you like – to the undiscovered potential of some resources. Resource-picking points to the role of strategic factor markets in explaining firm behavior and competitive advantage.

Strategic factor markets: Barney (1986) characterized markets for resources as strategic factor markets. Discounting luck, firms may only acquire resources below their net present value by forming heterogeneous expectations about resource value. Otherwise, prospective buyers bid up the price to the resource's net present value and the seller appropriates the value from the resource (Capron and Shen, 2007). Much subsequent research on strategic factor markets has focused on the origins of differential expectations about resources. Makadok and Barney (2001) analyse differences in the information acquisition strategies of firms, while Denrell, Fang and Winter (2003) point to entrepreneurial serendipity to explain the acquisition of undervalued resources. A second line of inquiry has focused on co-specialization among heterogeneous resources (Adegbesan, 2009; Lippman and Rumelt, 2003; Teece, 1986). Even with perfect information, heterogeneous firms may place different values on a complementary resource in a strategic factor market. With resource heterogeneity among buyers, gains from resource trade are not dissipated in a competitive bidding process and at least some of the resource value is appropriated by the buyer.

Bargaining: Work on strategic factor markets points to the more general problem of bargaining resource owners (Peteraf, 1993). Bargaining among resource owners has attracted a great deal of attention in recent contributions to the RBV. Coff (1997, 1999) argues that value appropriation among resource owners (e.g., employees, shareholders, suppliers) fundamentally depends on the bargaining power of each resource owner. He shows how resource mobility systematically influences the bargaining position of resource owners. Lippman and Rumelt (2003) and Adgbesan (2009) draw on (co-operative) game theory to analyse how co-specialization among resources systematically changes the outside options for resource owners and thereby determines their relative bargaining positions. MacDonald and Ryall (2004) add to this emerging stream of literature by establishing the necessary conditions for value appropriation. They highlight the importance of competition for a scarce resource among different resource coalitions for value appropriation. Blyler and Coff (2003) add a social dimension to the bargaining problem by stressing the role of social capital for attaining and leveraging bargaining power.

Empirical work

Despite its broad theoretical appeal and strong influence on managerial education and practice, the empirical track record of the key tenets of the RBV has so far been somewhat modest (Priem and Butler 2001a, 2001b). Hoopes and Madsen (2008) argue that the RBV lacks a cumulative body of work showing how firms differ in their resource bases. In survey articles on the empirical support for the RBV, Armstrong and Shimizu (2007) and Newbert (2007) find only modest support for the key tenets of the RBV that connect resource characteristics to sustained profitability; see also Crook et al. (2008) for a meta study that finds more robust support. Arend (2006) argues (1) that resources that meet the VRIO criteria are usually only identified *ex post*, making the explanation circular; (2) the RBV is mainly used as a convenient framing device and specific implications of the view are seldom tested; (3) the link between resources and performance is not carefully examined, for example, in terms of organizational variables that mediate this link; (4) key resources are hard to measure, particularly those 'socially complex' and 'tacit' resources that the view often focuses on (Dierickx and Cool, 1989; Barney, 1991) and (5) the gains from superior resources may not be captured at the firm level – but rather be captured by individual resources (Coff 1997, 1999; Lippman and Rumelt, 2003) – in which case firm performance cannot be the dependent variable.

Other resource-based research streams

The above resource-based ideas constitute what may be seen as the core of the RBV. These are ideas that primarily draw on mainstream economics.

However, many of the ideas that have popped up in the evolution of the RBV are not so easily aligned with, for example, the basic micro-economics, such as notions involving process, learning, innovation, evolution and tacit knowledge. Research streams closely related to the core RBV have emerged to deal with these more dynamic issues. They encompass the 'knowledge-based view of the firm' (Kogut and Zander, 1992), the 'evolutionary theory of the firm' (Nelson and Winter, 1982), the 'capabilities view of the firm' (Langlois, 1992) and the 'dynamic capabilities view' (Teece, Pisano and Shuen, 1997). These streams, which Gavetti and Levinthal (2004) call the 'low-church RBV', draw on the product development and knowledge management literatures in management, evolutionary economics, Schumpeterian thought, the organizational learning literature, work on leadership and alliances and business history.

While overall there is the same emphasis on firms as collections of heterogeneous resources, the low-church RBV focuses on building, accumulating, transforming, managing, learning about, combining and recombining resources, and, in particular, the services that can be derived from them. Dynamics and learning are heavily emphasized. Moreover, the low-church RBV unambiguously concentrates on resources or assets that are knowledge-based, social in the sense that they are somehow linked to a collectivity of interacting agents, and tend to put much emphasis on the tacit nature of the knowledge that is alleged to reside in such interaction.

A particularly influential contribution is that by Teece, Pisano and Shuen (1997). They argue that superior performance comes from a firm's capacity to change its resource base in the face of Schumpeterian competition and environmental change. Dynamic capabilities are defined as the firm's ability to integrate, build and reconfigure internal and external competences to address rapidly changing environments (Teece et al., 1997, p. 516). Importantly, dynamic capabilities reflect past learning processes, as they are a learned pattern of collective activity through which the organization systematically generates and modifies its operational routines in pursuit of improved performance. This basic definition has been subsequently refined and extended, but what unites different approaches and definitions is the insistence on an organizational ability to alter its resource base. Thus, Helfat et al. synthesize prior conceptual work by defining a dynamic capability as 'the capacity of an organization to purposefully create, extend, and modify its resource base' (2007, p. 4). Accordingly, dynamic capabilities may perform different tasks that alter the resource base, such as new product development, alliance formation or post-acquisition integration (Eisenhardt and Martin, 2000).

Recent work on dynamic capabilities has increasingly stressed the role of organizational processes for understanding how firms alter their resource base. Teece (2007) opens up the black box of dynamic capabilities by relating the concept to organizational processes of sensing and seizing business opportunities and the constant (re)alignment of resources, compare with Helfat and Peteraf (2009). A firm's sensing ability critically depends on the organizational systems and individual capacities to learn and to identify, filter, evaluate and shape opportunities. Once a business opportunity is identified, the organizational structure, procedures and incentives influence whether and how a firm seizes the opportunity and creates a new strategic path.

The resource-based view and entrepreneurship: What are the connections?

What is entrepreneurship?

In the entrepreneurship curriculum of many business schools, the phenomenon under investigation has often been 'small-business management'. Entrepreneurs are pictured as the managers of small, family-owned businesses or start-up companies. Entrepreneurship consists of routine management tasks, relationships with venture capitalists and other sources of external finance, product development, marketing and so on. Unfortunately, this notion of entrepreneurship is sufficiently elastic to be practically meaningless. It appears to include virtually all aspects of small or new business management, while excluding identical tasks when they are performed within a large or established business. Put differently, if entrepreneurship is simply a set of management activities, or any management activity that takes place within a particular type of firm, then it is unclear why we should bother to add this label to those activities.

It is in fact common, particularly within the management literature, to associate entrepreneurship with boldness, daring, imagination or creativity (Lumpkin and Dess, 1996). Such accounts emphasize the personal, psychological characteristics of the entrepreneur. Entrepreneurship in this conception is a specialized activity that some individuals are particularly well equipped to perform. Probably the best-known concept of entrepreneurship in economics is Joseph Schumpeter's idea of the entrepreneur as innovator. Schumpeter's entrepreneur introduces 'new combinations' – new products, production methods, markets, sources of supply, or industrial combinations – shaking the economy out of its previous equilibrium through a process Schumpeter termed 'creative destruction'. Entrepreneurship can also be conceived as 'alertness' to profit opportunities. This concept has been elaborated most fully by Israel Kirzner (1973), who follows Austrian economist Friedrich Hayek (1968/1978) in describing competition as a discovery process: the source of entrepreneurial profit is superior foresight, the discovery of something (new products, cost-saving technology) unknown to other market participants. The simplest case is that of the arbitrageur, who discovers a discrepancy in present prices that can be exploited for financial gain. In a more typical case, the entrepreneur is alert to a new product or a superior production process and steps in to fill this market gap before others.

Success, in this view, comes not from following a well-specified maximization problem, but from having some knowledge or insight that no one else has, notably in future changes in technologies, preferences, regulation, new markets, new sources of supply and so on. As Salerno (1993, p. 123) argues, entrepreneurs 'are those who seek to profit by actively promoting adjustment to change. They are not content to passively adjust their ... activities to readily foreseeable changes or changes that have already occurred in their circumstances; rather, they regard change itself as an opportunity to meliorate their own conditions and aggressively attempt to anticipate and exploit it'.

In generating superior foresight, entrepreneurs rely on the knowledge they hold. Thus Shane (2000) demonstrates how experiential knowledge, which he takes to include 'prior knowledge about markets', 'prior knowledge about how to serve markets', 'prior knowledge of customer problems', etc., influences the opportunities that entrepreneurs discover.

A general understanding of entrepreneurship that integrates the above notions, and used in the following is that entrepreneurship is the exercise of ability and willingness to perceive new economic opportunities and to introduce specific ways of seizing these opportunities into the market in the face of uncertainty (Knight, 1921; Wennekers and Thurik 1999).

The RBV and Entrepreneurship

Given the above characterization of entrepreneurship, it would immediately seem that there are multiple connections to the RBV. Like the RBV, entrepreneurship is about exploiting superior information or insight for the purpose of earning a profit, preferably over an extended period of time. Thus, entrepreneurial outcomes are also competitive outcomes, that is, they lead to the production of goods or services at lower costs or qualities that are higher than those of the competition (Mosakowski, 1998). In order to exploit an opportunity, an entrepreneur usually has to assemble a set of resources, at least one of which (namely his own specific insight) is specialized to the opportunity. He will often have to modify the resource-base as he pursues the opportunity. The insight is sometimes so much inside the head of the entrepreneur that he may find it difficult to communicate to outside parties, such as venture capitalists and other financiers. As stressed in the 'effectuation approach' of Sarasvathy (2008), entrepreneurs usually don't begin from an analytical industry or segment analysis à la Porter or Kotler; they begin with the resources, including network contacts, that they have 'at hand'. Similarly, the RBV stresses that strategy begins from an analysis of the resources that the firm controls rather than from Porterian industry analysis (Barney, 1986).

Thus, idiosyncrasy, tacit knowledge, uncertainty, dynamics, resource assembly and changes in the resource-base seem central to entrepreneurship – as it does to resource-based strategy! As RBV scholar Kathleen Conner (1991, pp. 133–4) perceptively noted two decades ago:

> In a resource-based view, discerning appropriate inputs is ultimately a matter of of entrepreneurial vision and intuition: the creative act underlying such vision is a subject that so far has not been a central focus of resource-based theory development.

Given this, it is somewhat surprising that the RBV and entrepreneurship research have, in fact, made rather little contact.

Never the twain shall meet?

However, there are some good reasons for this lack of contact. Consider first the situation from the point of view of the RBV. The key point of interest in the RBV is sustained competitive advantage; that is, a firm's (note: not an entrepreneur's) ability to create and appropriate more value than the competition on a sustained basis. First, notice that this means that the RBV is primarily about outlier firms, those few exceptional firms that are actually persistently successful. In contrast, entrepreneurship is about the creation of any firm, from the Mom & Pop store on the corner to a new breakthrough corporation based on cutting-edge theory. And some would argue that the entrepreneurship field is really about any entrepreneurial act, by individuals or firms, whether emerging or established. Second, various lists have been compiled of the criteria that resources must meet in order to yield rents in equilibrium, such as the VRIN criteria of Barney (1991). However, there is a retrospective character to such lists: their main function is to perform a kind of sort among the firm's resources to see if any conform to the criteria. Equipped with the list, a manager can ascertain every resource in the firm to check if any of them conform to the criteria on the list.

However, the list does not explicitly tell a manager how to go about *creating* strategic resources. Also, the list is not a guide to the identification of opportunities, the exploitation of which may later be turned into advantages; in contrast, entrepreneurship is all about being forward-looking. Thus, the core RBV analysis simply lacks a story about the creation of competitive advantage. All it seems to have is the admonition that managers should try to use their superior inside information so as to pick those resources in strategic factor markets that are currently undervalued (Denrell et al., 2003; Makadok and Barney, 2001; Rumelt, 1987).

Now consider the situation from the point of view of the entrepreneurship field. Entrepreneurship research has characteristics, even biases; namely it concentrates on new firm formation (start-ups), it focuses on individual entrepreneurs and it highlights the discovery activities of these individuals.

With respect to the first characteristic, Gartner and Carter (2003) declare that they '... consider the processes of organization formation to be the core characteristics of entrepreneurship', and many appear to agree with them. However, this would seem imply that already-formed organizations cannot engage in entrepreneurial actions. But there is no simple inherent reason why entrepreneurship thus defined cannot be exercised by established firms. Established firms regularly discover and exploit new opportunities. In fact, Schumpeter (1942) argued that entrepreneurship should be thought of as a firm-level phenomenon; see also Baumol (1990). If entrepreneurship researchers have nevertheless often tied together new firm formation and entrepreneurship, this is presumably because of new firm formation being an important driver of economic growth.

A second characteristic of the entrepreneurship literature is the concentration on individuals. Organizations enter the analysis mainly as instruments of the entrepreneur's vision. This contrasts with the evidence that a substantial number of new ventures are founded by entrepreneurial *teams*; that is, a group of entrepreneurs with a common goal that can only be realized by certain combinations of entrepreneurial actions (Harper, 2008).

The third characteristic of the more recent entrepreneurship literature is what is arguably an over-concentration on opportunity discovery. Following

Scott Shane's work (2003), management research on entrepreneurship has made entrepreneurship virtually synonymous with opportunity discovery. However, there is clearly much more to entrepreneurship than the discovery of opportunities, namely the exploitation of those opportunities through assembling and deploying a bundle of relevant resources, such as complementary assets related to production, sales and marketing.

Two examples of papers that forge linkages between the RBV and entrepreneurship

One of the first papers to deal with the relation between (the high-church) RBV and entrepreneurship is Elaine Mosakowski's 'Entrepreneurial Resources, Organizational Choices and Competitive Outcomes' (1998). She defines 'entrepreneurial resources' as the 'propensity of an individual to behave creatively, act with foresight, use intuition, and be alert to new opportunities' (1998, p. 625), and argues that such resources can be distributed in two ways in firms: either they are held by a single manager-entrepreneur, or they are distributed across individuals in an entrepreneurial team. However, her main interest is in understanding the organizational embeddedness of such resources rather than their contribution to competitive advantage.

Sharon Alvarez and Lowell Busenitz (2001) are more forthcoming regarding how the RBV and entrepreneurship relate to one another. They seek to extend the RBV by introducing 'entrepreneurial recognition' – defined as both the recognition of opportunities and opportunity-seeking behaviour – as a resource. They also treat the 'process of combining and organizing resources as a resource' (2001, p. 756). They analyse entrepreneurship thus understood in terms of the Peteraf (1993) framework. Thus, entrepreneurial recognition and resource organization are heterogeneous because they are based on different information, personal backgrounds, heuristics and so on; they are given to *ex post* limits to competition, because they are rooted in path-dependent processes that are difficult to emulate and because they embody much tacit knowledge; and they are highly immobile, because they are typically linked to specific resource with which they co-specialize. Except for a few very general remarks Alvarez and Busenitz do not offer a discussion of Peteraf's final criterion, specifically that there must be *ex ante* limits to competition.

Strategic entrepreneurship

The field of strategic entrepreneurship (SE) is a fairly recent one. Mainly associated with scholars like Michael Hitt and Duane Ireland, its central idea is that opportunity-seeking and advantage-seeking – the former the central subject of the entrepreneurship field, the latter the central subject of the strategic management field – are processes that need to be considered jointly. Establishing this link is particularly important in dynamic environments where advantages may be short-lived. SE involves going beyond the focus on start-ups, characteristic of the entrepreneurship field, and paying explicit attention to the established firm as a source of entrepreneurial actions. It also involves paying explicit attention to the *creation* of competitive advantages, a weak spot of the strategic management field.

In one of the early conceptualizations of strategic entrepreneurship Hitt and Ireland (2000) propose six different domains of intersection between strategic management and entrepreneurship: innovation; organizational networks; internationalization; organizational learning; top management teams and governance; and growth, flexibility and change. As this list indicates, the focus in this stream is on the enactment of entrepreneurial strategies 'to continuously create competitive advantages that lead to maximum wealth creation' (Hitt et al., 2002, p. 2). There is a strong emphasis on the top management team and its strategic intent (Ireland et al., 2001; Ireland, Kuratko and Covin, 2003). However, not all entrepreneurial actions are the result of firms having enacted an entrepreneurial strategy. Entrepreneurial behaviors can emerge from lower levels of an organization (Burgelman, 1983), but this does not yet seem to have been incorporated in this research stream.

Ireland et al. (2001, 2003) discuss the determinants of organizational level 'wealth creation': an entrepreneurial mindset, entrepreneurial culture and leadership, managing resources strategically, and applying creativity and developing innovation. However, many different variables at different levels of analysis are invoked in this research stream as determinants of wealth creation. A particularly influential construct is that of 'entrepreneurial orientation', which originates before the advent of strategic entrepreneurship (Lumpkin and Dess, 1996). An entrepreneurial orientation '… refers to the strategy-making practices that businesses use to identify and launch corporate ventures' (Dess and Lumpkin, 2005, p. 147), and is is measured by five key entrepreneurial variables, namely autonomy, innovativeness, risk taking, proactiveness and competitive aggressiveness (Dess and Lumpkin, 2005, p. 147). Firms differ with respect to these variables (Ireland et al., 2003). Broadly defined, innovation is perhaps the most examined element of entrepreneurial orientation.

Conclusions

This chapter has examined the relations between strategic management, exemplified by the RBV, and the entrepreneurship field. While the RBV has concentrated on competitive advantages and their protection, the entrepreneurship field raises questions about the very origin of those advantages. Of course, not all opportunities become competitive advantages: they may exploited, the competition finds out, imitation ensures, etc., and the profit opportunity is competed away. But some do, and to the extent that strategy is concerned with competitive advantages (and not just their sustainability), more attention needs to be paid to essentially entrepreneurial acts of creating or discovering opportunities.

Given the strongly complementary nature of the RBV and entrepreneurship, the existing amount of contact is not exactly overwhelming. There are many signs, however, that this is changing. Scholars associated with the RBV and its dynamic capabilities offspring are increasingly becoming interested in managerial cognition; they address those capabilities that dynamically act to change the firm's resource-base; they discuss the tradeoffs between exploiting existing activities and resources and exploring new activities and uses of existing resources; and so on. These developments have been going for almost 15 years. Although they may have most explicitly related to innovation research, entrepreneurship and innovation overlap very strong. For almost as long a group of scholars have been gathering under the 'strategic entrepreneurship' banner and have made strides forward in the attempt to link entrepreneurship to established firms (rather than just start-ups). They result of all this is that both strategy and entrepreneurship are changing. In fact, Baker and Pollock argue that 'strategy is succeeding in its takeover of the academic field of entrepreneurship' (2007, p. 297). This may be overstating it, but it does point to the existence of a much closer liaison between strategy and entrepreneurship – to the benefit of both.

Further reading

Anyone interested in the RBV should familiarize herself with the classical research papers, in particular Wernerfelt (1984), Barney (1986, 1991), and Peteraf (1993). These are quite accessible and are readable by most reasonably advanced students. More recent, and difficult, papers are Lippman and Rumelt (2003), Denrell, Fang and Winter (2003), and Adegbesan (2009). The founding paper on core competences is Prahalad and Hamel (1990) and the founding dynamic capabilities paper is Teece, Pisano and Shuen (1997). Foss and Stieglitz (2011) summarizes the resource-based literature of various stripes. Foss (1997) is a collection of classical RBV papers, although it may now be a bit outdated.

In entrepreneurship, it pays to study one of the classics, notably Schumpeter (Schumpeter, 1934b, 1942) or Kirzner (1973). Most students will find these somewhat tough going, particularly because they presuppose substantial knowledge about economics. More managerially oriented contributions by very influential scholars in the recent entrepreneurship literature are Shane (2003) and Sarasvathy (2008), representative of the 'opportunity discovery' and 'effectuation' approaches, respectively. The strategic entrepreneurship literature is discussed in Foss and Lyngsie (forthcoming).

Questions for discussion

A key concept in the RBV is the notion of a strategic factor market; that is, those markets where firms acquire resources that are necessary for realizing their strategies (Barney, 1986). Is entrepreneurship a resource that can be purchased on a strategic factor market?

Entrepreneurs are usually thought of as individuals. In contrast, strategic management usually highlights top management teams. Discuss to what extent it makes sense to think of entrepreneurship as something that is exercised by a managerial team.

Discuss the meaningfulness of the notion of 'sustained competitive advantage' in the presence of (ongoing) entrepreneurship.

Part III
Integrating Micro and Macro Perspectives

CHAPTER 10

Critical Realism and Entrepreneurship

Kevin Mole

Critical realism is a philosophical system that seeks to explain the underlying causes of social phenomena. It derives from work by the philosopher Roy Bhaskar and has been employed by sociologists like Margaret Archer; other writers interested in this area range from Tony Lawson in economics to Stephen Ackroyd, Steve Fleetwood, Tony Mingers, Alistair Mutch and Mike Reed in management.

Critical realism has its roots in Marxism, sharing the view that social structures are necessary to an explanation of events. Critical realism offers the researcher an overview of a situation that focuses on the mechanisms that are activated in order for a particular event to happen. Some critical realists have argued that existing perspectives lack explanatory power (Fleetwood and Hesketh, 2006). Rather than the predictions sought in a positivist approach, which finds correlations between variables, or an interpretivist view of the micro environment where the understanding pertinent to an individual is described, critical realists take a position in between the positivists and interpretivists, accepting not only that there is a world outside of our interpretation but also that our interpretation matters. Critical realists seek to find the links between the macro and the micro to explain complex phenomena in terms of the mechanisms that are present to make an event happen.

Within the philosophy of science, and central to social science, has been a well-established debate concerning the theoretical division of structure and agency (Archer, 1995; Giddens, 1979). Archer (1995) took the philosophy of critical realism and developed a general model of change using structure, agency and culture for social science. The discussion around structure and agency centres on the extent to which we can shape our destiny, versus the extent to which our destiny is shaped for us. Agency refers to the ability of individuals (or groups) to shape their environment, whether intentionally or not. Structure refers to the environment or context, often including material constraints (McAnulla, 2002). This general model is useful for looking at the interaction between structure and agency.

Archer suggests that individuals make choices within the constraints and enablements of structure. When you awake in the morning possibilities are open to you. You might decide today is the day to start a new business or today is too good to waste on work. At the same time, if you have children, you have to care for them. If you decide not to go to work today, this might threaten your job security. We all have the power to decide aspects of our lives and we all have obligations that may be imposed from outside. In social science, these two aspects, our power and our obligations, reflect structure and agency. In turn, what we decide to do may have an impact on the structural context. Archer's approach has been used within entrepreneurship: in a study of institutional entrepreneurship (Leca and Naccache, 2006), in a historical analysis of institutional change (Mutch, 2007) to examine regional and entrepreneurship policy (Hart, 2007), in a critical realist approach to social capital within business start-up (Lee and Jones, 2008) and in a comment on the theory of entrepreneurship (Mole and Mole, 2010).

It is the purpose of this chapter to review the critical realist approach and to reflect it back to entrepreneurship. To do this the chapter examines the tenets of critical realism, how Archer has used critical realism to model change, how Bhaskar suggests it should be applied in the social sciences and how Mutch (2007) used it in his analysis of institutional change, before looking forwards. First the paper examines the tenets of critical realism.

A realist view of social reality

Critical realism (CR) takes a realist view about the nature of social reality. This means that there is a reality independent of our knowledge of it. The desk in front of me has a hard wooden surface and when I leave this room it will continue to have that hard surface; it is not simply my interpretation of the desk that matters, the desk is something 'out there' to be explained that exists independently of me.

In addition, social reality is layered. There are three levels in CR explanations: the empirical, the actual and the real. At the level of the 'empirical' occur events that are measured. The psychologist administers the personality test. The survey researcher obtains responses to the questions she posed on innovation. Of course, events also occur when they are not measured. The person has a personality irrespective of the test, the firms not surveyed also had innovations, and it might be that if we had better measures we could explain more. This is the level called 'the actual': here events happen irrespective of our knowledge of them. But there is an even deeper level, a level of 'the real'. This is a level where there are forces that exist as tendencies and possibilities. A parent who is self-employed enables their child to have a greater likelihood to start their own business (Blanchflower and Oswald, 1998) but the child does not have to start a business. Empirical findings suggest a mechanism that causes children of the self-employed to be more likely to start a business. Is it tacit knowledge obtained from close observation of their parents? Is it the presence of a guide and mentor? Is it knowledge that the self-employed parents will support the choice to start a business? These possible causal (sometimes called generative) mechanisms that CR seeks are at the domain of the real. These are the key deeper explanations that CR seeks to reveal: mechanisms exist that can cause events to happen under certain circumstances. Thus, an outcome (is the result of) = a mechanism + (acting in a certain) context (Pawson and Tilley, 1997).

Collectively, these three layers of social life comprise the depth ontology. As an example of the three layers, consider me making a cup of instant coffee for my friend. The jar of coffee enables me to make this cup of coffee; when I boil the kettle of water and make the coffee then the cup of coffee is an event, but only when I take the coffee to my friend can she drink the cup of coffee. The jar of coffee and the kettle of water are mechanisms, the cup of coffee is the actual, but only when it gets to my friend can she empirically 'measure' it. When we are looking to explain something we try to realize the mechanisms that make it happen. In this instance, the jar of coffee and the kettle of water had to be present for the event to happen.

The depth ontology of CR gives it the unique claim to a deeper explanation of social life, and by extension entrepreneurship. It does this by uncovering causal (generative) mechanisms. But of particular interest for entrepreneurship scholars is the attention given to change.

Morphogenesis

No discussion of CR within social science would be complete without a discussion of the approach of Archer (1995). Consistent with CR, Archer provided a general framework of change within social science that has the capacity to provide a framework for entrepreneurship (Mole and Mole, 2010; Mutch, 2010).

Consistent with the depth ontology, Archer (1995) argued that structure and agency are interdependent but ontologically different. In particular, structure is more enduring than agency. She suggested a cycle of change over time; see Figure 10.1 (McAnulla, 2002). We start at time T1, structural conditioning. Here agents are faced with existing structures that both constrain and enable their actions. These have resulted from the past actions of agents and they set the conditions for agents to act. They influence the interests that people have in terms of jobs, educational opportunities and the like. Then at time T2–T3 social interaction takes place. Agents have the power to affect outcomes. At this point agents (including groups) interact to further their interests in conflict or co-operation with other agents. At time T4 these actions have produced consequences, both intended and unintended, which may impact on the initial structures either to change them (morphogenesis) or to reinforce them (morphostatis).

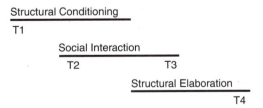

Figure 10.1 The Morphogenetic Cycle
Source: Archer (1995)

In turn this provides the structural context for agents – and so the cycle resumes. Structure, therefore, is the result of the past actions of agents. While these are interdependent it is possible to separate them for analysis, hence the term analytical dualism. Archer also suggested in a subsequent book that culture also constrains and enables agents in the same way as structure (Archer, 1996).

Archer (1995) isolated these structural factors to show that they have emergent properties even when agents were unknowing about them (Porpora, 2007). Porpora argued that agents can be exploited without their knowledge. An explanation of a phenomenon in social science may combine material elements (or structural emergent processes), ideational elements or (cultural emergent properties) and the agency of the person or group of people or (personal emergent properties). By isolating and studying these emergent properties it is possible to study how the context shapes the actions of agents. Although there are a multitude of these morphogenetic sequences, it is possible, because they are in a different relationship to time, to give an account of how structure and agency link over time. With this toolkit of analytical dualism, Cruickshank (2003) suggested that researchers should draw on a general realist ontology of structural emergent processes (SEPs), cultural emergent processes (CEPs) and personal emergent processes (PEPs). This takes us to the problem of developing methodology in CR.

The problem of science

Bhaskar (1975, 1979) argued that science works by scientists creating conditions that reveal underlying causes. Conventionally, science is thought to look for relationships that always hold (if x then y); the philosopher Hume called these constant conjunctions. If entrepreneurs are always well-financed then over many instances the expectation might be that being well-financed is a prerequisite for being an entrepreneur. However, Bhaskar (1975, 1979) suggested that science works in a different way. The scientist devises an experiment to create an artificial environment that isolates the particular phenomena that they want to study. How the scientist designs their study is critical. The ability to control the context sufficiently in science is what makes experimental scientific advance possible. The problem in social science and entrepreneurship is that most of our research takes place in an open system, in the uncontrolled social world. Positivist social science has relied on the notion of constant conjunctions in the real world. If those businesses that have limited liability (x) are more likely to grow (y) then positivists will establish that limited liability causes growth. Researchers do find this consistently (Storey, 1994), but what reasons link limited liability and growth? This stresses prediction at the expense of explanation (Fleetwood and Hesketh, 2006). But even the prediction falls down because social science takes place within open systems. There is more than limited liability and there are all sorts of other extraneous factors. For example, Alan Hughes (2009) argued that the effect of business support was negligible because a correlation between regional performance and spending on business support was not found. There would be a profusion of outside influences on both concepts; however, that would not be controlled for in this very open system. From a realist perspective, such work is flawed.

Thus, for example, our 'laws' and regularities that predict the future of the economy miss the most important changes, like the credit crunch (Lawson, 1997). Instead, the task of the researcher is to uncover causal mechanisms and, by organizing concepts, be able to show their essential features (Keat and Urry, 1975).

Researchers cannot be content with studying everyday practices or conversations because these miss the essential ingredients that make them possible. For example, going to the bank presupposes a banking system. Researchers need to reveal the social mechanisms that create these practices. This is not to say that people's actions are explained entirely from the external structures that surround them.

Although CR accepts that people's beliefs and understandings of a situation affect their behaviour, that is not all. Archer put people's social concerns and understanding as central to any explanation of why people act as they do. In other words, causes do not determine actions, they manifest themselves as tendencies; yet people's interpretations of their situation cannot be taken as truth either, since agents are fallible (Archer, 2007). They may try to put their projects into practice, yet their social situations can differ from how they interpret them (Outhwaite, 1998). Simply interviewing participants will not necessarily reveal mechanisms, either.

Mechanisms have to be identified. In Marx's writing, capitalism was distinguished by a 'central structural mechanism' that caused it to differ from all other systems (May, 2001). While the ownership of capital is an all-embracing mechanism, mechanisms can be more mundane. Pawson and Tilley (1997) investigated the mechanisms for change triggered by putting CCTV in a car park. They suggest a number of possible mechanisms that would reduce car park crime, including a 'caught in the act' mechanism that deters theft and a 'nosy parker' mechanism that encourages more people to be around, which, in turn, deters theft.

Retroduction

To try to explain the social world, critical realists have introduced retroduction. Retroduction is a mode of thinking that tries to answer the question: what properties must exist for ___ to exist and to be what ___ is? (Danermark et al., 2002). The impression is of uncovering the layers of an onion. Danermark et al. give a number of examples of studies that, while not necessarily being critical realist, use an approach similar to retroduction. Zygmund Bauman (1989) investigated what had to be in place to make the Holocaust possible. Having rejected purely German or Jewish explanations, Bauman argues that the structure of rational modern society made it possible. In particular, the characteristic of this society is that it is governed by a 'gardening culture' (Bauman, 1989). This is a cultural aspect that creates strategies to create and maintain order. In a garden, you remove what does not fit the orderly pattern. Racism was one sign of this culture. Secondly, characteristic of modern society is bureaucracy and routinized work, which distances one's actions and reduces responsibility for one's actions to playing a role. These (deeper) characteristics were fundamental to making it possible for the Holocaust to exist, but note that these mechanisms do not determine that it would happen. Bureaucracy and a gardening culture may exist but they are not sufficient for the Holocaust to occur.

An empirical recipe book

It is not clear what constitutes a CR study. There are a number of approaches to performing empirical research within CR (Cruickshank, 2003; Danermark et al., 2002; Hartwig, 2007; Sayer, 2000). The confusion over what constitutes a CR study is particularly unhelpful for academic researchers and journal editors alike. Since it is not clear or accepted within the academic community it has to legitimate itself (Vincent, 2008). To counter this problem and give guidance to those starting a CR project, Bhaskar set out a staged approach to conducting an applied CR study. The applied model has the acronym RRREI(C) standing for resolution, redescription, retroduction, elimination, identification and correction. The C is in brackets to denote that this is a new recursive cycle, which improves the study. The applied CR model is discussed in the next section and it is used as a yardstick to explore the CR-inspired study of Mutch (2007). The model denotes stages in the research process, starting with resolution.

Resolution – one starts with a complex event or situation of interest in an open system (i.e. not an experiment). This event is resolved into its separate components. For example, firm growth is a complex event with a number of causes. Firm growth might be influenced by factors to do with the market, the entrepreneur, their attitudes, capabilities and the nature of the industry within which the firm competes.

Redescription – the components are redescribed scientifically, in terms that are theoretically significant. The market might be redescribed in terms of the market growth or its maturity. The entrepreneur's attitudes might be described in terms of entrepreneurial orientation or their background might be conceived of as reflecting investments in human capital. This indicates the concepts that are important for the event.

Retroduction – this is the stage where antecedents are inferred. What caused the events to happen? This involves working out how mechanisms may have been triggered and the interaction between mechanisms to produce the event. What causes growth in a firm? There might be a need to grow to meet a minimum efficient scale, or the demand from customers in a fast growing market might increase demand. At this stage, Pawson and Tilley (1997) suggested a number of mechanisms that might influence the behaviour of people in their car park watched by CCTV.

Elimination – at this stage we might be able to reduce the number of mechanisms because they do not apply. If a growing firm was in a mature market that exhibited little growth, then we would be able to disregard this aspect. This process appears to be one where we are thinking of what is necessary for the event to occur. In this aspect, counterfactual thinking might be helpful (Danermark et al., 2002). Could you imagine a firm growing without a labour market? Could a firm have fewer employees and still be a growing firm? What would stop a firm from growing? Would it stop growth if the market were saturated with products? In this way we can get to grips with the mechanisms that underlie the events that are studied. In Bauman's (1989) work recall that he eliminated explanations based on German and Jewish aspects at this stage because he felt that they were too specific.

Identification – then you try to tease out the evidence for each of the mechanisms. This leads to the identification of the causal mechanism at work. Once this is identified it then becomes the phenomenon that we seek to explain. So if we found that minimum efficient scales were critical for new firms to grow, then we might then have to think about what causes them to be important, perhaps with a discussion of the way technology is produced (Schumacher, 1993).

Correction – The initial theory is updated with the new knowledge gained from this process. The tendencies producing the event are deduced retrospectively. This is iterative in the sense that our knowledge of the world is always fallible. Hartwig (2007) suggests that the model gives grounds to attribute '*natural necessity and necessary truth*' (2007, p. 196). By thus going through these stages the critical realist suggests that the underlying factors that cause firm growth would be revealed, for example. This is a general approach to critical realist explanation.

The classic study

Alistair Mutch uses Archer's approach to critical realism, in particular her attention to reflexivity, to analyse the way in which Sir Andrew Barclay Walker introduced the new arrangement of the tied landlord to the brewing industry in Victorian England. Using a business history approach connects well with Archer's view that structure shifts over a long time (Mutch, 2007).

Mutch's paper focussed on the institutional entrepreneur, a figure from institutional theory that uses his or her agency to change and legitimate new institutions. So the entrepreneur is not only acting as a business person to improve his or her earnings but is also legitimating new ways of doing things. Mutch uses a historical example that is consistent with CR.

Also consistent with CR, and rather typical of the papers in the *Journal of Critical Realism*, Mutch uses a case study. A case study is an approach that has been likened by the expert on case studies, Robert K. Yin, to an experiment (Yin 2009). It is this aspect that Sayer used to suggest that case studies are how critical realism is normally studied (Sayer, 2000).

Mutch (2007) asks: How do some people become institutional entrepreneurs, resisting the social conformity that underlies much of institutional theory? His answer lies in the agency of the institutional entrepreneur; crucial to this agency is the ability of the individual to be reflexive (Archer, 2003; Giddens, 1979). Giddens (1979) discusses differences between agents in terms of their knowledge and their openness to new knowledge.

Yet Mutch argues that Giddens' agent is too powerful and appears to have few constraints. In response he concentrates on reflexive agency in terms of an internal conversation (Archer, 2003; Emirbayer and Mische, 1998). Emirbayer and Mische (1998), in a classic article entitled 'What is agency?' argued that agents formulate their ideas and projects from an internal conversation. Archer builds upon this to suggest that there are different types of internal conversations. These different types conduct their conversations in terms of an interplay between 'contexts' and 'concerns'. Following an exploratory study of 40 interviews, Archer (2003) suggests that there are four types of reflexives: 'communicative reflexives', who tend to discuss concerns with others and seek to maintain their position; 'autonomous reflexives', who conduct their internal conversation in relative isolation; 'meta reflexives', who tend to reflect not only on their concerns but also on how they reflect; and 'fractured reflexives', who had difficulties with their internal conversation (and so with formulating projects). We focus on the autonomous reflexives because they seem to be consistent with entrepreneurship.

Archer found that autonomous reflexives were more likely to be self-employed, so it is they whom Mutch (2007) believes to be institutional entrepreneurs. Autonomous reflexives make decisions based on

the lone exercise of a mental activity, which its practitioners recognise as being an internal dialogue with themselves and one which they do not need and do not want to be supplemented by external exchanges with other people. (Archer, 2003, p. 210)

Mutch (2007) argues that these are society's strategists. Since, these autonomous reflexives were more likely to have moved and had breaks in their context, they were more likely to have broken ties that others (communicative reflexives) had not. These autonomous reflexives were more likely to strike out on their own and come up against the enablements and constraints in their lives. Mutch therefore argues that institutional entrepreneurs will probably exhibit this type of reflexivity.

By using a case from history, Mutch acknowledged the problem of inferring types of understanding from historical records. He suggests that we should not entirely rely on interviews for the evidence, quoting Archer (1995). He defends his choice of historical methods by suggesting that there is compensating documentary evidence and that it was a clear example of successful institutional entrepreneurship. As an example of CR in action the case study is a classic method.

Mutch (2007) shows that Andrew Barclay Walker introduced an organizational innovation of the public house manager to the pub trade in Liverpool. Previous to this innovation, pubs were run by tenanted managers who were tied to a brewer, Walker's change was to simply employ managers as one would employ managers of a coalmine. Mutch suggests that this change was indeed an institutional innovation. By connecting Walker's life story with elements of Archer's reflexivity Mutch suggests that this change reflected the reflexivity of Walker. Mutch finds evidence of individualism in the few letters written where he would expect communicative reflexives to write a great deal, he finds interest in work in the intense use of ledgers and evidence of contextual discontinuity in Walker's Scottish background. In addition, Mutch suggests that the Scottish background and the family network of business and property are of significance in the way that the innovation was implemented. He ascribed the notion of 'the outsider' as a prerequisite for not taking the accepted way of doing things for granted and the family connections with coal mining for the particular method of managing the public houses.

Mutch (2007) has analysed a change in the institution from T1 (structural conditioning) where the landlord is a tenanted manager through to T2–T3 (social interaction) where the new innovation occurs to T4 where the institution has changed (structural elaboration). He adopts the morphogenetic approach.

Mutch (2007) started with a complex event. He re-described this in scientific terms, using terms such as autonomous reflexive, 'outsiderness', contextual discontinuity. In addition Mutch mentions Walker's Scottish background and network, and connections with other institutions. He then identifies the evidence for the mechanisms: the evidence of individualism in the few letters written and the contextual discontinuity.

One might argue that in the research paper there is little evidence for alternative retroduced paths. For example, in institutional theory it is argued that institutional ideas can leak from one industry to another. Greenwood and Suddaby (2006) cite the example of change in accounting firms, giving a purely institutional explanation. This raises the question of whether Mutch (2007) was only seeking to confirm his preferred explanation rather than going through the elimination procedure.

Mutch develops the notion of the autonomous reflexive to argue that we might understand why some entrepreneurs seek to change the accepted way of doing things. However, he concedes that for an institutional entrepreneur to be successful may require a number of other causal factors to be in place: networks and connections may be important in this respect. Therefore, the autonomous reflexive may be necessary but not sufficient.

In making his case, Mutch uses the case study method to try to identify the important elements of the case. However, his paper does not use retroduction to isolate the generative mechanisms involved. In his discussion, he touches on the issue of whether Liverpool in the 1850s was a receptive place for the innovation. Finally, he suggests that the institutional entrepreneur may put too much emphasis on the individual rather than the outcome of change being a combination of intended and unintended outcomes from an attempt to change institutions, as is suggested by Archer (1995).

Mutch (2007) used as a case study a change in institutions. He adopted Archer's approach towards structure and agency. In terms of Bhaskar's approach, he adopted most steps but was perhaps weak on the stage of elimination, leading to a potential charge of fitting the data to the theory. In illustrating Mutch's approach we can see an empirical CR study enacted in practice. Having shown this study the chapter turns to the criticisms of CR and Archer's (1995) morphogenetic cycle.

The critique

There are three main lines of criticism of CR of interest to management researchers. The first two are general critiques. The third is aimed specifically at Archer (1995). First, a critique of CR within management has come from a post-structural perspective (Contu and Willmott, 2005), which has been rebutted (Reed 2005a, 2005b). Second, a debate has centred on the contribution of quantitative methods to post-positivist explanation (Kemp and Holmwood, 2003; Holmwood, 2001). Third, in the critique of Archer, Anthony King and Margaret Archer debated the role of structure (King, 1999; Archer, 2000). We take each critique in turn.

Contu and Willmott (2005) made two points. First, they suggest that the critical realist approach is not new and is structural. They point to the 'adoption' of older studies by critical realists, such as Braverman's (1974) study of the labour process, to argue that these studies have been recognised under different perspectives. Second, they argued that it was not possible really to know that reality was stratified; however, Reed (2005a) pointed out that this just confused a question about our assumptions about reality (ontology) with ways to find out about the world (epistemology). One could just as easily ask Contu and Willmott how we know that discourse shapes reality, retorted Reed.

Another line of critique has focused on the issue of retroduction (Holmwood, 2001; Kemp and Holmwood, 2003). Holmwood (2001) takes issue with the abstraction of critical realism's depth ontology. He argued that if CR can distinguish between the domain of the 'real' and the domain of the 'actual' then its findings are not testable. Yet if we find that a real causal mechanism is not observed, should that not reduce our faith in its causal powers? The issue at which Holmwood (2001) takes aim is how we are going to establish that retroduction and abstract theorizing can produce trustworthy theory: 'how is what is logically or conceptually necessary to be established?' (Holmwood, 2001, p. 952).

Kemp and Holmwood (2003) are concerned with the critical realist assertion that there are no social science equivalents to the experiment. They question Bhaskar's suggestion that one should divorce prediction from explanation. Their argument is that there are regular occurrences of events, such as the link between having a parent who ran a business and starting one oneself. These links might provide temporary closures that are a social science equivalent to experiments. This approach sits fine with the approach of critical realists such as Lawson (1997) but Kemp and Holmwood (2003) further suggest that quantitative research should have a role in the testing of theories.

The debate between King (1999) and Archer (2000) concerns whether structure is necessary in social science. King takes issue with Archer's structure to argue from Collins (1981) that we do not need a macro-sociology or structure as an autonomous, independent realm. King argues that Archer (1995) discusses structures under three aspects: numerical, relational and bureaucratic. The numerical aspect comes from demography. Where Archer uses the literacy rate in Castro's Cuba, for example, the intent to improve literacy would show a greater degree of success depending on the proportions of literate members of society. Similarly, when role models for entrepreneurship are cited then a greater number of entrepreneurs in a local area would help to create more new firms (Lafuente, Vaillant and Rialp, 2007).

King set out to show that each of these types of structures could be seen, in an interpretist ontology, as resulting from 'other people', which undermined Archer's claim that structure is pre-existing, causal and autonomous. King also argued that the 'relational' structures where the sum of the individuals is autonomous of each individual but not more than them. Using Adam Smith's pin factory example, King suggested that the factory system is not greater than the individuals within it. The third example of social structure from Archer is the 'bureaucratic' structure. This suggests that there are roles that are embedded in the social structure such that one's occupation of them confers certain powers which existed prior to one taking on the role. King (1999) argued that these roles, such as bank manager, had been created in the past by individuals in the bank and re-created by today's bank employees. King (1999) believes that Archer (1995) misrepresents the interpretist tradition by classifying it in the same way as a rational choice approach and adopting an individualist view. King (1999) argued that a social constraint is very evident in the interpretist position. He claims,

> [t]o argue that the material conditions of a society are somehow independent of relations between individuals in a society is to produce a mystifying and pessimistic social theory, which excuses poverty and dispossession as the property of an objective system and, therefore, the responsibility of no-one. Material differences are the product of knowingly unequal material exchanges between people in the past which are repeated in further knowingly unequal exchanges in the present. Our material condition presents itself to us as individuals, like the role of the bank manager, as objective and autonomous, when in fact it is the outcome of beliefs and interactions of numerous individuals over time and space. From the interpretive tradition's rejection of a pre-existent and autonomous structure follows a refutation of any notion of objective causality in society but that does not mean dispensing the notion of social causality or constraint, altogether. Rather, it grounds that constraint in the practices and beliefs of individuals. (King 1999, p. 222)

Archer (2000) responded to King's argument by suggesting that the point of social structure is precisely that it provides limits to what is feasible. It shapes social action. Moreover, she cites Herbert Blumer as suggesting that social organization enters into action only through shaping the situation and supplying fixed sets of symbols (Blumer, 1963). This is enough for a social realist position. Archer points out that interpretist sociology suffers from a problem when it recognizes real but non-interpretist properties of society such as when King discusses the real distribution of wealth. Besides, these structures have effects whether the participants recognize them or not, contra King (1999).

The future direction for CR in entrepreneurship

The criticism of CR has not left it weakened. Archer's work is written very 'defensively' and thus the criticisms have not been strong.

The role of methods within CR is critical for its future. For example, within the ESRC funded 'Critical realism in Action' group led by Professor Paul Edwards and Steve Vincent there has been some difficulty in enticing scholars to come forward with more empirical work using CR. Much of the work surrounding CR seems to be discussions about the theory (Fleetwood and Hesketh, 2006; Mole and Mole, 2010; Vincent, 2008).

CR and prospective entrepreneurs

This is another section where we need to examine the promise of the perspective. In Mutch (2007) we see the view that the extent to which people are reflexive and how they reflect on their situation can determine their entrepreneurial outcomes. It is no good looking for institutional entrepreneurs among the ranks of those who make decisions in communication with their peers. To be an institutional entrepreneur you have to rely on your own judgement (Casson, 2003).

Mole and Mole (2010) suggest that entrepreneurs react to their situation and take action to change the institutional outcome to their benefit; yet at the same time the personal costs to the individual entrepreneurs may be high. You can succeed in changing an industry while your business fails and you become bankrupt. For example, a social franchise was successfully accepted by charities; yet its business model depended crucially on positive media coverage that was present in the initial Bristol area but not in the new franchisee's areas (Tracey et al., 2011). Thus, changing the structure and allowing new ways of working can be costly.

Further reading

The entry level guide to critical realism is Danermark et al. (2002). This makes it clear what is being attempted. Pawson and Tilley (1997) apply critical realism to evaluation and produce a reasonably accessible Context-Mechanism-Outcome model of explanation. Grix (2004) provides a clear overview of critical realism as a perspective in between interpretivism and positivism. An account that starts from the economics perspective and is more tolerant of quantitative methods generally is Lawson (1997). For those who are more familiar with politics Lewis (2002) is a brief and clear reference. Those who want to get the real thing might start with Bhaskar (1975, 1978). In sociology Archer (1995) sets out the arguments in favour of CR. The CR bible is Archer et al. (1998) *Critical Realism: Essential Readings*.

Questions for discussion

What is structure and how does it help explain the levels of new firm start-ups?
What structural, cultural and personal factors would you think affect the decision of a person to start their own business?
How might you construct a critical realist inspired study of small firm growth?

CHAPTER 11

Critical Theories of Entrepreneurship

André Spicer

Introduction

Today many people throughout society who do not own and run businesses are being encouraged to think about themselves as entrepreneurs: architects, medics, school teachers, librarians, social activists, subsistence farmers and even school children are encouraged to be more entrepreneurial. It seems that enterprise has become a one size fits all solution to the many woes of the social world. And this situation is championed by most theories of entrepreneurship. These theories assume that entrepreneurship is something which is good, necessary and always produces desirable results. For sure, entrepreneurship does produce many benefits for individuals, groups and broader society. However, this is not the end of the story. By focusing on all the good aspects associated with entrepreneurship, we turn a blind eye to many of its more questionable aspects. We miss the fact that entrepreneurship does not just involve grand business success and economic growth but also can entail economic failure for individuals and even whole nations. Because many mainstream perspectives on entrepreneurship are so committed to a rosy picture of entrepreneurship, they often miss what is the overwhelming reality for most entrepreneurs: struggle, hardship, business failure, anxiety and lack of freedom.

In this chapter I try to address some of these missing parts in the story of entrepreneurship. I do this by outlining a critical theory of entrepreneurship. This is a body of theory which tries actively to question entrepreneurship and the role it plays in the broader economy. Critical theories examine how entrepreneurship is linked with broader patterns of power and domination. Critical studies have tended to investigate the following broad questions: how entrepreneurship is a kind of discourse which gives us a limited way of talking and thinking about the world, what the effects of this are, the structural constraints around who can and cannot be an entrepreneur, how people ignore or resist notions of enterprise, and the affective dimensions of entrepreneurship. I look at some of the shortcomings of this perspective, and what future directions of research it opens up and what it might suggest to budding entrepreneurs.

Critical theory: An overview

The critical study of entrepreneurship springs from the field of critical management studies; for a review see Alvesson, Bridgeman and Willmott (2009).

Critical management studies (CMS) has a history of at least 30 years. It is now a well-established perspective from which to examine managerial processes. CMS took significant inspiration from the Frankfurt School of Critical Theory (Alvesson and Willmott, 1992). One way to think about critical theory is as a type of knowledge in contrast to existing perspectives. This develops Jürgen Habermas's argument that forms of knowledge are not value free, but are underpinned by human interests (1971, pp. 301–317). Habermas points out that there are three broad sets of interest underpinning human knowledge (1971, pp. 308–311). The first set of interests is based on instrumental-technocratic knowledge. The aim of this kind of knowledge is ultimately to be able to manipulate and control aspects of social life. This approach is reflected in functionalist studies of entrepreneurship. These studies try to predict what causes entrepreneurial behavior and then control for it. The second set of interests is based on hermeneutic-interpretive knowledge. The aim of this kind of knowledge is to create mutual understanding. This is reflected in interpretive studies of entrepreneurship that seek to conceptualize how entrepreneurs make meaning out of the world and perceive opportunities.

The third set of interests is based on critical knowledge. This kind of knowledge aims at fundamentally transforming the objects of analysis with the aim of emancipation from existing modes of domination. In the case of entrepreneurship, this involves knowledge that fundamentally questions the whole concept of enterprise. It does this in order to create some distance from our assumptions about entrepreneurialism. Critical theorists hope to get us fundamentally to rethink the entrepreneur.

Critical theory prompts us to rethink the entrepreneur in a number of ways. First, it seeks dialectically to challenge many of our pre-existing assumptions (Benson, 1977). Doing this involves pointing out many of the already existing contradictions that haunt organizations. One example of such a tension is the incessant desire for growth and the ecological limits that entrepreneurs come up against. This usually requires the critical theorist to go looking for the 'darker side' of business life such as mistakes, misconducts and disasters (Vaughan, 1999). Furthermore, critical approaches recognize that this dark side is by no means an aberration from normal functioning. Rather, it is actually produced by entrepreneurial activity. In other words, exploitation, environmental degradation and alienation are by no means minor divergences from some kind of more rational norm. Rather, they are the norm.

Second, critical theorists seek to reveal the existing political presuppositions that lurk below the discussion of entrepreneurship. Most people studying entrepreneurship would claim that politics is not something that should cloud our value-free analysis of what causes someone to be entrepreneurial and what the consequences of this are. A critical theorist would point out that such a claim to value-free knowledge is a delusion at best and an ideological move at worst. This is because all forms of research are underpinned by some more or less acknowledged politics. All researchers have a sense of what is more or less valuable, what the purpose of their knowledge is and how things should be in the future. As we will see, most entrepreneurship researchers are often committed to some project of advancing what Peter Drucker (1985) called an 'entrepreneurial society'. This might involve encouraging entrepreneurship or helping entrepreneurs to be more successful. The political assumption here is that entrepreneurship is a good thing that needs to be wholeheartedly encouraged. By highlighting the implicit political assumptions and commitments, it is possible to demonstrate how this apparently value-free body of knowledge is actually directed and informed by political commitments. In the field of entrepreneurship research, some versions of neo-liberalism or even libertarianism often infuse the research. Critical approaches not only make these mute political assumptions speak, but also introduce alternative political positions that are sorely lacking in debates. Typically, critical studies push forward a progressive political agenda that is 'broad(ly) left, pro-feminist, anti-imperialist, environmentally concerned' (Parker, 2002, p. 117). Thus a critical approach to knowledge is marked by an explicit confrontation with political commitments underlying research.

Third, CMS also seeks to confront the implicit assumptions around knowledge production that have often led to a very narrow account of entrepreneurship. In an influential account of CMS, Valarie Fournier and Chris Grey (2000) argue that CMS is tied up with three commitments with regard to knowledge production. For them, critical knowledge should fundamentally destabilize our knowledge claims. This involves three critical moves: a reflexive epistemology that questions how our methodological assumption structure and in some ways shape how we see our very object of inquiry (i.e. entrepreneurship), a de-naturalizing ontology that seeks to show how objects of inquiry (entrepreneurs) are constructed through ongoing social processes and a political anti-performativity that seeks to un-tether knowledge production from means–ends calculation. While this schematic is by no means the only account of CMS, it does provide an orientation to knowledge production that fundamentally challenges many of the assumptions that are routinely assumed in the study of business and management. It pushes us to question how we know our object of analysis, how this object came into being, and the purpose of our knowledge.

Fourth, critical theories seek to intervene in the subject that they study. As we have already seen, Fournier and Grey (2000) suggest that critics should break the link between knowledge production and a performative agenda. By this they mean that knowledge should not just be sought due to means–ends calculations such as producing more efficient or effective outputs, whether that be for the scientists or some group they are serving such as policy makers or an occupational community. However, as we have already pointed out, many attempts to develop critical knowledge rest upon a political project. Developing knowledge becomes a process of seeking to advance that agenda in one way or another. This makes critical knowledge performative – not in the sense that it is based on means–ends calculation, but in the sense that it seeks to actively intervene in the discourse around a subject in order to disturb and challenge it fundamentally (Spicer, Alvesson and Karreman, 2009). Thus, we could say that critical knowledge involves an intervention in debates to open out the often stultifying and technocratic talk which usually bog them down. There are a range of possible strategies as to how this might be pursued. For instance, Spicer and colleagues (2009) suggest six potential strategies: an affirmative stance through proximity to an object of analysis, which allows the identification of potential points of revision; an ethic of care, which provides space for subjects views and addresses the ambiguities in these views; a pragmatic orientation, which seeks to find particular points of tension within discourses in order to unsettle them; a focus on potentialities, which involves looking for already existing alternatives that have been excluded from dominant discourses; and a normative orientation, which seeks systematically to clarify and assert the grounds on which judgements about the 'good' are asserted. This demands entrepreneurship researchers work more closely with the real experiences of entrepreneurs, and by doing so recognize many of the ambiguities and potentials that lurk beneath the surface. It also pushes entrepreneurship researchers to offer normative standards with which to understand and indeed change entrepreneurship. To be clear, this list of potential strategies of intervention is by no means complete. It is supposed to act more like an invitation for considering modes of possible critique.

We are now in a position to bring together some of the elements of a broad critical approach. Critical studies recognize that all knowledge is underpinned by some kind of human interest and a particular orientation towards emancipatory interests. This means acknowledging that studies of entrepreneurship are not value free. Rather, they are underpinned by a set of what Habermas called 'human interests'. As we have already pointed out in the introduction, the most common of these are instrumental-technocratic interests (what we called functionalism) that seek to predict and control for entrepreneurialism. There is a small but increasing group of studies built on hermeneutic-interpretive knowledge (what we called interpretivism).

These studies try to trace the processes of understanding and interpretation involved in entrepreneurship. A critical approach would instead seek to champion a commitment to emancipatory knowledge. This entails a confrontation with the implicit political position underpinning any research on entrepreneurship. More than this, critical studies often imply a clear commitment to broadly progressive politics. Such political commitment requires us to delve into the darker sides of entrepreneurialism that are so often ignored. Tallying up this darker side involves acknowledging that the rather rosy picture of the entrepreneurial success story we are so often given does not represent the reality of entrepreneurship. Rather, it often involves frequent failure, false starts and various forms of oppression and exploitation. As well as unearthing such progressive politics, critical studies consider the conditions of knowledge production: the critical theorist must ask how our attempts to develop knowledge about the entrepreneur are shaped by particular orientations – often to positivist, naturalizing, and performative knowledge. We should also ask how we might be able to change these goals by adopting a reflexive, de-naturalizing and non-performative approach to knowledge. By adopting this alternative orientation, a different approach to studying entrepreneurs begins to emerge: it relies on reflexive knowledge, which questions and unsettles how we have come to know particular areas of research; it de-naturalizes the entrepreneur by showing how the entrepreneur is a product of a particular historical and cultural juncture rather than a natural and universal figure; it develops non-performative knowledge which is not clearly yoked to the goals of advancing an entrepreneurial society or making entrepreneurs more successful. Finally, a critical theory involves advancing knowledge that seeks to interrupt and reconfigure existing knowledge around a particular discourse. In our case, this means that critical studies of entrepreneurship seek to interrupt and reconfigure discourses of enterprise and entrepreneurialism. This does not mean a wholesale repudiation of the entrepreneur. Rather, it involves knowledge that will fundamentally reconfigure how we understand the entrepreneur and what we think entrepreneurship involves.

The contribution of critical theory to entrepreneurship research

The critical approaches to entrepreneurship largely began with researchers who began to apply the critical approach we described above to what they called 'enterprise culture'. During the 1990s, a group of largely British-based researchers noted that talk about entrepreneurship had spread out of its heartland and come to infuse many aspects of social life. Corporate employees, public servants, professionals and people in the non-profit sector were being encouraged to act more entrepreneurially. The core characteristics of this enterprise culture involved pressure to be calculating and risk taking, approaching oneself as a business and seeking out opportunities to make oneself more marketable (Keat and Abercrombie, 1991; Heelas and Morris, 1992). Perhaps the most notable change this brought about was a transformation in the language people used in a range of settings. Socio-linguists such as Norman Fairclough (1995) noted that during the 1980s and 1990s there was a rapid spread and generalization of the talk about people being entrepreneurial and enterprising. The language of enterprise came to infuse institutions from schools to hospitals, factories to retail outlets, the development sector to those with environmental concerns. What was vital here was that certain systems of discourse that represented the entrepreneur as unfailingly positive became ever more widespread. Enterprise was systematically applied as the catch-all solution to nearly any aspect of social life.

The rise of enterprise culture involved not only an innocent change in how we talked about the social world but also a more deep-seated relations of 'socio-cultural power'. Some researchers argued that perhaps the most important expression of these changing relations of socio-cultural power were shifts in the way actors understood their very sense of self. Those studying 'governmentality' argued that the rise of entrepreneurship discourse led to people to seeing themselves as rational self-calculating subjects who weigh up the costs and benefits of their every action and ceaselessly pursue entrepreneurial opportunities (Burchell, 1993; du Gay and Salaman, 1992; Rose, 1992). This process of the internalization of the discourse of enterprise has been examined in a range of studies that demonstrate how workers in a variety of contexts come to think of themselves as 'enterprising subjects'. This entails people seeing themselves as having particular entrepreneurial characteristics, such as the drive relentlessly to seek out opportunities, take risks and come up with innovative combinations and connections. The crucial point is that these figures do not necessarily need to be actual entrepreneurs who start up a new business. They can also be people doing work that we would usually see as being very non-entrepreneurial. For instance, researchers have charted the rise of entrepreneurial identities in large corporations (Fournier, 1998), among middle management (du Gay, Salaman and Rees, 1996; Badham et al., 2003), professionals (Doolin, 2003), public sector employees (du Gay, 2004), government policy making (Perren and Jennings, 2005) and society more generally (Ogbor, 2000). Throughout each of these studies, the major insight is that the rise of enterprise discourse has led to changes in how employees think about their work and themselves. They increasingly see themselves as responsible risk takers rather than routine rule followers.

This body of research on the spread of enterprise culture has yielded some remarkably consistent findings. First, it has shown that enterprise is a relatively coherent discourse that emphasizes risk taking, calculation and economizing, and presents these points in an unfailingly positive way. Second, it has sought repeatedly to argue that enterprise culture has effects that are not just caused by structural changes in multinational capitalism but also increased enthusiasm for neo-liberal policy in many governments. The rise of enterprise culture involves a significant change in the symbolism, understandings and perceptions of people in an economy. In short, enterprise culture has a vital and irreducible cultural dimension. Third, the effects of enterprise culture are largely 'ideational' in nature, insofar as they change how people talk and think about themselves and the social world. Instead of seeing themselves as mere workers or professionals, they become 'entrepreneurs'. Finally, the rise of an enterprise culture produces important changes in how people understand themselves and what they are able and not able to do. This occurs through the reconstruction of 'subject positions' that carefully delimit the scope of possible actions people can and cannot carry out. These critical approaches to entrepreneurship certainly make some important additions to existing interpretive work on the topic. This body of work demonstrates that entrepreneurship is more than just a process of making meaning: it is also a process of making and producing relations of domination. The literature on enterprise culture has convincingly argued that the language of enterprise has spread throughout various sectors of the British economy and in some cases transformed how we operate and speak. Such transformations call into question how subjects act and think about themselves. This research shows us that entrepreneurship and entrepreneurialism has an impact that goes beyond the boundaries of the organization and actually draws many people into thinking about themselves as entrepreneurs or at least having entrepreneurial qualities.

Enterprise discourse: A classic study

Although there have been many studies of examining enterprise discourse, perhaps the most influential of these is Paul du Gay's (1996) book *Consumption and Identity at Work*. At the outset, I should note that this book is not a study of 'entrepreneurs' as we would traditionally conceive of them. Rather, du Gay looks at how the discourse of enterprise has shifted into particular employment settings and how that has changed how employees experience of themselves. This involves developing an account of how occupational identity has been transformed during the 1980s and 1990s in the United Kingdom. In particular, he is interested in how the global restructuring of the production resulted in the culture of enterprise becoming particular influential throughout modern British workplaces. He asks how the rise of this culture of enterprise has impacted people's understanding of themselves at work, and how this enterprise culture has been used and consumed by employees.

Du Gay sets out on his investigation of the rise of enterprise in the workplace by contextualizing it in terms of a broader sense of identity crisis in western societies such as the United Kingdom. He notes that many of the stable reference points we use to construct our sense of self have been increasingly called into question through broader processes of social change such as the rise of post-industrialism in the west, the decline of traditional 'working class' employers such as manufacturers and an increasing orientation towards the service sector and consumption. This has created an 'identity crisis' for the working subject.

To investigate this identity crisis, du Gay draws on post-structural theories that approach identity as being constructed by discourses. He notes that these discourses become important 'governmental technologies' that shape how people understand their own identity and engage with the social world. He then asks the question of how discourses construct and regulate employees' identities in the contemporary workplace. He points out that this happens in contemporary workplaces through 'corporate cultures'. This brings him to an investigation of a work context where corporate cultures have become particularly widespread and influential – retail. To do this he undertook an ethnographic study of work in four chains of retail stores in the United Kingdom. His investigation of these service settings reveals that the management of these two contexts sought to engage employees through instilling a culture of entrepreneurialism. This involves encouraging employees to think of themselves as being entrepreneurs when they are at work (even though they are not actually starting a business). The theme of the enterprising worker was highly influenced by much pop management literature, which emphasized how companies can build success through developing cultures of excellence. Employees are encouraged to see themselves as risk-takers, opportunity spotters and so on. More importantly they are encouraged to respond to the sovereign consumer.

Du Gay also found that employees frequently did not accept this new entrepreneurial identity – they did not just see themselves as being entrepreneurs. Rather, they sought tactically to negotiate this identity by drawing on other identities that they found outside the workplace in the spheres of consumption. What this indicates is that while enterprise discourse may become an important way that companies seek to manage even the most lowly members of their workforce, it is always open for contestation and challenge.

In later work, du Gay (2000, 2007) seeks to extend his insights gained from the study of the retail shop floor into the context of the restructuring of the public sector. Here he investigates how many public servants have been encouraged to see themselves as entrepreneurs and risk takers. He notes that this cuts against the grain of the bureaucratic ethos that had been nurtured in many public sector organizations. Instead of distancing himself from this ethos, du Gay notes many of the important values and benefits associated with it, such as un-enthusiastic and rational assessments of cases. What this stream of work shows us is that the ethos of entrepreneurialism has spread far outside of its homeland of small business activity. Today it appears that nearly anyone and everyone is encouraged to think about themselves and experience themselves as 'entrepreneurs'. This often happens through the propagation of entrepreneurial cultures that encourage people to think about themselves as being 'enterprising'. This can result in significant changes in employee subjectivity in a way that makes them more amenable to the contemporary workplace. But it also can become a significant source of resistance. What du Gay offers us is a comprehensive study of how discourses of entrepreneurship have become increasingly introduced into apparently non-entrepreneurial contexts, how these discourses shape identity, how they can act as a form of power and domination and how they might be resisted.

Criticism of critical theories of entrepreneurship

Despite the success of critical theories in examining enterprise discourse and how it has reshaped power relations, there have been a number of questions raised about some of the shortcomings in the critical literature on enterprise culture. In particular, researchers have raised three significant objections to the critique of enterprise discourse: it discounts how enterprise discourse might be given new meaning through processes of consumption or actively resisted by actors in an organization, it ignores the more material and social structural aspects associated with entrepreneurship discourse and it sees enterprise discourse as being too coherent and integrated, thereby missing the ambiguities and uncertainties which are in some ways implicit within the discourse of entrepreneurialism. Each of these limitations opens up significant scope for further analysis of the working of entrepreneurship discourses and the extension and revision of research in the area. In what follows, I will look in more detail at these three criticisms and the areas of research they open up.

The first criticism of many studies of enterprise culture is that they attribute too much power to entrepreneurial discourse and largely ignore how actors may not be particularly affected by the entrepreneurial discourse in some cases, actively resist it in others and seek to modify and reconstruct the discourse in still other cases (Armstrong, 2005; Fournier, 1998). For instance, in their analysis of seminal work on discourse of enterprise, Fournier and Grey claim that 'enterprise is treated deterministically' (1999 p. 117). By this they mean there is an assumption in many studies of enterprise culture that it constructs new 'entrepreneurial' subject positions that circumscribe power relations. They point out that in many cases enterprise culture can become an object of contention and even protest.

The second criticism of studies of the discourse of enterprise is exactly how 'ideational' the changes associated with enterprise cultural actually are. Critics like Peter Armstrong (2005) have argued that discourses of enterprise often have important dimensions that are not totally reducible to discourse. These include changes in the way rules are structured as well as the distribution of resources. Armstrong points out that instead of seeing enterprise as a discourse that has increasingly infused all aspects of social life, it should be treated as an 'ideology', which many parts of the population do not necessarily buy into but has nonetheless had a profound impact on government policy, thereby transforming the distribution of resources in broader society. Armstrong argues that by ignoring aspects that fall outside of the distribution of resources such as government funding, researchers have been largely unable to document how changes in discourse might also be connected or indeed embodied within shifts in the distribution of more material configurations.

Alongside questions about the deficient account of agency and the anaemic account of social structures, existing critical studies of entrepreneurship have been called into question for largely ignoring the affective dimension of enterprise discourse (Jones and Spicer, 2009). By this, I mean that existing accounts have largely focused on the conscious technologies, such as language, typically associated with enterprise. They have missed the role that emotions and excitement play in making people so enthusiastic about entrepreneurialism. Existing work in entrepreneurship tends to approach entrepreneurial affect as the emotions of entrepreneurs that in some ways shape their patterns of cognition (Goss, 2005). But the affective dimension is broader than this. It involves preconscious responses that work at the level of emotion, bodily everyday life and sense. By largely discounting this aspect, researchers have rendered themselves largely unable to account for the ways that enterprise can work though capturing people at the level of desire, but can also work through various bodily forms. Providing an accurate account of this dimension would require researchers to explore how discourses of enterprise work through harnessing desire, organizing bodily capacities and shaping their sense in a particular way.

Future directions of research

While existing studies that take a critical approach to the entrepreneur provide some interesting findings, they also pose some new questions for further research. The first involves questions around how we can think about entrepreneurial activity that uses the concept of entrepreneurship in novel and strange ways. This involves considering how some groups have reworked the idea of being an entrepreneur in a way that moves away from utility creation to the creation of new modes of sociality. Examples of this kind of process abound, ranging from social entrepreneurs who find new ways of connecting people, to political entrepreneurs who are able to create new coalitions and linkages between unlikely groups, to institutional entrepreneurs who build new institutional forms. The question this would involve asking is how we might modify our existing theories of entrepreneurship when creating innovative connections rather than maximizing utility is the core goal.

Furthermore, it would force us to confront situations where entrepreneurs need to bring together what are often conflicting different worlds of activity such as social change and building a market (Stark, 2009). Finally, we might ask how some actors using a term such as 'social entrepreneur' might find themselves trapped in what can often be experienced as insoluble binds.

The second new line of research opened up by critical approaches to entrepreneurship is how actors negotiate the various structural constraints they face. In particular, I highlighted that much entrepreneurial activity happens outside of the realm we would consider to be proper and acceptable enterprise. Further research would explore how budding entrepreneurs work with these marginal positions: How do they challenge their marginality in some cases? How might they exploit their marginality in other instances? How might they seek to work between the spaces of marginality and being accepted? Such questions might be pursued by looking in more depth at the strategies that are employed by groups who are typically marginalized by existing entrepreneurial discourses.

The third future line of research we would like to suggest involves a deeper exploration of the affective dimension of entrepreneurship. We already know that desires, emotions and bodily experiences like 'gut feeling' are a central part of what the entrepreneur does. However, we know less about the affective work that goes into entrepreneurial activity. One the one side, this involves considering how entrepreneurs often work with affects and sense in particular ways. This might involve asking how do entrepreneurs seek not just to make sense in particular industries, but also disrupt this sense. How does such disruption take place and what skills do entrepreneurs need to do this. In addition, we might also inquire into the kinds of social, emotional and aesthetic labour required by entrepreneurs. This might reveal the rich pallet of abilities and skills that are required in the work of entrepreneurship. But it might also show some of the more destructive and curtailing aspects of contemporary work imposed by the entrepreneurial labour process. For instance, we may come across significant forms of self-exploitation, pent-up experiences of frustration and the control being exercised by other agents. Asking these kinds of questions might lead us to think about the work and activity that actually goes into making discourses of enterprise work.

Implications for entrepreneurs

Critical theory clearly seeks to question the idea of enterprise and entrepreneurship. It aims to show that entrepreneurship is not all wine and roses, and that there is a significant negative side as well. However, I should stressing that critics focus on the category and discourse of entrepreneurship – not individual entrepreneurs. The central question that critical theorists ask is why has the category of the entrepreneur been applied to an ever increasing range of actors.

What critical theory then does is force us to question whether the concept or category of the entrepreneur is actually useful in particular contexts. Moreover, it encourages us to think about what some of the more negative aspects might be of identifying ourselves as entrepreneurs. Thus the first clear implication of critical theory for entrepreneurs is that they need to be more circumspect about entrepreneurial talk and the very identity of the entrepreneur.

This involves recognizing that this talk does not apply in all settings. For instance, many people we might think of as entrepreneurs often succeed because they identify more strongly as scientists or engineers than as entrepreneurs. An example here is the well-known vacuum cleaner designer James Dyson, who talks about himself primarily as a designer not an entrepreneur. Pushing all possible other professional and occupational identities aside in favour of the entrepreneur is a dangerous move. Perhaps a little scepticism will help us to see that entrepreneurship and entrepreneurialism may be a useful solution in some cases, but it can also be a disastrous option in other settings. Thus by loosening our attachment to notions of enterprise, a critical approach helps us to see that entrepreneurialism is only one potential approach to economic activity among a whole range of others.

As well as adding a touch of scepticism, critical studies of entrepreneurship also help us to recognize many of the darker sides of enterprise. By pointing out that entrepreneurship is not necessarily a set of good things, but also involves failure, (self) exploitation, waste, conformity and delusion, we hope to remind budding entrepreneurs that many of the problems that they might experience are not because of some innate problem within themselves. Rather, these issues are more systematic and common among many entrepreneurs. Indeed, a large part of the experience of working as an entrepreneur involves these darker and perhaps more negative experiences. By recognizing this, we hope that entrepreneurs will be able not only to make sense of some of the difficulties that they face, but also to realize when many of the myths of entrepreneurship could actually be destroying them. This might help to loosen the grip of what can often be highly corrosive ideas about entrepreneurship and entrepreneurialism which can lead people to squandering their own resources as well as those of friends and families in attempts to be 'entrepreneurial'. Thus, the second practical implication of critical approaches is that they help us to recognize and perhaps more clearly understand the darker side of organizational life.

In addition to getting us thinking about the darker side of entrepreneurship, I also hope that a critical approach pushes us to consider how entrepreneurship is something which can potentially be done differently. Critical theories try to push us to see that there are many people who think about themselves as being entrepreneurial. What critical theory seeks to encourage is a more serious investigation of these particular settings. When looking at how entrepreneurial activities play out in the public sector and the third sector, critical theory encourages a broader definition of what counts as entrepreneurism. This would help to move us away from the fixation on business creation and utility creation towards broader processes involved in creating opportunities and coming up with new combinations of the means of social production. Such a step would push us to take lessons from other kinds of entrepreneurs such as institutional entrepreneurs, political entrepreneurs, cultural entrepreneurs or social entrepreneurs. This forces the budding entrepreneur to ask themselves to look for lessons in unusual places. For instance, they may learn from social movements that create social change or artists who shift cultural boundaries. But it also encourages entrepreneurs to see their activities as not just establishing a business but seeking to change aspects of social, cultural or political life. Perhaps it may encourage entrepreneurs to recognize that starting a business is only one among many ways that broad economic change can be pursued. There are many other organizational forms, ranging from the social enterprise to the social movement, that can possibly effect such changes. Thus the third practical implication of a critical theory of entrepreneurship is to help budding entrepreneurs think beyond existing models of enterprise and consider what alternative modes of building organizations will help them to affect the kind of change they hope to achieve.

Further reading

Armstrong, P., *Critique of Entrepreneurship* (Basingstoke: Palgrave Macmillan, 2005).
Du Gay, P., *Consumption and Identity at Work* (London: Sage, 1996).
Jones, C. and A. Spicer, *Unmasking the Entrepreneur* (Cheltenham: Edward Elgar, 2009).

Questions for discussion

What are some of the dark sides of entrepreneurship that are usually ignored by more mainstream theories?
What is mean by enterprise discourse?
Can you think of some examples where enterprise discourse has appeared in un-expected settings (e.g. education, large corporations, non profits, government, the military)?
How do you think people might resist enterprise discourse?
Can you think of examples of cases where entrepreneurs do not think of themselves in terms of 'enterprise discourse'?

CHAPTER 12

Pragmatism, Reality and Entrepreneurship: Entrepreneurial Action and Effectuation Perspectives

Tony J. Watson

Introduction

Studying any aspect of social or economic life confronts us with a variety of different perspectives, approaches or 'paradigms'. The study of entrepreneurship is no different from any other field in this respect. The intention of this chapter is to argue for two closely related 'perspectives' which – in the spirit of Pragmatist philosophical thinking – are concerned with getting to grips with the practical realities of entrepreneurship. One of these, the 'entrepreneurial action' perspective, is much broader than many others. It can, in fact, incorporate the insights of other perspectives, including the second one featured in this chapter, the 'effectuation' perspective. Most importantly, the entrepreneurial action perspective overcomes the distinction between 'micro' and 'macro' perspectives. One of its defining features is its continuous relating of the 'micro' and the 'macro' aspects of entrepreneurship.

First, I will explain the some of the key principles of Pragmatist philosophy, using the term 'pragmatic realism' to emphasize the realist dimension of this way of thinking about the world ('realism' having been introduced earlier in Chapter 10). I shall then explain how these ideas have been applied to social science, showing that a pragmatically-realist social science can incorporate interpretive ideas (introduced in Chapter 4) without slipping into the non-realism of much contemporary 'interpretivism'. Having established these methodological and theoretical foundations, I shall explain the Pragmatist view of human beings as creative, exchanging and emergent animals before deriving from this the key concepts of *entrepreneurial action, emergent life orientations* and *the entrepreneurial actor*. The entrepreneurial action perspective will then be linked to the effectuation perspective developed by Sarasvathy (2008). These two perspectives, it will be argued, make the study of entrepreneurship a broader and more 'open' undertaking than it has previously tended to be. For now, let's examine the Pragmatist thinking that underpins both the entrepreneurial action and the effectuation perspectives.

Pragmatic realism: Much more than 'another perspective'

Pragmatism is not just another narrow perspective on social life. It is a whole way of thinking about knowledge and its relationship to human activities. Entrepreneurship is just one of those activities. This does not mean that an invitation is being issued to reject theory and any consideration of principles and values and to proceed by adopting whatever methods or concepts are convenient or expedient. The word 'pragmatism' is used in this sense in everyday conversation but the word has a different meaning in philosophy. I shall therefore give the word a capital letter – Pragmatism – to make it clear that the ideas being applied in this chapter are ones associated, originally, with a particular school of philosophy and, second, with a style of social science that was shaped by Pragmatist ideas and that has at its heart a concern with relating the micro with the macro in social and economic analysis. Its purpose is to produce analyses of the social world that have the potential to inform the thinking and practices of the citizens of modern democratic societies.

The classical Pragmatist philosophers are Charles Peirce (1839–1914), William James (1842–1910) and John Dewey (1859–1914), and although each of these had distinctive views we can see certain common themes running through their work. The most important of these is the idea that we should evaluate scientific knowledge not in terms of how accurately it tells us 'what is the case' in the world but, instead, in terms of how well it informs human actions in the world. Neither a fully formed 'correct' theory nor a complete understanding about any aspect of the world is ever possible because reality is far too complicated for that. We therefore strive to develop knowledge about the world which is better than what we had before, or is better than rival pieces of knowledge, in terms of its value as a guide to human actors trying to deal with that world. The 'guiding principle of pragmatism', Joas says, is that truth is no longer to do with getting a correct 'representation of reality in cognition'; 'rather, it expresses an increase of the power to act in relation to an environment' (1993, p. 21). James spoke of theories being 'instrumental'; they are 'mental modes of adaptation to reality, rather than revelations [about the world]' (quoted by Mills, 1966, p. 227). Dewey put this very clearly by arguing that 'the aim of knowledge is not to represent the world but to cope with it' (quoted by Mounce, 1997, p. 177).

This position is very clearly a realist one. If there was not a social 'real world' out there beyond our apprehension of it, then any kind of social science knowledge with relevance to human practices would be impossible. Different individuals and different groups might have different 'takes' on reality – but that is not the same thing as claiming that there are multiple realities in society (we will return to this point later when considering the notion of the social construction of reality). This stance is one shared by the critical realists, whose position was explained in Chapter 10. Critical realists attempt to identify 'generative mechanisms' and 'causal powers' operating in society. Those who adopt what I am calling a pragmatic realist position would not necessarily reject an interest in such matters. They would, however, regard these notions of mechanisms and powers as intellectual devices used in the struggle to 'come to terms with reality' as opposed to their being things with a solid reality or 'ontology' of their own.

Pragmatism and the sociological imagination

There is an affinity between Pragmatism and the ideas of the great economic historian, political theorist and sociologist, Max Weber (1947, 1949). Radkau (2009), in his monumental biography, shows that reality was a central concept in Weber's thinking. Reality is complex, contradictory, ambiguous and, ultimately, unknowable. Yet social science has to 'get to grips with reality' (a phrase that appears at various points in Radkau's account of Weber's life and thinking). The concepts, models, types and theories that the social scientist develops are simply means of engaging with the infinite complexity of the 'nature' of the world and the nature of the human being. The essentially problematic relationship between means and ends in social life is a leitmotif in Weber's work and his passionate moral and political engagement with the political, economic and cultural issues of the age. This meant that social science must not become an end itself; social research and theorizing is a means towards practical engagement with social, political and economic issues of the time.

Weberian and Pragmatist ideas were most effectively brought together in the work of Charles Wright Mills (1916–1962) and its central concern with the relationship between the micro and the macro aspect of societies and history. Mills advocated the application of the 'sociological imagination' to social, political and economic matters (he explains that he is addressing the social science community generally in spite of his use of the word 'sociology' here). One of the most powerful ideas in the social sciences, he says, is the distinction between social structure and personal milieu (Mills, 1956). The social sciences should help people 'grasp what is going on in the world, and to understand what is happening in themselves at minute points of the intersection of biography and history within society' (Mills, 1990, p. 14). Mills called for the social scientist to develop a capacity to 'shift from one perspective to another, and in the process to build up an adequate view of a total society and its components' (1990, p. 14). This requires the imagination to combine 'ideas that no one expected were combinable', a 'playfulness of mind' and a 'fierce drive to make sense of the world' (1990, p. 14). From this, we can take the message that a socially fruitful study of entrepreneurship would be one that looked across, but also beyond, the range of 'perspectives' covered in the present text to find conceptual resources that might be imaginatively utilized to study entrepreneurial actors and how their actions and their lives are both shaped by their social contexts and, in themselves, contribute to the shaping of social worlds.

The vital need to ground interpretive processes in an objectively real world

In spite of what has just been said, one cannot do worthwhile studies of something like entrepreneurship simply by collecting conceptual bits and pieces from here and there. If we are going to look at entrepreneurship in a way which relates the micro and the macro realities of social life, we need to develop some clear working assumptions and a set of pragmatically helpful analytical concepts. Chapter 4 of this book examined what is called the 'interpretive' way of studying entrepreneurship. Interpretivism is treated in this volume as a micro approach to studying the social world. In his massive contribution to political, economic and social science, Weber showed that it was necessary to examine meaning-making or interpretive processes in social life. He insisted, though, that these micro and subjective matters must always be related to the larger macro and objective structural and cultural tendencies of societies and history. His sociological work is often described as 'interpretive'. Indeed he called part of his work 'interpretive sociology'. But it would be a serious mistake to call him interpretivist in the sense that has now become common. Just like Berger and Luckmann (1967) half a century later, he was striving to bring together what we might call the objective and the subjective aspects of social life as well as the micro and macro. 'His intention', Freund explains, 'was certainly not to assign a higher place to interpretation than to explanation' (1972, p. 91): 'He took the view that to study the development of an institution solely from the outside, without regard to what [the human being] makes of it, is to overlook one of the principal aspects of social life' (Freund, 1972 p. 89). Weber argued for considering the objectively existing 'real' world as well as subjective meaning-making subjective factors. He gave neither one primacy over the other.

A key problem with 'interpretivism', from a Pragmatist point view, is that valuable concepts like, social construction, narrative, rhetoric, identity and discourse are being pumped up into 'master ideas' rather than being utilized as analytical devices that can be pulled together to create conceptual frameworks for the study of particular areas of social life. The difficulty, to put it simply, is that aspects of reality are being treated as approaches to reality. This is unfortunate because while one cannot but recognize the multiplicity of aspects to reality one can only ever take a single approach to anything at any given moment. But, just a minute, did I say 'reality' again here?

As was explained in Chapter 10, what I would call a 'turn back' to realism has occurred in reaction to interpretivism. Neither the critical realism discussed in that chapter nor the Pragmatic Realism introduced here have any difficulty with looking at interpretive and social construction processes, meanings, narratives and the rest. These terms refer to aspects of the real social world; yes, an objectively existing real world. This is the real world encountered by a couple of informants in my current research work who have become bankrupt after their businesses failed to survive economic recession. It is the reality of another informant who was made redundant by the business he worked for and which has not survived global competitive pressures. The 'personal troubles', as Mills (1956) called them, of these people can only be understood in terms of 'public issues' arising within the reality of changing social, political and economic circumstances. These are realities that human beings have to face, regardless of what lenses are in their spectacles, regardless of what they wish to be the case and regardless of everything they have tried to do to avoid their current predicaments. The interpretivist or social constructionist lens-wearer might well object to this analysis as 'objectivist' and as failing to recognize that notions like 'bankruptcy' and 'redundancy' are social constructions. They might also want to insist that there are multiple realities in the world, as opposed to a single 'real world'.

The realist response to the first point made by our interpretivist is 'Yes of course "bankruptcy" is a humanly invented institution emerging out of processes of social construction'. But that does not stop bankruptcies and redundancies being part of a real world (reality being for Berger and Luckmann things which we cannot 'wish away'). It is too often forgotten that Berger and Luckmann (1967) created the term 'the social construction of reality' to examine the relationship between the objective and the subjective aspects of the social world (note that the title of Part II of their book is 'Society as Objective Reality'). On the second point, about 'multiple realities', the realist response might be 'Yes and no.' A realist could accept that there are multiple subjective realities, with the failed entrepreneurs having a different 'take' on what happened to their business from the banker who withdrew their loan facility. So, in this sense, yes, we can differentiate between the 'reality of the banker' and the 'reality of the bankrupt business partners'. But the realist social scientist cannot leave it at that. It is part of their job to study such matters as the involvement of different people, in this case bankers and business owners, in the shared objective reality of a particular political economy, business culture, State, network of relationships and so on. How can we do social science if we abandon the notion of people's involvement in a shared and objective real world? How can we study any aspect of society and economy if we get trapped by the 'epistemic fallacy' (Bhaskar, 1979) of collapsing ontology ('what is') into epistemology ('what we know')? Not only that, but how could we possibly set about trying to change any aspect of our social existence?

Human beings as creative, exchanging and emergent social animals

Different 'perspectives' on entrepreneurship make their own assumptions about what is traditionally called 'human nature'. Assumptions need to be made on this matter if we are going to study social activities and structures because social actions, processes and institutions have emerged over the species' history to deal with aspects of what I will call here the nature of being human. The term 'human nature' is too associated with that type of argument in which, say, entrepreneurial initiatives are explained simplistically in terms of alleged qualities of human individuals – the desire for wealth, say, the drive for power or the need for achievement (McClelland, 1961). If we are careful to avoid this kind of reductionism, it is possible to identify certain fairly basic assumptions about 'the nature of being human' which will be helpful to us in our study of entrepreneurship. Remember, this is not a matter of identifying here some essentially true or correct assumptions about human beings. It is applying the Pragmatic principle of identifying assumptions which will enable us to cope better with the realities of the world than if we work with other assumptions. And Pragmatic thinking offers a particular assumption about human beings that is especially helpful for our present purposes.

Joas says that the Pragmatists 'maintain that all human action is caught in the tension between unreflected habitual action and acts of creativity' (1996, p. 129). 'Creativity', he continues, 'is seen as something which is performed within situations which call for solutions', and this, he suggests, 'permits us to apply the idea of creativity to the full spectrum of human action' (1996, p. 144). The pragmatists, he concludes, understand human action as 'situated creativity'. We are encouraged to see human beings as creative animals. That creativity is not unbounded, however. It will have different effects in different circumstances. It does suggest, however, that insofar as creativity is an element of entrepreneurial action, it has the potential to emerge in human beings generally – given situations which are conducive to it. Such an approach is advocated by Steyaert (2007) and by Johannisson (2011) who wish to associate 'entrepreneuring' with 'everyday life and not with heroic achievements', re-establishing it as 'a fundamental human activity, central in man's ongoing quest of identity and meaning of life'.

The implication of a Pragmatist view of the world is that it would be wise to move away from the standard and individualistic 'framing' of so much business, management and entrepreneurship thinking, which treats human beings as creatures with 'needs' that 'motivate' them to behave in certain ways. Instead, we think of people as sense-making and project-oriented creatures who 'in the light of how they interpret their situations ... make exchanges with others to deal with their material and emotional circumstances' (Watson, 2006, p. 30). When human beings arrive in the world, they are not like young foals, which are very quickly up on their legs and are soon young versions of a fully-formed horse. We could say, in fact, that the human being never becomes a fully formed 'person'. They are 'unfinished animals' (Gehlen, 1940) who are always in a state of emergence, constantly working on who they are, in their own eyes and the eyes of others. They are helped in this by the institutions and cultures around them of course but this, from very early on, involves negotiation, exchange or 'trading'. The degree of creativity that is to be seen in their exchanging activities is, as was stressed above, a situated creativity. The Pragmatists were not concerned, we must remember, about the 'correctness' or otherwise of ideas like this. Instead they believed that if we worked with these kinds of assumption about the 'nature of being human' we were more likely to be effective in our social practices than if we worked with other assumptions.

Working with a view of the human animal as a creative and emergent being who continuously exchanges with others to shape their identities and life orientations, we can now move to conceptualize entrepreneurship, as one socially and historically 'situated' manifestation of the human propensity towards creative exchange.

Focusing on entrepreneurial action

To the Pragmatist, definitions of phenomena are simply adaptive devices, rather than more-or-less 'correct' takes on the world. This is especially the case in science. The scientist creates concepts in order to complete a given investigative project. Concepts are working definitions, devised to help the investigator get to grips with an aspect of reality. A concept of entrepreneurship is not a more-or-less correct definition of what entrepreneurship 'is'. It is, rather, a more-or-less helpful working definition of a type of action, which, one hopes, will enable us to understand better the more creative, innovative or imaginative aspects of 'doing business'. I propose the following as a useful conceptual way forward for the study of entrepreneurship.

Entrepreneurial action (or 'entrepreneurship' or 'entrepreneuring') is the making of creative or innovative exchanges (or 'deals') between the entrepreneurial actor's home business (or 'enterprise') and other parties with which the enterprise trades.

'Entrepreneurship', 'entrepreneuring' and 'entrepreneurial action' are treated here as more-or-less synonymous. Entrepreneurship has an attractive connotation of 'making' or 'creating'. Barnhart's etymological account of the suffix 'ship' goes back to the Old English 'sceppan' or 'scieppan' meaning to 'create, form, shape' something (Barnhart, 1988, p. 998). Entrepreneuring has appeal too, with its emphasis on enterprising activities as processes (Steyaert 2007). This is comparable to processual thinking about 'managing' rather than 'management' and 'organizing' rather than 'organization' (Watson, 2006; Weick, 1979). 'Entrepreneurial action' is favoured here partly because of its fit with Weber's key focus on 'social action' and Pragmatism's fundamental action orientation. More important, though, is that the term 'has the edge' when it comes to ensuring that we look at something that some people sometimes *do* in the social and economic world, as opposed to trying to understand what certain 'special' people are *like*.

Beyond the matter of the key term to be used, there are three dimensions to the entrepreneurial action perspective that make it open to a wider range of activities than do many other perspectives. It helps broaden the scope of our studies in three ways:

1.   The entrepreneurial action perspective has at its heart the notion of creative, innovative, imaginative deal-making. The starting point for this is the idea that a propensity to exchange is a species-characteristic of the human being. In certain circumstances, however, we see people exchanging by making business deals that have a particularly novel or innovate dimension to them. This is best seen as a matter of degree. And this means that no business move is to be seen as totally entrepreneurial. By the same token, a business totally lacking an entrepreneurial dimension is unlikely to be found. By talking about a form of exchange activity we are able to recognize the role that elements of enterprising deal-making might, and indeed do play in professional, governmental and 'social enterprise' spheres. Some of the most strikingly innovative 'business' activities that I have seen in my current research are within a small town law firm, for example.

2.   The concept of entrepreneurial action incorporates the idea of 'the enterprise' in the form of the entrepreneurial actor's 'home business'. This latter term is used instead of talking about the individual's 'own' business, to decouple the idea of the entrepreneurial actor from the idea of the business owner. The entrepreneurial deal makers in a business are often its owners. It is not helpful, however, to allow the definition-making process to close down the possibility that the 'creative' force in an enterprise might come from other than its owner(s). The link between ownership and entrepreneuring is something to be investigated, rather than something to be taken for granted from the start. This point is related to the broader one of bringing the organizational dimension into our way of thinking about entrepreneurship. The standard focus on the individual entrepreneur has led to an under-emphasis on the extent to which entrepreneurship is a social activity. This is avoided here by considering 'the enterprise' as much as 'the entrepreneur'. Doing so does not, however, preclude the possibility that an 'enterprise' could well be a one-person one, with the individual incorporating the standard functional division of labour within their own working day.

3.   The proposed concept takes us back to the underpinning principle of exchange. Whether we are looking at a one-person operation or a large corporation, we must recognize that its continuation into the long term is dependent on exchange relationships with a whole range of what are often called 'stakeholders' (Freeman, 1984). It is more helpful, I believe, to call these suppliers, customers, employees, State authorities and media organizations, and the rest resource dependent parties or 'constituencies' (Hillman, Withers and Collins, 2009; Pfeffer and Salancik, 1978; Watson, 2006). The term 'stakeholder' implies a degree of emotional attachment to an enterprise of these various parties that is rather unrealistic. There is also an implication of status or power equivalence, even a hint of 'partnership', in the stakeholder notion. Nevertheless, it is a reality of running enterprises that they can only continue into the future if a whole series of exchanges are to be made and remade with this range of parties (Watson, 1995). However brilliant an individual might be at making key or 'big' business deals, their undertaking will soon come to grief if successful deals are not also made across the whole range of parties with whom the enterprise exchanges – from employees to suppliers and from investors to newspaper reporters. This means that we can expect to see entrepreneurial actions occurring from time to time across the range of managerial functions; whenever, that is, particularly innovative or creative deals are done by managers with the particular constituencies they connect to – employees, suppliers and the rest.

The move that has been made here, in the spirit of Pragmatism, has the potential to rescue the idea of entrepreneurship for the social sciences. Various notions of entrepreneurship, generally centring on 'entrepreneurs' rather than on exchange processes, float about in contemporary culture in a mist of ambiguity and ambivalence. Some people speak with admiration of entrepreneurs; others with clear distaste. Some speak of entrepreneurs as 'big people'; others speak of them as 'small people'. Sometimes they are the starters of businesses; sometimes they are buyers and sellers of businesses. The ambivalence – the mixture of approval and disapproval – seen to exist in the culture alongside this considerable ambiguity could well encourage us to abandon completely any notion of using entrepreneurship as a formal concept to help us with socially worthwhile research on the 'innovative-exchange' aspect of business life. In fact, this might be very wise with regard to the notion of 'the entrepreneur'. The shift we need to make, pragmatically, is to focus on entrepreneurship as a type of action and only then to look at the people who engage in it.

Entrepreneurial actors and life orientations

The creativity that is at the heart of entrepreneurial action is always 'situated', as we stressed earlier. It is situated, at the macro level, in a particular period of history, within a particular type of political economy and within a set of other structural and cultural circumstances ranging from the current state of labour markets and interest rates to the current patterns of demand and consumer tastes. But it is also situated, at the micro level, in the biographies, personal circumstances and aspirations of those who engage in entrepreneurial actions. A useful concept here, building on the concept of 'orientation to work', a key idea in industrial sociology (Goldthorpe et al., 1968; Watson, 2011c), is that of *emergent life orientation*.

Emergent life orientations are the meanings attached by an individual at a particular stage of their life to their personal and social circumstances: meanings that predispose them to act in particular ways with regard to their future, including their relationship to work and consumption.

This concept is related to the notion of human beings as 'project-oriented' creatures (as opposed to motive-driven or need-led animals) that was introduced earlier. The concept links people's interpretations of their life situation with the actions in which they engage. A version of the concept was used to show how certain shifts in the life priorities of a property-developer entrepreneurial actor, involving a shift from an urban to a rural life style, was linked to the changing life orientations of potential customers for properties in the country area to which they were moving, as part of a shift in lifestyle on their parts (Fletcher and Watson, 2006). What we might call the consumption aspect of the potential house buyers' life orientations matched the work aspect of the property developer's life orientation, thus creating a business opportunity for him. But, again insisting that 'micro' matters like these must always be related to 'macro' factors, we must recognize that none of this could have occurred had there not been significant economic and land-use changes in that rural area in the first place.

Macro factors don't just take the form of material circumstances within which entrepreneurial action occurs. The interpretations that people make of their very selves (their self-identities), their pasts and their present life situations are powerfully influenced by both very broad and very specific cultural and discursive factors (Watson, 2008). These include various narratives that people grow up hearing and that they meet in literature, news and entertainment media every day. For some people, they will include the various images of 'entrepreneurs' that the individual sees in the culture around them and may decide to emulate – or avoid for that matter.

For some time, academic observers argued that macro-level entrepreneurial *discourses* were important factors in micro-level entrepreneurial initiative taking (du Gay, 1996). Detailed research across a range of different entre-preneurial activities has completely changed this understanding (Bolton and Houlihan, 2005; Fenwick, 2002; Halford and Leonard, 2006; Storey, Salaman and Platman, 2005). It is clearly quite possible for people to act in an enter-prising manner without any apparent significant attachment to ideologies or discourses of enterprise. The business partner of one self-proclaimed 'entre-preneur' that I closely studied, for example, was in no doubt that her colleague (and cousin) would have acted no differently in his business life had he never come across the expressions 'enterprise' and 'entrepreneurship' (Watson, 2009). He used these linguistic devices in his outward-facing identity work, his 'presentation of self' to others (Goffman, 1958) but his business creativ-ity was much more significantly situated in his ethnic and family backgrounds than in any 'discourse' of entrepreneurship. One could only understand the pattern of actions in this business by setting them within the realities of his family having been expelled from Uganda in the 1970s, the death of his father and uncle, a clash which came about with other family members who briefly took over the running of the business, and so on. These factors played a part alongside a range of others; from the state of the national economy at the time of the business's growth and aspects of current popular culture that encouraged an interest in the goods and services that the business offered to customers and clients. And, to go even further in situating entrepreneurial action in this way, we must always consider the would-be entrepreneurial actor's personal social and business competences. These are factors that will inevitably contribute to the shaping of an individual's work–life orientation and the way in which an adopted orientation encourages them to undertake one kind of work or business activity rather than another.

A key study in the Pragmatist tradition: Effectuation and entrepreneurship

The personal competences or 'expertise' of any individual involved in entre-preneurial activities is one of the various 'means' to entrepreneurial success that are emphasized in the effectuation perspective. This is a way of looking at and thinking about entrepreneurship derived from empirical studies of entre-preneurial activities carried out by Sarasvathy (2001, 2008). This research led Sarasvathy to turn away from the 'causation model' that frames mainstream entrepreneurship thinking. In this model, entrepreneurial activity begins with goals which would-be entrepreneurs set for themselves. To achieve those goals or ('fulfil entrepreneurs' dreams' in the popular cliché, I would add) various *means* are sought. But careful and close examination of what actually hap-pens within entrepreneurial processes points towards an alternative model – an effectuation one. This suggests that entrepreneurial actors begin, not with goals or dreams, but with the *means* available to them for working effectively in the circumstances in which they find themselves. In emphasiz-ing the ways in which these entrepreneurial actors creatively deal with their circumstances the model resonates, as Sarasvathy notes, with Pragmatist thinking. And, going back to the detail of the model, once the entrepreneurial actor has identified the 'means' that are at their disposal, they act so as to bring about *effects* that these means make possible. It is these effects that we should pay closest attention to when studying entrepreneurial activity – not some putative cause of the activities engaged in. But what are these 'means' that are so important? They fall into three categories: who the person is (characteristics, abilities etc); what they know (education, experiences etc) and whom they know (social and professional networks).

In my own 'entrepreneurial action' research I have found, time and again, just like Sarasvathy, that I could understand much more fully how a business, or a venture within a business, had developed by looking at the ways in which the actors involved started with what they could do, what they knew and who they linked up with to help them be entrepreneurially effective (Watson, 2011b). Sarasvathy and her colleagues (Read et al. 2010), in trying to pull together a notion of 'effectual entrepreneurship' for a wide audience, refer to 'a common logic we have observed … across industries, geographies and time' (2010, p. ix). And, fully in line with Pragmatist principles, they argue that their readers will benefit in a practical way by applying this logic. Thus, a logic identified by scientific research becomes a logic that practitioners can be advised to follow. They recommend that entrepreneurial actors not focus on opportunities (which they are frequently exhorted to do) but, from the start, use what 'you have available' in terms of who you are, what you know and who you know; 'embrace surprises that arise from uncertain situations'; 'remain flexible rather than tethered to existing goals'; and form partnerships with appropriate 'people and organizations'.

The effectuation perspective is entirely compatible with the entrepreneurial action one. This is perhaps not surprising given that both perspectives work with a Pragmatist understanding of the social world. The entrepreneurial perspective is perhaps broader than the effectuation one and, in developing my own work, I am incorporating the effectuation insight into an extended entrepreneurial action framework (Watson, 2011b). One difference between the two approaches is that the effectuation writers retain a concept of 'the entrepreneur'.

Nevertheless, Read et al. make it clear that effectuation principles apply to 'new ventures' whether or not these are done 'for profit' and whether they are undertaken individually or within existing organisations (2010, p. x). And they do make use of the term 'entrepreneurial action'. There is thus no substantial difference between the two perspectives apart from the greater breadth of the entrepreneurial action one and the fact that the effectuation writers retain the tradition term the 'the entrepreneur'. The way they use this term, however, makes it fully interchangeable with the notion of the 'entrepreneurial actor'.

Pragmatic thinking: Potential dangers and criticisms

It is difficult to point to criticisms of a style of philosophical thinking and a type of social science that have been central to one's own thinking and activity over many years. Nevertheless I can point to one issue that repeatedly arises when people are presented with Pragmatist thinking: they reduce Pragmatism's central principal to the crude idea that knowledge is only judged to be worthwhile if it is 'useful'. They then attack Pragmatism on the grounds that it fails to deal with the question, 'useful to whom?' And people are right to oppose the simplistic and, indeed, dangerous notion that an idea or a piece of knowledge should be judged 'true' or 'worthwhile' if it is useful. For example, a 'big lie' of the type associated with Nazism in the twentieth century, or any piece of political propaganda for that matter, could be very useful to certain people. Similarly, bogus ideas about entrepreneurship could be very helpful to certain interest groups in contemporary society. This usefulness does not give such ideas validity. But the Pragmatist philosophers did not work with such a simplistic notion of 'usefulness'. There is a clear emphasis on the utility of knowledge in their writing. But they were thinking of the potential utility of knowledge, as we might put it, to members of society as a whole. The Pragmatist judges knowledge about, say, entrepreneurship in terms of how well it might inform the actions of anyone in society who might become involved with it as a would-be or actual entrepreneur, as a potential client or partner of an entrepreneur, as an investor, a policy-maker or an anti-capitalist political activist. Pragmatism judges knowledge in terms of how well it informs human action, not in terms of some vague or crude notion of usefulness.

Conclusions

It was argued earlier that one of the considerable advantages of the *entrepreneurial action* perspective is that it avoids the danger of 'closing off' issues that we need to investigate as a result of assumptions that we build into the conceptual apparatus we use. I argued, for example, that the link between ownership and entrepreneuring is something to be investigated and not something to be taken for granted from the start, by building ownership into the concept of entrepreneurship. The same can be said with regard to the question of whether or not there are people who are especially entrepreneurially inclined (as opposed to being heavily involved in entrepreneurial actions). Yet again, the extent to which particular or 'actual' entrepreneurial actions comply or not with public ideas of honesty and trustworthiness is a matter for investigation and not something to be defined into or out of consideration from the start. Further, to keep our minds open in our studies we should recognize that business 'start ups' may or may not involve anything more than minimal entrepreneurial action and, by the same token, that entrepreneurship itself may or may not involve starting a new business. We should be open to the idea that any particular entrepreneurial operator will often engage in entrepreneurial actions for only a part of their working day or week (alongside administration, problem-solving, selling and so on). Also, there is a lot still be learnt about the ways in which entrepreneurial actions are located in the division of labour at the executive level of the enterprise. Co-preneurship is a concept that sometimes arises here (Fitzgerald and Muske, 2002). However, as well as being etymologically awkward, this is one of those concepts that closes off, from the start, consideration of a variety of different empirical possibilities. We need to examine the various ways in which entrepreneurial, managerial and leadership tasks are shared (or are not shared) across the 'top team' of any particular enterprise (a family business or otherwise), rather than assuming that apparent co-venturers are necessarily all involved in entrepreneurial endeavours.

Pragmatist thinking helps us to keep our feet on the ground here, so to speak, by encouraging us to adopt working assumptions, concepts and theoretical devices that help us produce knowledge with a potential to inform the actions of all those in society who have an interest – material, intellectual or political – in the entrepreneurial dimension of economic life. To help here, use has been made of Mills's notion of the sociological imagination and Weber's concept of social action. More specifically the Pragmatists' concept of situated creativity has been exploited to take us towards a pragmatically helpful working concept of entrepreneurial action. This concept is firmly rooted in the assumption that, first, no aspect of social life can be understood without recognizing the constant interplay of micro and macro factors and, second, that exchange processes are central to social and economic life. The entrepreneurial action perspective is fully compatible with the effectuation perspective, with its similarly Pragmatism-inspired stress on entrepreneurial actors taking advantage of the circumstances in which they find themselves to develop businesses, as opposed to seeing them as visionary types of people pursuing 'dreams'.

I have proposed that we concentrate on entrepreneurial action rather than on 'entrepreneurs' and that when we look at individual actors we examine their *emergent life orientations*. This encourages us to recognize that an individual's engagement in entrepreneurial activities may happen to varying extents at different stages of their personal lives or their home business's circumstances. In a research transcript sitting on my desk as I write, for example, I see the following words, 'Am I an entrepreneur? I get asked that. Well, I certainly could have been called an entrepreneur between 1995 and 2000. Not now. But I'm getting bored at the moment with being just a rich and successful businessman. So I think I might go back to what I so enjoyed in that earlier deal-making period – for a while anyway'.

At this point, it must be said that entrepreneurship is far too important to leave either to so-called entrepreneurs themselves or to entrepreneurship academics. The role that entrepreneurial activities play in a society, economy and polity is a highly significant aspect of the very nature of that social order. This makes it an important aspect of life for social scientists to study, especially if they want their research and writing to influence the making of political decisions, as did Max Weber, the Pragmatist philosophers and Charles Wright Mills. Weber and Mills may not be known as entrepreneurship scholars (like Weber's associate and sometimes ally Joseph Schumpeter). But they both saw the part that entrepreneurial activities would or could play in the societies of their time as vitally important. Weber saw vigorous entrepreneurial activity as an important counter to tendencies towards the over-bureaucratisation of life in early twentieth-century Germany. Mills's worry was about the rise of large corporations and the control of society by a 'power elite' in later twentieth century America. These corporations were replacing the 'small entrepreneurs', which he believed had previously had a 'real part to play in the equilibrium of power' in American society (Mills, 1956, p. 260).

Is any of this relevant to the times in which the readers of the present book are living? Is the role of entrepreneurial activity a matter which we ought to be debating within our contemporary political processes? I would say yes, most certainly, pointing out that the British government that came to power in 2010 was one in which key members had argued powerfully for a more 'entrepreneurial' society. In the election campaign, the prime minister-to-be promised the electorate 'a country with entrepreneurs everywhere, bringing their ideas to life – and life to our great towns and cities' (*Guardian*, 2009). Whatever view we take of this political aspiration and its relationship to that government's preference for market-based economies, it is clear that entrepreneurial activities are of continuing relevance to the choices we make about the sort of society, economy and democracy we live in. Pragmatism sees social scientific knowledge as potentially vital in informing the choices that are made in modern democracies. The more effectively we develop that knowledge with regard to entrepreneurship, the better placed we will be as potential entrepreneurial actors, as customers of or suppliers to innovative enterprises, as opponents or supporters of business-based social innovation, or simply as concerned citizens in a democratic society.

Further reading

A fuller explanation of Pragmatism, realism and the need to shift away from studying 'entrepreneurs' to the study of 'entrepreneurial action' is in the first of two articles appearing in *Entrepreneurship and Regional Development* (Watson, 2011b). A second article (Watson, 2011a) presents a developed version of the entrepreneurial action perspective that incorporates the effectuation principle and applies the perspective to empirical field research. For a clear overview of effectuation thinking and many examples of effectual entrepreneurship in action see Read et al. (2010).

Questions for discussion

How many different meanings of the term 'entrepreneur' can you find when you look at its usage among people you know, in newspapers and on television programmes?

To what extent do you agree with the contention in this chapter that these usages are so varied, ambiguous and politically 'coloured' that, for serious study purposes, we need a more neutral term like 'entrepreneurial action'?

If you look closely at any business venture about which you can find detailed information, what part was played in its emergence by (a) who the principal entrepreneurial actors were, (b) what they knew and (c) whom they knew.

Conclusion

Kevin Mole

The most evident element of this edited collection is the wide variety of perspectives within entrepreneurship. Within this collection, there is little dominance of quantitative studies. In this book, the attempt has been to showcase the wide variety of approaches that are open to researchers when they seek to research within the field of entrepreneurship. Eleven different approaches were highlighted, each with its own take on what researchers seek to do when they investigate a subject.

The differences are difficult to understand without an appreciation of ontological and epistemological issues. There are clear distinctions between the way that interpretivists such as Fletcher view the world as socially constructed, and how realists such as psychologists and rational choice economists view the world as something outside of social concepts, even if all groups use concepts that are theory-laden; that is, that there are no facts outside of man-made concepts.

Some differences can be linked to different positions. The approaches have shown us different sides to entrepreneurship. While the edited collection was not concerned to highlight the latest research within entrepreneurship, the intepretivist work showed the importance of a narrative; how the narrative was constructed into a coherent story of the start-up event, with a beginning, middle and resolution; with the entrepreneur at the centre of events. Similarly in other work the myth of (?) the entrepreneur as an active agent is reinforced. This narrative structure was met again in the chapter on neo-institutionalism, where entrepreneurs used their narratives as an important element by which to gain material resources (Zott and Huy, 2007). Hence, the narratives had real effects.

Narratives were not something that concerned the economists in Chapter 2; they were much more interested in the incentives surrounding entrepreneurship. If taxes fell then more would join the ranks of those forming new firms. More interest in the economics literature is concerned with finance, the perceptions of entrepreneurial ability and the expected future profits of an undertaking (Evans and Jovanovic, 1989). But without the narrative and neo-institutional perspectives, an important part of the process of gaining finance would be missed.

The different approaches give us more depth in the knowledge of entrepreneurship. We have more knowledge combining the elements. The interpretive approach shows us how entrepreneurs make meaning out of their situation; the rational choice perspective assesses the potential for finance gaps in funding and the call for public policy intervention. While the rational choice economic approach discusses entrepreneurial ability (Evans and Jovanovic, 1989), the psychological approach can lead us to understand the cognitive abilities that enable some entrepreneurs to estimate their abilities (Chen et al., 1998). Other perspectives show that successful entrepreneurs vary their routines to find those that fit the environment (Breslin, 2010). This comparison offers the clearest example of how different ontological and epistemological positions have implications for what is studied and how it is studied.

More examples could be found from each of the chapters. When entrepreneurship remains as a field for interdisciplinary work, it can attract a wider set of interested scholars to enhance our knowledge of entrepreneurship (Sorenson and Stuart, 2008). To quote Tony Watson from the previous chapter:

> From this, we can take the message that a socially fruitful study of entrepreneurship would be one which looked across, but also beyond, the range of 'perspectives' covered in the present text to find conceptual resources which might be imaginatively utilised to study entrepreneurial actors and how their actions and their lives are both shaped by their social contexts and, in themselves, contribute to the shaping of social worlds.

Making this case, however, is difficult against the counter that an entrepreneurship free-for-all is a recipe for a poorly legitimated field that does not count as a sub-discipline of management. As students will know, the issue of what is seen as legitimate is a powerful source of social conformity (DiMaggio and Powell, 1983).

This debate between the legitimated strong paradigm and the creativity of the academic marketplace is not new and has taken place in many other subjects, including strategy (Bracker, 1980). The outcome probably lies between the two. What is important here is to preserve the ability to hear dissident voices from whatever position is taken so that those who identify themselves with particular perspectives, which is all of the academic community, do not simply talk among themselves but debate in a wider forum.

The future of the perspectives

Finally, what is the future for the different perspectives? The number of perspectives in the discipline has probably increased over time. Early approaches to small business emphasized empirical work (Romanelli, 1989; Storey, 1982) and some questioning of the notion of enterprise, as noted by Spicer (Burrows, 1991; du Gay, 1996; MacDonald and Coffield, 1991; Ram and Holliday, 1993) and the conditions within small firms (Goss, 1991), but a great deal was inspired by the economics of small businesses (Brock and Evans, 1989; Evans and Jovanovic, 1989).

Although within social science there was a broader critical response to enterprise, within business and management the emphasis in the early years was on the entity of the small firm.

However, in many business and management sub-disciplines there has been a movement away from a focus on the organization and entity, in this case small firms, towards the agency of those practising or acting (Santos and Eisenhardt, 2005; Sarasvathy, 2001, 2004; Tsoukas, 1994; Tsoukas and

Chia, 2002; Westhead, Ucbasaran, and Wright, 2005). This has been noticed within the chapters of this volume. Denise Fletcher noticed this shift from notions of the ethnicity to the way in which the ethnicity is negotiated and used in personal agency (see also Ram et al., 2008). The critical approach has always focussed on the discourse of entrepreneurship. This movement away from a focus on the entity towards the practice of entrepreneurship reflects, in part the rise of anti-foundationalism, which suggests that there is no world outside of our social construction (Grix, 2004). As the idea that the world is socially constructed has developed the emphasis has been towards how people use their knowledge of social constructions to re-invent themselves (Ram, 1999b; Watson, 2009).

In entrepreneurship, we have moved from the focus on the business to the process of developing an idea and taking it to a market, from the discovery of opportunity towards the exploitation of that opportunity (Shane and Venkataraman, 2000; Venkataraman, 1997). From the business to the process; hence, within the perspectives in this book we have seen the movement towards performing ritualistically to access resources (Zott and Huy, 2007).

So it is likely that there will be more perspectives associated with entrepreneurship rather than fewer. The notion that entrepreneurship was dominated by one paradigm is no longer tenable (Grant and Perren, 2002), although the standards of the positivists in terms of methodological strictures still hold force (King, Keohane and Verba, 1994). Even though this might be seen as a world of competing viewpoints, it would be a great shame to emphasize the competitive aspects rather than the co-operative aspects. As has been shown, there is much to be gained from the tolerance of difference; what is needed is the meeting place where the 'broad church' of entrepreneurial perspectives can come together.

This book has introduced students to the concept of perspectives within entrepreneurship and small business. We have shown that academics take different viewpoints with different assumptions. As such, they disagree over what entrepreneurship is, what we should investigate about it and how we should go about conducting that investigation. The study of entrepreneurship requires students and scholars to acknowledge these differences.

Scholars will continue to sit within perspectives. Few expect economists suddenly to decide that we should not predict, only try to explain retrospectively (Lawson, 1997), and no interpretivist is likely to use econometrics to understand why people start a new firm. Scholarship demands one accepts the ontological and epistemological assumptions of your perspective. Yet until recently, scholars could quite happily sit within their individual perspective silos ignoring all the other contributions in other perspectives. This is becoming less tenable. No longer should the new venture finance specialist ignore the ways in which entrepreneurs behave and position themselves to attract finance. The well-rounded scholar needs to recognize a wider discipline. In turn, that wider discipline may be able to contribute to our understanding more quickly on more fronts than ever before. It is a positive time to study entrepreneurship.

Bibliography

Acedo, F. J., C. Barroso and J. L. Galan (2006) The Resource-Based Theory: Dissemination and Main Trends. *Strategic Management Journal*, 27, 621–636.

Adegbesan, A. J. (2009) On the Origins of Competitive Advantage: Strategic Factor Markets and Heterogeneous Resource Complementarity. *Academy of Management Review*, 34, 463–475.

Adkins, L. (2002) *Revisions: Gender and Sexuality in Late Modernity*. Buckingham: Open University Press.

Ahl, H. (2002) The Making of the Female Entrepreneur. In *Jonkoping International Business School Dissertation Series*. Jonkoping: Jonkoping International Business School.

—— (2006) Why Research on Women Entrepreneurs Needs New Directions. *Entrepreneurship Theory and Practice*, 30, 595–621.

—— (2007) Sex business in the toy store: A narrative analysis of a teaching case. *Journal of Business Venturing*, 22, 673–693.

Ahlstrom, D. and G. D. Bruton (2006) Venture Capital in Emerging Economies: Networks and Institutional Change. *Entrepreneurship: Theory and Practice*, 30, 299–320.

Ahmadjian, C. L. and P. Robinson (2001) Safety in Numbers: Downsizing and the Deinstitutionalization of Permanent Employment in Japan. *Administrative Science Quarterly*, 46, 622–654.

Ajzen, I. (1988) *Attitudes, Personality and Behavior*. Milton Keynes: Open University Press.

Ajzen, I. (1991) The Theory of Planned Behavior. *Organizational Behavior and Human Decision Processes*, 50, 179–211.

Akerlof, G. A. (1970) The Market for 'Lemons': Quality uncertainty and the market mechanism. *Quarterly Journal of Economics*, 84, 488–500.

Aldrich, H., P. R. Reese, P. Dubini, B. Rosen and B. Woodward (1989) Women on the Verge of a Breakthrough: Networking Between Entrepreneurs in the United States and Italy. *Entrepreneurship and Regional Development*, 1, 339–356.

Aldrich, H. and T. Sakano (1995) Unbroken Ties: How the Personal Networks of Japanese Business Owners Compare to Those in Other Nations. In *Networks and Markets: Pacific Rim Investigations*, ed. M. Fruin, 17–45. New York: Oxford.

Aldrich, H. and C. Zimmer (1986) Entrepreneurship through Social Networks. In *The Art and Science of Entrepreneurship*, eds. D. Sexton and R. Smilor, 3–23. Cambridge MA: Ballinger Publishing Compan.

Aldrich, H. E. and M. C. Fiol (1994) Fools Rush In? The Institutional Context of Industry Creation. *Academy of Management Review*, 19, 645–670.

Aldrich, H. E., G. M. Hodgson, D. L. Hull, T. Knudsen, J. Mokyr and V. J. Vanberg (2008) In defence of generalized Darwinism. *Journal of Evolutionary Economics*, 18, 577–596.

Aldrich, H. E. and M. A. Martinez (2001) Many are Called, but Few are Chosen: An Evolutionary Perspective for the Study of Entrepreneurship. *Entrepreneurship Theory and Practice*, 25, 41–56.

Aldrich, H. E., B. Rosen and W. Woodward (1987) The Impact of Social Networks on Business Foundings and Profit: A Longitudinal Study. In *Frontiers of Entrepreneurship Research*, eds. N. C. Churchill, J. A. Hornaday, B. A. Kirchhoff, O. J. Krasner and K. H. Vesper. Wellesley, MA: Babson College.

Aldrich, H. E. and M. Ruef (2006) *Organizations evolving*. Thousand Oaks, CA: Sage.

Aldrich, H. E. and G. Wiedenmayer (1993) From traits to rates: An ecological perspective on organizational foundings. In *Advances in entrepreneurship, firm emergence, and growth*, eds. J. A. Katz and S. R. H. Brockhaus, 145–195. Greenwich, CN: JAI Press.

Allinson, C. W. and J. Hayes (1996) The cognitive style index: A measure of intuition-analysis for organizational research. *Journal of Management Studies*, 33, 119–135.

Alvarez, S. A. and L. W. Busenitz (2001) The Entrepreneurship of Resource-Based Theory. *Journal of Management*, 27, 755–775.

Alvesson, M., T. Bridgman and H. Willmott (2009) *The Oxford Handbook of Critical Management Studies*. Oxford: Oxford University Press.

Alvesson, M. and Y. Due Billing (2002) *Kon och organisation*. Lund: Studentlitteratur.

Alvesson, M. and K. Skoldberg (2000) *Reflexive Methodology: New Vistas for Qualitative Research*. London: Sage.

Alvesson, M. and H. Willmott. 1992. Critical Management Studies. London: Sage.

Anderson, A. R., S. L. Jack and S. D. Dodd (2005) The Role of Family Members in Entrepreneurial Networks: Beyond the Boundaries of the Family Firm. *Family Business Review*, 18, 135–154.

Arauzo, J. M. and M. C. Manjon (2004) Firm size and geographical aggregation: An empirical appraisal in industrial location. *Small Business Economics*, 22, 299–312.

Archer, M., R. Bhaskar, A. Collier, T. Lawson and A. Norrie (1998) *Critical Realism: Essential Readings*. London: Routledge.

Archer, M. S. (1995) *Realist Social Theory: The Morphogenetic Appraoch*. Cambridge: Cambridge University Press.

Archer, M. S. (1996) *Culture and Agency*. Cambridge: Cambridge University Press.

Archer, M. S. (2000) For structure: its reality, properties and powers: A reply to Anthony King. *The Sociological Review*, 48, 464–472.

Archer, M. S. (2003) *Structure, Agency and the Internal Conversation*. Cambridge: Cambridge University Press.

Archer, M. S. (2007) *Making our Way Through the World*. Cambridge: Cambridge University Press.

Arend, R. J. (2006) Tests of the Resource-Based View: Do the Empirics have any Clothes? *Strategic Organization*, 4, 409–421.

Armington, C. and Z. J. Acs (2002) The determinants of regional variation in new firm formation. *Regional Studies*, 36, 33–45.

Armitage, C. J. and M. Conner (2001) Efficacy of the theory of planned behaviour: A meta-analytic review. *British Journal of Social Psychology*, 40, 471–499.

Armstrong, C. E. and K. Shimizu (2007) A Review of Approaches to Empirical Research on the Resource-Based View of the Firm. *Journal of Management*, 33, 959–986.

Armstrong, P. (2005) *Critique of Entrepreneurship*. Basingstoke: Palgrave Macmillan.

Atkinson, P. (1990) *The Ethnographic Imagination: Textual Constructions of Reality*. London: Routledge.

Audretsch, D. B. and M. Keilbach (2004) Entrepreneurship Capital and Economic Performance. *Regional Studies*, 38, 949–959.

Audretsch, D. B. and M. Keilbach (2007) The Theory of Knowledge Spillover Entrepreneurship. *Journal of Management Studies*, 44, 1242–1254.

Badham, R., K. Garrety, V. Morrigan, M. Zanko and P. Dawson (2003) Designer Deviance: Enterprise and Deviance in Culture Change Programmes. *Organization*, 10, 707–730.

Baker, T. and T. S. Pollock (2007) Making the Marriage Work: The Benefits of Strategy's Takeover of Entrepreneurship for Strategic Organization. *Strategic Organization*, 5, 297–312.

Bandura, A. (1997) *Self-Efficacy: The Exercise of Control*. New York: W. H. Freeman and Company.

Barley, S. R. (2008) Coalface Institutionalism. In *The SAGE Handbook of Organizational Institutionalism*, eds. R. Greenwood, C. Oliver, K. Sahlin and R. Suddaby, 491–518. London: Sage.

Barney, J. B. (1986) Strategic Factor Markets: Expectations, Luck, and Business Strategy. *Management Science*, 32, 1230–1241.

Barney, J. B. (1991) Firm Resources and Sustained Competitive Advantage. *Journal of Management*, 17, 99–120.

Barnhart, R. K. (1988) *Chambers Dictionary of Etymology*. Edinburgh: Chambers.

Baron, R. A. (1998) Cognitive Mechanisms in Entrepreneurship: Why and When Entrepreneurs Think Differently than Other People. *Journal of Business Venturing*, 13, 275–294.

Baron, R. A. (2004) The Cognitive Perspective: A Valuable Tool for Answering Entrepreneurship's Basic "Why" Questions. *Journal of Business Venturing*, 19, 221–239.

Baron, R. A. (2007) Entrepreneurship: A Process Perspective. In *The Psychology of Entrepreneurship*, eds. J. R. Baum, M. Frese and B. R. A., 19–39. Mahwah, New Jersey: Lawrence Erlbaum Associates Inc.

Bates, T. (1994) Social Resources Generated by Group Support Networks may not be Beneficial to Asian Immigrant-Owned Small Businesses. *Social Forces*, 72, 671–689.

Battilana, J., J. J. Lok and W. W. Powell. 2009. Microfoundations of Institutions. In *EGOS call for papers sub-theme 21*.

Baum, J. A. C. and T. J. Rowley (2002) Companion to Organizations: An Introduction. In *The Blackwell Companion to Organizations,* ed. J. A. C. Baum, 1–34. Oxford: Blackwell.

Baum, J. A. C. and J. Singh (1994) Organizational Hierarchies and Evolutionary Processes: Some Reflections on a Theory of Organizational Evolution. In *Evolutionary Dynamics of Organizations*, eds. J. A. C. Baum and J. Singh, 3–22. New York: Oxford University Press.

Baum, J. R., M. Frese and J. A. Baron (2007a) The Psychology of Entrepreneurship. Mahwah NJ: Lawrence Erlbaum Associates Inc.

Baum, R. J., M. Frese, R. A. Baron and J. A. Katz (2007b) Entrepreneurship as an Area of Psychology Study: An Introduction. In *The Psychology of Entrepreneurship*, eds. J. R. Baum, M. Frese and R. A. Baron, 1–18. Mahwah, New Jersey: Lawrence Erlbaum Associates Inc.

Bauman, R. and S. L. Briggs (1990) Poetics and performance as critical perspectives on language and social life. *Annual Review of Anthropology*, 19, 59–88.

Bauman, Z. (1989) *Modernity and the Holocaust* Cambridge: Polity Press.

Baumol, W. J. (1990) Entrepreneurship: Productive, Unproductive and Destructive. *Journal of Political Economy*, 98, 893–921.

Baygan, G. and M. Freudenberg (2000) The Internationalisation of Venture Capital Activity in OECD Countries: Implications for Measurement and Policy.

Beck, U. (1992) *Risk Society*. London: Sage.

Becker, M. C. (2004) Organizational Routines: A Review of the Literature. *Industrial and Corporate Change*, 13, 643–677.

Becker, M. C. (2005) A Framework for Applying Organizational Routines in Empirical Research: Linking Antecedents, Characteristics and Performance Outcomes of Recurrent Interaction Patterns. *Industrial and Corporate Change*, 14, 817–846.

Beesley, V. (2005) *What is Feminism?* London: Sage.

Bennett, R. (2008) SME Policy Support in Britain Since the 1990s: What Have we Learnt? *Environment and Planning C-Government and Policy*, 26, 375–397.

Bennett, R. and P. Robson (2003) Changing use of External Business Advice and Government Supports by SMEs in the 1990s. *Regional Studies*, 37, 795–811.

Bennett, R. J., W. A. Bratton and P. J. A. Robson (2000) Business Advice: The Influence of Distance. *Regional Studies*, 34, 813–828.

Bennett, R. J. and C. Smith (2002) The Influence of Location and Distance on the Supply of Business Advice. *Environment and Planning A*, 34, 251–270.

Benson, J. K. (1977) Organizations – Dialectical View. *Administrative Science Quarterly*, 22, 1–21.

Berger, P. and T. Luckmann (1967) *The Social Construction of Reality*. New York: Anchor Books.

Berglund, K. and A. W. Johansson (2007) Entrepreneurship, Discourses and Conscientization in Processes of Regional Development. *Entrepreneurship and Regional Development*, 19, 499–525.

Bester, H. (1985) Screening vs Rationing in Credit Markets with Imperfect Information. *American Economic Review*, 75, 850–855.

Bevir, M. and R. A. W. Rhodes (2002) Interpretive Theory. In *Theory and Methods in Political Science*, eds. M. D. and S. G, 131–152. Basingstoke: Palgrave Macmillan.

Bhaskar, R. (1975) *A Realist Theory of Science*. Brighton: Harvester.

Bhaskar, R. (1979) *The Possibility of Naturalism*. Brighton: Harvester.

Biggiero, L. (2001) Self-organizing Processes in Building Entrepreneurial Networks: a Theoretical and Empirical Investigation. *Human Systems Management*, 20, 209–223.

Bird, B. (1988) Implementing Entrepreneurial Ideas: the Case of Intentions. *Academy of Management Review*, 13, 442–454.

Birley, S. (1985) The Role of Networks in the Entrepreneurial Process. *Journal of Business Venturing*, 1, 107–117.

Birley, S. 1996. The Start-Up. In *Small Business and Entrepreneurship*, eds. P. Burns and J. Dewhurst, 20–39. Basingstoke: Macmillan.

Birley, S., S. Cromie and A. Myers (1991) Entrepreneurial Networks: Their Emergence in Ireland and Overseas. *International Small Business Journal*, 9, 56–74.

Blaikie, N. 2000. *Designing Social Research*. Cambridge: Polity Press.

Blanchflower, D. G. and A. J. Oswald (1998) What Makes an Entrepreneur? *Journal of Labor Economics*, 16, 26–60.

Blumer, H. (1963) Society as Symbolic Interaction. In *Human Behaviour and Social processes: An Interactionist Approach*, ed. A. M. Rose, 179–192. Boston: Houghton Mifflin.

Blyler, M. and R. W. Coff (2003) Dynamic Capabilities, Social Capital, and Rent Appropriation: Ties that Split Pies. *Strategic Management Journal*, 24, 677–686.

Boisot, M. and J. Cohen (2000) Shall I Compare Thee to … an Organization? *Emergence*, 2, 113–135.

Boje, D. M. (2001) Introduction to Deconstructing Las Vegas. *M@n@gement*, 4, 79–82.

Bolton, S. C. and M. Houlihan (2005) The (Mis)Representation of Customer Service. *Work Employment and Society*, 19, 685–703.

Bouwen, R. (2001) Developing Relational Practices for Knowledge Intensive Organisational Contexts. *Career Development International* 6, 361–369.

Bowden, P. and J. Mummery. (2009) *Understanding Feminism*. New York: Acumen Press.

Boyd, N. G. and G. S. Vozikis (1994) The Influence of Self-efficacy on the Development of Entrepreneurial Intentions and Actions. *Entrepreneurship Theory and Practice*, 18, 63–77.

Bracker, J. (1980) The Historical Development of the Strategic Management Concept. *Academy of Management Review*, 5, 219–224.

Bradley, H. (2007) *Gender*. London: Polity Press.

Brandstätter, H. (1997) Becoming an Entrepreneur – a Question of Personality Structure? *Journal of Economic Psychology*, 18, 157–177.

Braverman, H. (1974) *Labor and Monopoly Capital: The Degradation of Work in the Twentieth Century*. New York: Monthly Review Press.

Breslin, D. (2008) A Review of the Evolutionary Approach to the Study of Entrepreneurship. *International Journal of Management Reviews*, 10, 399–423.

Breslin, D. (2010) Broadening the Management Team: An Evolutionary Approach. *International Journal of Entrepreneurial Behaviour and Research*, 16, 130–148.

Breslin, D. (2011) Reviewing a Generalized Darwinist Approach to Studying Socio-Economic Change. *International Journal of Management Reviews*, 13, 218–235.

Brittain, J. W. and J. H. Freeman (1980) Organizational Proliferation and Density Dependent Selection. In *The Organizational Life Cycle*, eds. J. Kimberely and R. Miles, 291–338. San Francisco: Jossey-Bass.

Brock, W. A. and D. S. Evans (1989) Small Business Economics. *Small Business Economics*, 1, 7–20.

Brockhaus, R. H. and P. S. Horwitz (1986) The Psychology of the Entrepreneur. In *The Art and Science of Entrepreneurship*, eds. D. Sexton and R. Smilor, 103–132. Cambridge, MA: Ballinger.

Bruderl, J. and P. Preisendorfer (1998) Network Support and the Success of Newly Founded Businesses. *Small Business Economics*, 10, 213–225.

Bruner, J. (1990) *Acts of Meaning*. Cambridge, MA: Harvard University Press.

Bruni, A., S. Gherardi and B. Poggio (2005) *Gender and Entrepreneurship: An Ethnographical Approach*. London: Routledge.

Buenstorf, G. (2006) How Useful is Generalized Darwinism as a Framework to Study Competition and Industrial Evolution? *Journal of Evolutionary Economics*, 16, 511–527.

Burchell, G. (1993) Liberal Government and Techniques of the Self. *Economy and Society*, 22, 267–282.

Burgelman, R. A. (1983) A Process Model of Internal Corporate Venturing in the Diversified Major Firms. *Administrative Science Quarterly*, 28, 223–244.

Burgelman, R. A. (1991) Intraorganizational Ecology of Strategy Making and Organizational Adaptation: Theory and Field Research. *Organization Science*, 2, 239–262.

Burr, V. (1995) *An Introduction to Social Construction*. London: Routledge.

Burrell, G. and G. Morgan (1979) *Sociological Paradigms and Organisational Analysis*. London: Heinemann.

Burrows, R. (1991) *Deciphering the Enterprise Culture*. London: Routledge.

Burt, R. S. (1992) *Structural Holes*. Cambridge, MA: Harvard University Press.

Busenitz, L. W. and J. B. Barney (1997) Differences Between Entrepreneurs and Managers in Large Organizations: Biases and Heuristics in Strategic Decision-Making. *Journal of Business Venturing*, 12, 9–30.

Butler, J. (1990) *Gender Trouble*. London: Routledge.

Butler, J. (2004) *Undoing Gender*. London: Routledge.

Bygrave, W. D. and M. Minitti (2000) The Social Dynamics of Entrepreneurship. *Entrepreneurship: Theory and Practice*, 24, 25–36.

Bygrave, W. D. and A. Zacharakis (2010) *The portable MBA in entrepreneurship*. New York: Wiley and sons.

Camagni, R. (1991) *Innovation Networks: Spatial Perspectives*. London: Belhaven Press.

Campbell, D. (1965) Variation, Selection and Retention in Sociocultural Evolution. In *Social Change in Developing Areas: A Reinterpretation of Evolutionary Theory*, eds. H. R. Barringer, G. I. Blanksten and R. W. Mack, 19–49. Cambridge, MA: Schenkman.

Campbell, D. (1974) Evolutionary Epistemology. In *The Philosophy of Karl Popper*, ed. Schilpp, P. A., 413–463. Lasalle: Open Court Publishing.

Capelleras, J. L. and K. F. Mole (2011) How Knowledge Spillovers Reduce Uncertainty for New Start-up Businesses: 'Buzz' and Business Advice in England and Spain. *Submitted to Journal of Economic Geography*.

Capelleras, J. L., K. F. Mole, F. J. Greene and D. J. Storey (2008) Do more Heavily Regulated Economies have Poorer Performing New Ventures? Evidence from Britain and Spain. *Journal of International Business Studies*, 39, 688–704.

Capron, L. and J.-C. Shen (2007) Acquisitions of Private vs. Public Firms: Private Information, Target Selection and Acquirer Returns. *Strategic Management Journal*, 28, 891–911.

Carroll, G. R. and M. T. Hannan (2000) *The Demography of Corporations and Industries*. Princeton, NJ: Princeton University Press.

Carroll, G. R. and A. Swaminathan (1992) The Organizational Ecology of Strategic Groups in the American Brewing Industry from 1975 to 1990. *Industrial and Corporate Change*, 1, 65–97.

Carter, S. and D. Jones-Evans (2006) Enterprise and Small Business. Harlow: FT Prentice-Hall.

Carter, S. and E. Shaw (2006) *Women's Business Ownership: Recent Research and Policy Development*. London: DTI Small Business Service.

Casson, M. and N. Wadeson (2007) Entrepreneurship and Macroeconomic Performance. *Strategic Entrepreneurship Journal*, 1, 239–262.

Casson, M. C. (2003) *The Entrepreneur: An Economic Theory*. Cheltenham: Edward Elgar.

Chandler, G. N. and S. H. Hanks (1994) Founder Competence, the Environment and Venture Performance. *Entrepreneurship Theory and Practice*, 18, 77–89.

Chell, E. and P. Tracey (2005) Relationship Building in Small Firms: The Development of a Model. *Human Relations*, 58, 577–616.

Chen, C. C., P. G. Greene and A. Crick (1998) Does entrepreneurial self-efficacy distinguish entrepreneurs from managers? *Journal of Business Venturing*, 13, 295–316.

Chia, R. (1995) From Modern to Postmodern Organizational Analysis. *Organization Studies*, 16, 579–604.

Chrisman, J. J., E. McMullan and J. Hall (2005) The Influence of Guided Preparation on the Long-Term Performance of New Ventures. *Journal of Business Venturing*, 20, 769–791.

Chua, J. H., J. J. Chrisman and L. P. Steier (2003) Extending the Theoretical Horizons of Family Business Research. *Entrepreneurship Theory and Practice*, 27, 331–338.

Churchill, N. C. and V. L. Lewis (1983) The Five Stages of Small Business Growth. *Harvard Business Review*, 61, 30–39and.

Clark, G. L., T. Palaskas, P. Tracey and M. Tsampra (2004) Market revenue and the scope and scale of SME networks in Europe's vulnerable regions. *Environment and Planning A*, 36, 1305–1326.

Clark, T. and G. Salaman (1998) Telling Tales: Management Gurus: Narratives and the Construction of Managerial Identity. *Journal of Management Studies*, 35, 137–161.

Clegg, S. R. (2008) Positivism and Post-Positivism. In *The Sage Dictionary of Qualitative Management Research*, eds. R. Thorpe and R. Holt, 155–157. London: Sage.

Code, L. (1998) Epistemology. In *A Companion to Feminist Philosophy*, eds. A. Jaggar and I. Young, 173–184. Oxford: Blackwell.

Coff, R. W. (1997) Human Assets and Management Dilemmas: Coping with Hazards on the Road to Resource-Based Theory. *Academy of Management Review*, 22, 374–402.

Coff, R. W. (1999) When Competitive Advantage Doesn't Lead to Performance: The Resource-Based View and Stakeholder Bargaining Power. *Organization Science*, 10, 119–133.

Cohen, M. D. and P. Bacdayan (1994) Organizational Routines are Stored as Procedural Memory – Evidence from a Laboratory Study. *Organization Science*, 5, 554–568.

Cohen, W. M. and D. A. Levinthal (1990) Absorptive Capacity: A New Perspective on Learning and Innovation. *Administrative Science Quarterly*, 35, 128–152.

Collins, R. (1981) On the Microfoundations of Macrosociology. *American Journal of Sociology*, 86, 984–1014.

Conner, K. (1991) A Historical Comparison of Resource-based Theory and Five Schools of Thought within Industrial Organization Economics: Do We Have a New Theory of the Firm? *Journal of Management*, 17, 121–154.

Contu, A. and H. Willmott (2005) You Spin me Round: The Realist Turn in Organization and Management Studies. *Journal of Management Studies*, 42, 1645–1662.

Cooper, A. C. (1986) Entrepreneurship and High Technology. In *The Art and Science of Entrepreneurship*, eds. D. Sexton and R. Smilor, 28–45. Cambridge, MA: Ballinger.

Cooper, A. C., F. J. Gimenogascon and C. Y. Woo (1994) Initial Human and Financial Capital as Predictors of New Venture Performance. *Journal of Business Venturing*, 9, 371–395.

Cooper, A. C., C. Y. Woo and W. C. Dunkelberg (1988) Entrepreneurs Perceived Chances for Success. *Journal of Business Venturing*, 3, 97–108.

Cordes, C. (2006) Darwinism in Economics: from Analogy to Continuity. *Journal of Evolutionary Economics*, 16, 529–541.

Cornelissen, J. P. and J. S. Clarke (2010) Imagining and Rationalizing Opportunities: Inductive Reasoning and the Creation and Justification of New Ventures. *Academy of Management Review*, 35, 539–557.

Cranny-Francis, A., W. Waring, P. Stavropoulos and J. Kirkby (2003) *Gender Studies: Terms and Debates*. New York: Palgrave Macmillan.

Crook, T. R., D. J. Ketchen, J. G. Combs and S. Y. Todd (2008) Strategic Resources and Performance: a Meta-Analysis. *Strategic Management Journal*, 29, 1141–1154.

Cruickshank, J. (2003) Underlabouring and Unemployment: Notes for Developing a Critical Realist Approach to the Agency of the Chronically Unemployed. In *Critical realism: the difference that it makes*, ed. J. Cruickshank, 111–127. London: Routledge.

Curran, J., R. Jarvis, R. A. Blackburn and S. Black (1995) Networks and Small Firms: Constructs, Methodological Strategies and Some Findings. *International Small Business Journal*, 11, 13–25.

Cyert, R. M. and J. G. March (1963) *A Behavioural Theory of the Firm*. Harlow: Prentice-Hall.

Czarniawska-Joerges, B. (1992) *Exploring Complex Organisations: A Cultural Perspective*. Newbury Park, CA: Sage.

Czarniawska, B. (2003) Social Constructionism and Organization Studies. In *Debating Organization Point-Counterpoint in Organization Studies*, eds. R. Westwood and S. R. Clegg, 128–139. Oxford: Blackwell.

Dachler, H. P., D. M. Hosking and K. J. Gergen (1995) *Relational Alternatives to Individualisation: Management and Organisation*. Aldershot: Avebury.

Dacin, T. M., J. Goodstein and R. W. Scott (2002) Institutional Theory and Institutional Change: Introduction to the Special Research Forum. *Academy of Management Journal*, 45, 45–57.

Danermark, B., M. Ekstrom, L. Jacobsen and J. C. Karlsson (2002) *Explaining Society: Critical Realism in the Social Sciences*. London: Routledge.

Darwin, C. R. (1859) *On the Origin of Species by means of Natural Selection or the Preservation of Favoured Races in the Struggle for Life*. London: Murray.

Davidsson, P. (2007) Method Challenges and Opportunities in the Psychological Study of Entrepreneurship. In *The Psychology of Entrepreneurship*, eds. J. R. Baum, M. Frese and R. A. Baron, 287–323. Mahwah, NJ: Lawrence Erlbaum Associates Inc.

Davidsson, P. and J. Wiklund (2001) Levels of Analysis in Entrepreneurship Research: Current Research Practice and Suggestions for the Future. *Entrepreneurship Theory and Practice*, 25, 81–99.

Davies, B. and R. Harré (1990) Positioning: The Discursive Production of Selves. *Journal for the Theory of Social Behaviour*, 20, 43–63.

Dawkins, R. (1976) *The Selfish Gene*. New York: Oxford University Press.

Dawkins, R. (1983) Universal Darwinism. In *Evolution from Molecules to Man*, ed. D. S. Bendall, 403–425. Cambridge: Cambridge University Press.

De Beauvoir, S. (1949) *The Second Sex*. London: Pan.

De Koning, A. J. (1999) Opportunity Formation as a Socio-cognitive Process. In *Frontiers of Entrepreneurship Research*, eds. P. D. Reynolds, W. D. Bygrave, S. Manigart, C. M. Mason, G. D. Meyer, H. J. Sapienza and K. G. Shaver. Wellesley, MA: Babson College.

Deakins, D. and M. Freel. (2006) *Entrepreneurship and Small Firms*. Maidenhead: McGraw Hill.

Delacroix, J. and G. R. Carroll (1983) Organizational Foundings – An Ecological Study of the Newspaper Industries of Argentina and Ireland. *Administrative Science Quarterly*, 28, 274–291.

Delacroix, J. and M. V. Rao (1994) Externalities and Ecological Theory: Unbundling Density Dependence. In *Evolutionary Dynamics of Organizations*, eds. J. V. Singh and J. A. Baum, 255–268. Cambridge, MA: Ballinger.

Delgado, M., M. E. Porter and S. Stern (2010) Clusters and Entrepreneurship. *Journal of Economic Geography*, 10, 495–518.

Delmar, F. and S. Shane (2004) Legitimating First: organizing Activities and the Survival of New Ventures. *Journal of Business Venturing*, 19, 385–410.

Demsetz, H. (1973) Industrial Structure, Market Rivalry, and Public Policy. *Journal of Law and Economics*, 16, 1–10.

Demsetz, H. (1982) Barriers to Entry. *American Economic Review*, 72, 47–57.

Dennett, D. (1995) *Darwin's Dangerous Idea*. New York: Simon and Schuster.

Denrell, J., C. Fang and S. G. Winter (2003) The Economics of Strategic Opportunity. *Strategic Management Journal*, 24, 977–990.

Denzin, N. K. (1979) The Interactionist Study of Social Organisation: A Note on Method. *Symbolic Interaction*, 2, 59–72.

Denzin, N. K. (1989) *Intepretive Interactionism*. Thousand Oaks, CA: Sage.

Denzin, N. K. (1997) *Interpretive Ethnography: Ethnographic Practices for the 21st Century*. Thousand Oaks, CA: Sage.

DePropris, L. (2000) Innovation And Inter-Firm Co-Operation: The Case Of The West Midlands. *Economics of Innovation and New Technology*, 9, 421–446.

Dess, G. G. and G. T. Lumpkin (2005) The Role of Entrepreneurial Orientation in Stimulating Effective Corporate Entrepreneurship. *Academy of Management Executive*, 19, 147–156.

Dick, B. and G. Morgan (1987) Family Networks and Employment in Textiles. *Work Employment and Society*, 1, 225–246.

Dierickx, I. and K. Cool (1989) Asset Stock Accumulation and the Sustainability of Competitive Advantge. *Management Science*, 35, 1504–1511.

DiMaggio, P. J. (1988) Interest and Agency In Institutional Theory. In *Institutional Patterns and Organizations: Culture and Environment*, ed. L. G. Zucker, 3–21. Cambridge, MA: Ballinger.

DiMaggio, P. J. and W. W. Powell (1983) The Iron Cage Revisited: Institutional Isomorphism and Collective Rationality in Organizational Fields. *American Sociological Review*, 48, 147–161.

Dimov, D. (2010) Nascent Entrepreneurs and Venture Emergence: Opportunity Confidence, Human Capital, and Early Planning. *Journal of Management Studies*, 47, 1123–1153.

Dobbs, M. and R. T. Hamilton (2007) Small Business Growth: Recent Evidence and New Directions. *International Journal of Entrepreneurial Behaviour and Research*, 13, 296–322.

Dodd, S. D. and A. R. Anderson (2007) Mumpsimus and the Mything of the Individualistic Entrepreneur. *International Small Business Journal*, 25, 341–360.

Doolin, B. (2003) Narratives of Change: Discourse, Technology and Organization. *Organization*, 10, 751–770.

Down, S. (2006) *Narratives of Enterprise: Crafting Self-Identity in a Small Firm*. Cheltenham: Edward Elgar.

Downing, S. (2005) The Social Construction of Entrepreneurship. *Entrepreneurship Theory and Practice*, 29, 185–204.

Drakopoulou Dodd, S., S. L. Jack and A. R. Anderson (2002) Scottish Entrepreneurial Networks in the International Context. *International Small Business Journal*, 20, 213–219.

Drakopoulou Dodd, S., S. L. Jack and A. R. Anderson (2006) The Mechanisms and Process of Entrepreneurial Networks: Continuity and Change. In *Advances in Entrepreneurship, Firm Emergence and Growth*, eds. J. Wiklund, D. Dimov, J. A. Katz and D. A. Shepherd, 107–145. Elsevier.

Drakopoulou Dodd, S. and E. Patra (2002) National Differences in Entrepreneurial Networking. *Entrepreneurship and Regional Development*, 14, 117–134.

Drucker, P. (1985) *Innovation and Entrepreneurship*. London: Butterworth-Heinemann.

Du Gay, P. (1996) *Consumption and Identity at Work*. London: Sage.

Du Gay, P. (2000) *In Praise of Bureaucracy: Weber, Organization, Ethics*. London: Sage.

Du Gay, P. (2004) Against 'Enterprise' (but not against 'Enterprise', for that would make no sense). *Organization*, 11, 37–57.

Du Gay, P. (2007) *Organizing Identity: Persons and Organizations After Theory*. London: Sage.

Du Gay, P. and G. Salaman (1992) The Cult(ure) of the Customer. *Journal of Management Studies*, 29, 614–633.

Du Gay, P., G. Salaman and B. Rees (1996) The Conduct of Management and the Management of Conduct: Contemporary Managerial Discourse and the Constitution of the 'Competent' Manager. *Journal of Management Studies*, 33, 263–282.

Durham, W. H. (1991) *Coevolution: Genes, Culture and Human Diversity*. Stanford: Stanford University Press.

The Economist (2007) Public v private equity: The business of making money In *economist.com*. http://www.economist.com/node/9440821 (last accessed 27 June 2011).

Eisenhardt, K. M. (1989) Building Theories from Case Study Research. *Academy of Management Review*, 14, 532–550.

Eisenhardt, K. M. (1991) Better Stories and Better Constructs: The Case for Rigor and Comparative Logic. *Academy of Management Review*, 16, 620–627.

Eisenhardt, K. M. and M. E. Graebner (2007) Theory Building from Cases: Opportunities and Challenges. *Academy of Management Journal*, 50, 25–32.

Eisenhardt, K. M. and J. A. Martin (2000) Dynamic capabilities: What are they? *Strategic Management Journal*, 21, 1105–1121.

Ellis, C. and A. Bochner (1996) *Composing ethnography*. London: Sage.

Emirbayer, M. and A. Mische (1998) What is Agency? *American Journal of Sociology*, 103, 962–1023.

England, K. V. L. (1994) Getting Personal: Reflexivity, Positionality and Feminist Research. *Professional Geographer*, 46, 80–89.

Evans, D. and B. Jovanovic (1989) An Estimated Model of Entrepreneurial Choice under Liquidity Constraints. *Journal of Political Economy*, 97, 808–827.

Fairclough, N. (1995) *Critical Discourse Analysis*. London: Longman.

Felin, T. and N. J. Foss (2009) Organizational Routines and Capabilities: Historical Drift and a Course-Correction Toward Microfoundations. *Scandinavian Journal of Management*, 25, 157–167.

Fenwick, T. J. (2002) Transgressive Desires: New Enterprising Selves in the New Capitalism. *Work Employment and Society*, 16, 703–723.

Fitzgerald, M. A. and G. Muske (2002) Co-preneurs: An Exploration and Comparison to other Family Businesses. *Family Business Review*, 15, 1–15.

Fleck, J. (2000) Artefact – Activity: the Coevolution of Artefacts, Knowledge and Organization in Technological Innovation. In *Technological Innovation as an Evolutionary Process*, ed. J. Ziman, 248–266. Cambridge: Cambridge University Press.

Fleetwood, S. and A. Hesketh (2006) HRM-performance research: Under-theorized and lacking explanatory power. *International Journal of Human Resource Management*, 17, 1977–1993.

Fletcher, D. E. (2002) *Understanding the Small Family Business*. London: Routledge.

Fletcher, D. E. (2003) Framing Organisational Emergence: Discourse, Identity and Relationship. In *New Movements in Entrepreneurship*, eds. C. Steyaert and D. Hjorth, 125–142. Cheltenham: Edward Elgar.

Fletcher, D. E. (2006) Social Constructionist Ideas and Entrepreneurship Inquiry. *Entrepreneurship and Regional Development*, 18, 421–440.

Fletcher, D. E. (2007) 'Toy Story': The Narrative World of Entrepreneurship and the Creation of Interpretive Communities. *Journal of Business Venturing*, 22, 694–672.

Fletcher, D. E. (2011) Undertaking Interpretive Work in Entrepreneurship Research In *Perspectives in Entrepreneurship*, eds. K. F. Mole and M. Ram. Basingstoke: Palgrave Macmillan.

Fletcher, D. E. and T. J. Watson (2006) Social Change in the Countryside: The Role of Entrepreneurship and Shifting Life Orientations in Processes of Counter-Urbanisation. In *Entrepreneurship as Social Change, Third Movements in Entrepreneurship book*, eds. C. Steyaert and D. Hjorth, 145–164. Cheltenham: Edward Elgar.

Forbes, D. P. (1999) Cognitive Approaches to New Venture Creation. *International Journal of Management Reviews*, 1, 415–439.

Foreman-Peck, J. (1985) Seedcorn or Chaff? New Firms and Industrial Performance in the Interwar Economy. *Economic History Review*, 38, 402–422.

Foss, N. J. (1997) *Resources, Firms and Strategies*. Oxford: Oxford University Press.

Foss, N. J. and T. Knudsen (2003) The Resource-based Tangle: Towards a Sustainable Explanation of Competitive Advantage. *Managerial and Decision Economics*, 24, 291–307.

Foss, N. J. and J. Lyngsie. forthcoming. Strategic Entrepreneurship. In *Handbook of Organisational Entrepreneurship*, ed. D. Hjorth. Cheltenham: Edward Elgar.

Foss, N. J. and N. Stieglitz. forthcoming. Modern Resource-based Theories. In *Handbook on the Economics and Theory of the Firm*, eds. M. E. Dietrich and J. Kraff. Cheltenham: Edward Elgar.

Foucault, M. (1972) *The Archeology of Knowledge*. London: Tavistock.

Fournier, V. (1998) Stories of Development and Exploitation: Militant Voices in an Enterprise Culture. *Organization*, 5, 55–80.

Fournier, V. and C. Grey (2000) At the Critical Moment: Conditions and Prospects for Critical Management Studies. *Human Relations*, 53, 7–32.

Fraser, S. (2009) Is there Ethnic Discrimination in the UK Market for Small Business Credit? *International Small Business Journal*, 27, 583–607.

Fraser, S. and F. J. Greene (2006) The Effects of Experience on Entrepreneurial Optimism and Uncertainty. *Economica*, 73, 169–192.

Fraser, S., F. J. Greene and K. F. Mole (2007) Sources of Bias in the Recall of Self-Generated Data: The Role of Anchoring. *British Journal of Management*, 18, 192–208.

Fraser, S., D. Storey, J. Frankish and R. Roberts (2002) The Relationship Between Training and Small Business Performance: An Analysis of the Barclays Bank Small Firms Training Loans Scheme. *Environment and Planning C-Government and Policy*, 20, 211–233.

Freeman, R. E. (1984) *Strategic Management: A Stakeholder Approach*. Boston MA: Pitman.

Freidan, B. (1963) *The Feminine Mystique*. New York: Norton.

Freund, J. (1972) *The Sociology of Max Weber*. Harmondsworth: Penguin.

Friedland, R. and R. R. Alford. (1991) Bringing Society Back In: Symbols, Practices, and Institutional Contradictions. In *The New Institutionalism in Organizational Analysis*, eds. W. W. Powell and P. J. DiMaggio, 232–263. Chicago: University of Chicago Press.

Friedman, M. (1953) *Essays in Positive Economics*. Chicago: University of Chicago.

Garfinkel, H. (1967) *Studies in Ethnomethodology*. Englewood Cliffs, NJ: Prentice Hall.

Gartner, W. B. (1988) Who is an Entrepreneur? is the Wrong Question. *American Journal of Small Business*, 12, 11–32.

Gartner, W. B. (1990) What are we Talking About when we Talk about Entrepreneurship? *Journal of Business Venturing*, 5, 15–28.

Gartner, W. B. (1993) Words Lead to Deeds: Towards an Organisational Emergence Vocabulary. *Journal of Business Venturing*, 8, 231–239.

Gartner, W. B. (2010) A New Path to the Waterfall: A Narrative on a use of Entrepreneurial Narrative. *International Small Business Journal*, 28, 6–19.

Gartner, W. B. and N. M. Carter. (2003) Entrepreneurial Behavior and Firm Organizing Processes In *Handbook of Entrepreneurship Research*, eds. Z. J. Acs and D. B. Audretch, 195–221. Boston: Kluwer Academic Publishers.

Gartner, W. B., N. M. Carter and G. E. Hills. (2003) The Language of Opportunity. In *New Movements in Entrepreneurship*, eds. C. Steyaert and D. Hjorth, 103–124. Cheltenham: Edward Elgar.

Garvan, T. N. and B. O'Cinneide (1994a) Entrepreneurship Education and Training Programmes: A Review and Evaluation – Part 1. *Journal of European Industrial Training*, 18, 3–10.

Garvan, T. N. and B. O'Cinneide (1994b) Entrepreneurship Education and Training Programmes: A Review and Evaluation – Part 2. *Journal of European Industrial Training*, 18, 13–21.

Gatley, S., R. Lessem and Y. Altman (1996) *Comparative Management: A Transcultural Odyssey*. London: McGraw Hill.

Gavetti, G. and D. A. Levinthal (2004) The Strategy Field from the Perspective of Management Science: Divergent Strands and Possible Integration. *Management Science*, 50, 1309–1318.

Geertz, C. (1973) *The Interpretation of Cultures: Selected Essays*. New York.

Gehlen, A. (1940) *Der Mensch. Seine Natur und seine Stellung in der Welt* [Man, his nature and place in the world]. Berlin: Junker and Dünnhaupt.

Gergen, K. J. and M. M. Gergen. (1993) Toward Reflexive Methodologies. In *Research and reflexivity*, ed. F. Steier, 76–95. London: Sage.

Gergen, K. K. (1999) *An Invitation to Social Construction*. London: Sage.

Giddens, A. (1979) *Central Problems in Social Theory* London: Macmillan.

Giddens, A. (1987) *Social Theory and Modern Sociology*. Cambridge: Polity Press.

Giddens, A. (1991) *Modernity and Self-Identity: Self and Society in the Late Modern Age*. Cambridge: Polity Press.

Giddens, A. (1994) Elements of the Theory of Structuration. In *The Polity Reader in Social Theory*, ed. T. P. Staff, 79–88. Cambridge: Polity Press.

Gilad, B. and P. Levine (1986) Entrepreneurial Supply. *Journal of Small Business Management*, 24, 45–51.

Gist, M. E. (1987) Self-Efficacy: Implications for Organizational-Behavior and Human-Resource Management. *Academy of Management Review*, 12, 472–485.

Gnyawali, D. R. and D. S. Fogel (1994) Environments for Entrepreneurship Development: Key Dimensions and Research Implications. *Entrepreneurship Theory and Practice*, 18, 43–63.

Goffman, E. (1958) *The Presentation of Self in Everyday Life*. Harmondsworth: Penguin.

Goffman, E. (1961) *Encounters: Two Studies in the Sociology of Interaction*. London: Macmillan.

Goldthorpe, J. H., D. Lockwood, F. Bechhofer and J. Platt (1968) *The Affluent Worker: Attitudes and Behaviour*. Cambridge: Cambridge University Press.

Goss, D. (1991) *Small Business and Society*. London: Routledge.

Goss, D. (2005) Schumpeter's Legacy? Interaction and Emotions in the Sociology of Entrepreneurship. *Entrepreneurship Theory and Practice*, 29, 205–218.

Granovetter, M. (1985) Economic Action and Social Structure: The Problem of Embeddedness. *American Journal of Sociology*, 91, 481–510.

Granovetter, M. S. (1973) Strength of Weak Ties. *American Journal of Sociology*, 78, 1360–1380.

Grant, P. and L. Perren (2002) Small Business and Entrepreneurial Research. *International Small Business Journal*, 20, 185–211.

Greene, F. and K. Mole (2006) Defining and Measuring the Small Business. In *Enterprise and small business*, eds. S. Carter and D. Jones-Evans, 7–29. Harlow: FT Prentice Hall.

Greene, F. J., K. F. Mole and D. J. Storey (2004) Does More Mean Worse? Three Decades of Enterprise Policy in the Tees Valley. *Urban Studies*, 41, 1207–1228.

Greene, F. J., K. F. Mole and D. J. Storey (2008) *Three Decades of Enterprise Culture*. London: Palgrave Macmillan.

Greenwood, R. and C. R. Hinings (1996) Understanding Radical Organizational Change: Bringing Together the Old and the New Institutionalism. *Academy of Management Review*, 21, 1022–1054.

Greenwood, R., C. Oliver, K. Sahlin and R. Suddaby (2008) Introduction. In *The SAGE Handbook of Organizational Institutionalism*, eds. R. Greenwood, C. Oliver, K. Sahlin and R. Suddaby, 1–46. London: Sage.

Greenwood, R. and R. Suddaby (2006) Institutional Entrepreneurship in Mature Fields: The Big Five Accounting Firms. *Academy of Management Journal*, 49, 27–48.

Greiner, L. E. (1998) Evolution and Revolution as Organizations Grow. *Harvard Business Review*, 76, 55–64.

Greve, A. (1995) Networks and Entrepreneurship – An Analysis of Social Relations, Occupational Background, and Use of Contacts During the Establishment Process. *Scandinavian Journal of Management*, 11, 1–24.

Greve, A. and J. Salaff (2003) Social Networks and Entrepreneurship. *Entrepreneurship and Regional Development*, 28, 1–23.

Grix, J. (2004) *The Foundations of Research*. Basingstoke: Palgrave Macmillan.

Guardian (2009) David Cameron Speech in Full. In *The Guardian*. http://www.guardian.co.uk/politics/2010/may/11/david-cameron-speech-full-text (last accessed 27 June 2011).

Habermas, J. (1971) *Knowledge and Human Interests*. Boston MA: Beacon.

Halford, S. and P. Leonard (2006) Place, space and time: Contextualizing workplace subjectivities. *Organization Studies*, 27, 657–676.

Hamilton, E. (2006) Whose Story is it Anyway? Narrative Accounts of the Role of Women in Founding and Establishing Family Businesses. *International Small Business Journal*, 24, 253–271.

Hanna, V. and K. Walsh (2002) Small Firm Networks: A Successful Approach to Innovation? *R and D Management*, 32, 201–207.

Hannan, M. T. and J. Freeman (1977) Population Ecology of Organizations. *American Journal of Sociology*, 82, 929–964.

Hargadon, A. B. and Y. Douglas (2001) When Innovators Meet Institutions: Edison and the Design of the Electric Light. *Administrative Science Quarterly*, 46, 467–501.

Hargrave, T. J. and A. H. Van de Ven (2006) A Collective Action Model of Institutional Innovation. *Academy of Management Review*, 31, 864–888.

Harper, D. A. (2008) Towards a Theory of Entrepreneurial Teams. *Journal of Business Venturing*, 23, 613–626.

Hart, M. (2007) Evaluating EU regional policy. *Policy Studies*, 28, 295–308.

Hartmann, H. (1983) Capitalism: Patriarchy and Job Segregation by Sex. In *The Signs Reader*, eds. E. Abel and E. K. Abel, 193–225. Chicago: Chicago University Press.

Hartsock, N. (1990) Foucault on Power: A Theory for Women? In *Feminism / Post-modemism*, ed. L. Nicholson, 157–172. London: Routledge.

Hartwig, M. (2007) *A Dictionary of Critical Realism*. London: Routledge.

Haveman, H. A. and R. J. David (2008) Ecologists and Institutionalists: Friends or Foes? In *The SAGE Handbook of Organizational Institutionalism*, eds. R. Greenwood, C. Oliver, K. Sahlin and R. Suddaby, 573–595. London: Sage.

Hayek, F. A. (1968/1978) Competition as a Discovery Procedure. In *New Studies in Philosophy, Politics and Economics*, ed. F. A. Hayek, 179–90. Chicago: University of Chicago Press.

Heelas, P. and P. Morris (1992) *The Values of Enterprise Culture: A Moral Debate*. London: Routledge.

Helfat, C. E., S. Finkelstein, W. Mitchell, M. A. Peteraf, H. Singh, D. J. Teece and S. G. Winter (2007) *Dynamic Capabilities: Understanding Strategic Change in Organizations*. Oxford: Blackwell.

Helfat, C. E. and M. A. Peteraf (2009) Understanding Dynamic Capabilities: Progress along a Developmental Path. *Strategic Organization, 7*, 91–102.

Hiatt, S. R., W. D. Sine and P. S. Tolbert (2009) From Pabst to Pepsi: The Deinstitutionalization of Social Practices and the Creation of Entrepreneurial Opportunities *Administrative Science Quarterly, 54*, 635–667.

Hillman, A. J., M. C. Withers and B. J. Collins (2009) Resource Dependence Theory: A Review. *Journal of Management, 35*, 1404–1427.

Hills, G. E., G. T. Lumpkin and R. P. Singh (1997) Opportunity Recognition: Perceptions and Behaviours of Entrepreneurs. In *Frontiers of Entrepreneurship Research*, eds. P. D. Reynolds, W. D. Bygrave, N. M. Carter, P. Davidsson, W. B. Gartner, C. M. Mason and P. P. McDougall. Wellesley, MA: Babson College.

Hirdman, Y. (2001) *Genus – om det Stabilas Föränderliga Former*. Malmö: Liber Press.

Hisrich, R., J. Langan-Fox and S. Grant (2007) Entrepreneurship Research and Practice – A Call to Action for Psychology. *American Psychologist, 62*, 575–589.

Hitt, M. A. and R. D. Ireland (2000) The Intersection of Entrepreneurship and Strategic Management Research. In *Handbook of Entrepreneurship*, eds. D. L. Sexton and H. A. Landstrom, 45–63. Oxford: Blackwell.

Hitt, M. A., R. D. Ireland, S. M. Camp and D. L. Sexton (2002) *Strategic Entrepreneurship: Creating a New Mindset*. Oxford: Blackwell.

Hoang, H. and B. Antoncic (2003) Network-Based Research in Entrepreneurship – A Critical Review. *Journal of Business Venturing, 18*, 165–187.

Hodgson, G. M. and T. Knudsen (2004) The Firm as an Interactor: Firms as Vehicles for Habits and Routines. *Journal of Evolutionary Economics, 14*, 281–307.

Hodgson, G. M. and T. Knudsen (2010) *Darwin's Conjecture: The Search for General Principles of Social and Economic Evolution*. Chicago: University of Chicago Press.

Hollis, M. (1994) *The Philosophy of Social Science*. Cambridge: Cambridge University Press.

Holmes, M. (2007) *What is Gender?* London: Sage.

Holmwood, J. (2001) Gender and Critical Realism: A Critique of Sayer. *Sociology, 35*, 947–965.

hooks, b. (1981) *Ain't I a Woman: Black Women and Feminism*. Boston, MA: South End Press.

Hoopes, D. G. and T. L. Madsen (2008) A Capability-Based View of Competitive Heterogeneity. *Industrial and Corporate Change, 17*, 393–426.

Hughes, A. (2009) Hunting the Snark: Some Reflections on the UK Experience of Support for the Small Business Sector. *Innovation: Management, Policy and Practice, 11*, 114–126.

Hull, D. L. (1988) *Science as a Process*. Chicago: University of Chicago Press.

Human, S. and K. Provan (1996) External Resource Exchange and Perceptions of Competitiveness Within Organizational Networks: An Organizational Learning Perspective. In *Frontiers of Entrepreneurship Research*, eds. P. D. Reynolds, S. Birley, J. E. Butler, W. D. Bygrave, P. Davidsson, W. B. Gartner and P. P. McDougall. Wellesley, MA: Babson College.

Hurst, E. and A. Lusardi (2004) Liquidity Constraints, Household Wealth and Entrepreneurship. *Journal of Political Economy, 112*, 319–347.

Iakovleva, T. and L. Kolvereid (2009) An Integrated Model of Entrepreneurial Intentions. *International Journal of Business and Globalisation, 3*, 66–80.

Ingham, G. (1970) *The Size of Industrial Organization and Work Behaviour*. Cambridge: Cambridge University Press.

Ireland, R. D., M. A. Hitt, S. M. Camp and D. L. Sexton (2001) Integrating Entrepreneurship Actions and Strategic Management Actions to Create Firm Wealth. *Academy of Management Executive*, 15, 49–63.

Ireland, R. D., D. F. Kuratko and J. G. Covin (2003) Antecedents, Elements and Consequences of Corporate Entrepreneurship Strategy. In *Best Paper Proceedings Annual Meeting of the Academy of Management*. Seattle Washington.

Irigaray, L. (1985) *This Sex which is not One*. Ed. and trans. C. Porter and C. Burke. Ithaca, NY: Cornell University Press.

Isaksen, E. (2006) Early Business Performance. Initial Factors Effecting New Business Outcomes. PhD, Bodø Graduate School of Business.

Jack, S. L. (2005) The Role, Use and Activation of Strong and Weak Network Ties: A Qualitative Analysis. *Journal of Management Studies*, 42, 1233–1259.

Jack, S. L. and A. R. Anderson (2002) The Effects of Embeddedness on the Entrepreneurial Process. *Journal of Business Venturing*, 17, 467–487.

Jagose, A. (1996) *Queer Theory: An Introduction*. New York: New York University Books.

Jeanes, E. (2007) Gender Injustice: An International Comparative Analysis of Equality in Employment. *Gender Work and Organization*, 14, 302–304.

Jennings, P. L., L. Perren and S. Carter (2005) Guest Editors' Introduction: Alternative Perspectives on Entrepreneurship Research. *Entrepreneurship Theory and Practice*, 29, 145–152.

Joas, H. (1993) *Pragmatism and Social Theory*. Chicago: University of Chicago Press.

Joas, H. (1996) *The Creativity of Action*. Chicago: University of Chicago Press.

Johannisson, B. (1996) The Dynamics of Entrepreneurial Networks. In *Frontiers of Entrepreneurship Research*, eds. P. D. Reynolds, S. Birley, J. E. Butler, W. D. Bygrave, P. Davidsson, W. B. Gartner and P. P. McDougall, 253–267. Wellesey MA: Babson College.

Johannisson, B. (1998) Personal Networks in Emerging Knowledge-based Firms: Spatial and Functional Patterns. *Entrepreneurship and Regional Development*, 10, 297–313.

Johannisson, B. (2007) Pioneering new Fields of Entrepreneurship Research. *Entrepreneurship and Regional Development*, 19, 451–452.

Johannisson, B. (2011) Towards a Practice Theory of Entrepreneuring. *Small Business Economics*, 36, 135–150.

Johannisson, B. and M. Mønsted (1997) Contextualizing Entrepreneurial Networking. *International Journal of Management and Organization*, 27, 109–137.

Johannisson, B. and A. Nilsson (1989) Community Entrepreneurs: Networking for Local Development. *Entrepreneurship and Regional Development*, 1, 3–19.

Johannisson, B., M. Ramirez-Pasillas and G. Karlsson (2002) The Institutional Embeddedness of Local Inter-firm Networks: A Leverage for Business Creation. *Entrepreneurship and Regional Development*, 14, 297–315.

Johansson, A. W. (2004) Narrating the Entrepreneur. *International Small Business Journal*, 22, 273–293.

Jones, C. and A. Spicer (2005) The Sublime Object of Entrepreneurship. *Organization*, 12, 223–246.

Jones, C. and A. Spicer (2009) *Unmasking the Entrepreneur*. Cheltenham: Edward Elgar.

Jones, S. (2009). Under the Influence? Symbolic Violence in UK HE Entrepreneurship Education. In *31st Institute for Small Business and Entrepreneurship (ISBE) Conference*. Liverpool.

Josselson, R. and A. Lieblich (1995) *Interpreting Experience: The Narrative Study of Lives*. Thousand Oaks, CA.: Sage.

Jovanovic, B. (1982) Selection and the Evolution of Industry. *Econometrica*, 50, 649–670.

Kahneman, D., P. Slovic and A. Tversky (1982) *Judgment under Uncertainty: Heuristics and Biases*. New York: Cambridge University Press.

Karatas-Ozkan, M. and W. D. Murphy (2010) Critical Theorist, Postmodernist and Social Constructionist Paradigms in Organizational Analysis: A Paradigmatic Review of Organizational Learning Literature. *International Journal of Management Reviews*, 12, 453–465.

Karra, N., P. Tracey and N. Phillips (2006) Altruism and Agency in the Family Firm: Exploring the Role of Family, Kinship and Ethnicity. *Entrepreneurship Theory and Practice*, 30, 861–877.

Katz, J. A. (1992) A Psychological Cognitive Model of Employment Status Choice. *Entrepreneurship Theory and Practice*, 17, 29–37.

Keat, R. and N. Abercrombie (1991) *Enterprise Culture*. London: Routledge.

Keat, R. and J. Urry (1975) *Social Theory as Science*. London: Routledge.

Keeble, D. (1997) Small firms, Innovation and Regional Development in Britain in the 1990s. *Regional Studies*, 31, 281–293.

Keeble, D., C. Lawson, B. Moore and F. Wilkinson (1999) Collective Learning Processes, Networking and 'Institutional Thickness' in the Cambridge Region. *Regional Studies*, 33, 319–332.

Kemp, S. and J. Holmwood (2003) Realism, Regularity and Social Explanation. *Journal for the Theory of Social Behaviour*, 33, 165–187.

Kenney, M. and D. Patton (2005) Entrepreneurial Geographies: Support Networks in Three High-Technology Industries. *Economic Geography*, 81, 201–228.

King, A. (1999) Against Structure: A Critique of Morphogenetic Social Theory. *The Sociological Review*, 47, 199–227.

King, G., R. O. Keohane and S. Verba (1994) *Designing Social Inquiry: Scientific Inference in Qualitative Research*. Princeton: Princeton University Press.

Kirzner, I. M. (1973) *Competition and Entrepreneurship*. Chicago: University of Chicago.

Kirzner, I. M. (1997) Entrepreneurial Discovery and the Competitive Market Process: An Austrian Approach. *Journal of Economic Literature*, 35, 60–85.

Klyver, K. and K. Hindle (2007) The Role of Social Networks at Different Stages of Business Formation. *Small Business Research*, 15, 22–38.

Knight, F. H. (1921) *Risk, Uncertainty and Profit*. New York: Houghton Mifflin.

Knott, A. M., D. J. Bryce and H. E. Posen (2003) On the Strategic Accumulation of Intangible Assets. *Organization Science*, 14, 192–207.

Kogut, B. and U. Zander (1992) Knowledge of the Firm, Combinative capabilities, and the Replication of Technology. *Organization Science*, 3, 383–397.

Kolvereid, L. (1996) Organizational Employment versus Self-Employment. Reasons for Career Choice Intentions. *Entrepreneurship Theory and Practice*, 20, 23–31.

Kolvereid, L. and B. W. Åmo (2007) Entrepreneurship among Graduates from Business School. In *Handbook of Research in Entrepreneurship Education. Volume 2. A contextual perspective*, ed. A. Fayolle, 207–218. Cheltenham: Edward Elgar.

Kolvereid, L. and E. Isaksen (2006) New Business Start-up and Subsequent Entry into Self-Employment. *Journal of Business Venturing*, 21, 866–885.

Kor, Y. Y. and J. T. Mahoney (2000) Penrose's Resource-Based Approach: The Process and Product of Research Creativity. *Journal of Management Studies*, 37, 109–139.

Kristeva, J. (1982) *Desire in Language: A Semiotic Approach to Literature and Art*. New York: Columbia University Press.

Krueger, N. F. (1993) The Impact of Prior Entrepreneurial Experience on Perceived New Venture Feasibility and Desirability. *Entrepreneurship Theory and Practice*, 18, 5–21.

Krueger, N. F. and D. V. Brazeal (1994) Entrepreneurial Potential and Potential Entrepreneurs. *Entrepreneurship Theory and Practice*, 18, 91–104.

Krueger, N. (2003) The Cognitive Psychology of Entrepreneurship. In *Handbook of Entrepreneurship Research. An Interdisciplinary Survey and Introduction*, eds. Z. J. Acs and D. B. Audretsch, 105–140. Dordrecht: Kluwer.

Kuhn, T. S. (1996) *The Structure of Scientific Revolutions*. Chicago: University of Chicago Press.

Lafuente, E., Y. Vaillant and J. Rialp (2007) Regional Differences in the Influence of Role Models: Comparing the Entrepreneurial Process of Rural Catalonia *Regional Studies*, 41, 779–795.

Langlois, R. N. (1992) Transaction-cost Economics in Real Time. *Industrial and Corporate Change*, 1, 99–127.

Larson, A. and J. A. Starr (1993) A Network Model of Organization Formation. *Entrepreneurship Theory and Practice*, 17, 5–15.

Law, S. (1992) Crystal Eastman *Pace Law Review*, 12, 529–542.

Lawrence, T. B. and R. Suddaby (2006) Institutions and Institutional Work. In *Handbook of Organization Studies*, eds. S. R. Clegg, C. Hardy, T. B. Lawrence and W. R. Nord, 689–711. London: Sage.

Lawrence, T. B., R. Suddaby and B. Leca (2009) Introduction: Theorizing and Studying Institutional Work. In *Institutional Work: Actors and Agency in Institutional Studies of Organizations*, eds. T. B. Lawrence, R. Suddaby and B. Leca. Cambridge: Cambridge University Press.

Lawson, T. (1997) *Economics and Reality* London: Routledge.

Leca, B. and P. Naccache (2006) A Critical Realist Approach to Institutional Entrepreneurship. *Organization*, 13, 627–651.

Lechner, C. and M. Dowling (2003) Firm Networks: External Relationships as Sources for the Growth and Competitiveness of Entrepreneurial Firms. *Entrepreneurship and Regional Development*, 15, 1–26.

Lee, D. Y. and E. W. K. Tsang (2001) The Effects of Entrepreneurial Personality, Background and Network Activities on Venture Growth. *Journal of Management Studies*, 38, 583–602.

Lee, R. and O. Jones (2008) Networks, Communication and Learning during Business Start-up The Creation of Cognitive Social Capital. *International Small Business Journal*, 26, 559–594.

Levitt, S. D. and S. J. Dubner (2007) *Freakonomics: A Rogue Economist Explores the Hidden Side of Everything*. London Penguin.

Lewis, P. A. (2002) Agency, Structure and Causality in Political Science: A Comment on Sibeon. *Politics*, 22, 17–23.

Linan, F. and Y. W. Chen (2009) Development and Cross-Cultural Application of a Specific Instrument to Measure Entrepreneurial Intentions. *Entrepreneurship Theory and Practice*, 33, 593–617.

Lincoln, Y. S. and E. G. Guba (1985) *Naturalist Inquiry*. Thousand Oaks, CA: Sage.

Lindgren, M. and N. Wåhlin (2001) Identity Construction among Boundary-Crossing Individuals. *Scandinavian Journal of Management*, 17, 357–377.

Lippman, S. A. and R. P. Rumelt (1982) Uncertain Imitability: An Analysis of Interfirm Differences in Efficiency under Competition. *Bell Journal of Economics*, 13, 418–438.

Lippman, S. A. and R. P. Rumelt (2003) A Bargaining Perspective on Resource Advantage. *Strategic Management Journal*, 24, 1069–1086.

Littunen, H. (2000) Entrepreneurship and the Characteristics of the Entrepreneurial Personality. *International Journal of Entrepreneurial Behaviour and Research*, 6, 195–308.

Loasby, B. J. (2007) A Cognitive Perspective on Entrepreneurship and the Firm. *Journal of Management Studies*, 44, 1078–1106.

Locke, E. A. and J. R. Baum (2007) Entrepreneurial Motivation. In *The Psychology of Entrepreneurship*, eds. J. R. Baum, M. Frese and R. A. Baron, 93–112. Mahwah, NJ: Lawrence Erlbaum Associates Inc.

Lounsbury, M. and M. A. Glynn (2001) Cultural Entrepreneurship: Stories, Legitimacy, and the Acquisition of Resources. *Strategic Management Journal*, 22, 545–564.

Lumpkin, G. T. and G. G. Dess (1996) Clarifying the Entrepreneurial Orientation Construct and Linking it to Performance. *Academy of Management Review*, 21, 135–172.

MacDonald, G. and M. D. Ryall (2004) How Do Value Creation and Competition Determine Whether a Firm Appropriates Value? *Management Science*, 50, 1319–1333.

MacDonald, R. and F. Coffield (1991) *Risky Business: Youth and the Enterprise Culture*. Basingstoke: Falmer Press.

Macpherson, A. and R. Holt (2007) Knowledge, Learning and Small Firm Growth: A Systematic Review of the Evidence. *Research Policy*, 36, 172–192.

Maguire, S., C. Hardy and T. B. Lawrence (2004) Institutional Entrepreneurship in Emerging Fields: HIV/AIDS Treatment Advocacy in Canada. *Academy of Management Journal*, 47, 657–679.

Makadok, R. (2001a) A Pointed Commentary on Priem and Butler. *Academy of Management Review*, 26, 498–499.

Makadok, R. (2001b) Toward a Synthesis of the Resource-Based and Dynamic-Capability Views of Rent Creation. *Strategic Management Journal*, 22, 387–401.

Makadok, R. (2010) The Interaction Effect of Rivalry Restraint and Competitive Advantage on Profit: Why the Whole Is Less Than the Sum of the Parts. *Management Science*, 56, 356–372.

Makadok, R. and J. B. Barney (2001) Strategic Factor Market Intelligence: An Application of Information Economics to Strategy Formulation and Competitor Intelligence. *Management Science*, 47, 1621–1638.

Malthus, T. R. (1798) *An Essay on the Principle of Population*. London: J. Johnson.

March, J. (1991) Exploration and Exploitation in Organizational Learning. *Organization Science*, 2, 71–87.

Marlow, S. (2002) Self-employed Women: A Part of or Apart from Feminist Theory? *International Journal of Entrepreneurship and Innovation*, 2, 23–37.

Marlow, S. 2009. The Myth of the Underperforming Female Entrepreneur. In *Enterprising Matters*. Institute for Small Business and Entrepreneurship.

Marlow, S., S. Carter and E. Shaw (2008) Constructing Female Entrepreneurship Policy in the UK: is the US a Relevant Benchmark? *Environment and Planning C-Government and Policy*, 26, 335–351.

Marlow, S., C. Henry and S. Carter (2009) Exploring the Impact of Gender upon Women's Business Ownership Introduction. *International Small Business Journal*, 27, 139–148.

Marsh, D. and P. Furlong (2002) A Skin not a Sweater: Ontology and Epistemology in Political Science. In *Theory and Method in Political Science*, eds. D. Marsh and G. Stoker, 17–41. Basingstoke: Palgrave Macmillan.

Marsh, D. and G. Stoker (2002) Theory and Methods in Political Science. Basingstoke: Palgrave Macmillan.

Martin, J. (2003) Feminist Theory and Critical theory: Unexplored Synergies. In *Studying Management Critically*, eds. M. Alvesson and H. Willmott, 66–91. London: Sage.

Mason, C. and R. Harrison (1999) Venture Capital: Rationale, Aims and Scope. *Venture Capital*, 1, 1–46.

Matthews, C. H. and S. B. Moser (1995) Family Background and Gender: Implications for Interest in Small Firm Ownership. *Entrepreneurship and Regional Development*, 7, 365–377.

May, T. (2001) *Social Research: Issues, Methods and Process*. Buckingham: Open University Press.

McAdam, M. and S. Marlow (2009) Walk like a Women, Talk like a Man? Constructing Identities in the Context of the High Technology Business Incubator. In *Paper to the 26th EURAM Conference*. Liverpool.

McAnulla, S. (2002) Structure and Agency. In *Theory and Methods in Political Science*, eds. D. Marsh and G. Stoker, 271–291. Basingstoke: Palgrave Macmillan.

McClelland, D. C. (1961) *The Achieving Society*. New York: Simon and Schuster.

McGuinness, S. and M. Hart (2004) Mixing the Grant Cocktail: Towards an Understanding of the Outcomes of Financial Support to Small Firms. *Environment and Planning C-Government and Policy*, 22, 841–857.

McKelvey, B. (1982) *Organizational Systematics: Taxonomy, Evolution, Classification*. Berkeley: University of California Press.

McRobbie, A. (2009) *The Aftermath of Feminism*. London: Sage.

Mead, G. H. (1934) *Mind Self and Society*. Chicago: University of Chicago Press.

Menzies, T. V. (2004) Are Universities playing a Role in Nurturing and Developing High-Technology Entrepreneurs? *International Journal of Entrepreneurship and Innovation*, 4, 149–157.

Meyer, J. W. (2008) Reflections on Institutional Theories of Organizations. In *The SAGE Handbook of Organizational Institutionalism*, eds. R. Greenwood, C. Oliver, K. Sahlin and R. Suddaby, 790–812. London: Sage.

Meyer, J. W. and B. Rowan (1977) Institutionalized Organizations: Formal Structure as Myth and Ceremony. *American Journal of Sociology*, 83, 340–363.

Miettinen, O., O. Mazhelis and E. Luoma (2010) Managerial Growth Challenges in Small Software Firms: A Multiple-Case Study of Growth-Oriented Enterprises. In *Software Business*, eds. P. Tyrvainen, S. Jansen and M. A. Cusumano, 26–37.

Mills, C. W. (1956) *The Power Elite*. New York: Oxford University Press.

Mills, C. W. (1966) *Sociology and Pragmatism: the Higher Learning in America*. New York: Oxford University Press.

Mills, C. W. (1990) *The Sociological Imagination*. Harmondsworth: Penguin.

Minitti, M., P. Arenius and N. Langowitz (2005) *Global Entrepreneurship Monitor 2004 Report on Women and Entrepreneurship*. Wellesey MA: Babson College.

Mirchandani, K. (1999) Feminist Insight on Gendered Work: New Directions in Research on Women and Entrepreneurship. *Gender, Work and Organisation*, 6, 224–235.

Mises, L. V. (1949) *Human Action*. New Haven, CT: Yale University Press.

Mitchell, R., L. Busenitz, T. Lant, P. McDougall, E. Morse and B. Smith (2002) Toward a Theory of Entrepreneurial Cognition: Rethinking the People side of Entrepreneurship Research. *Entrepreneurship Theory and Practice*, 27, 93–104.

Mokyr, J. (2000) Evolutionary Phenomena in Technological Change. In *Technological Innovation as an Evolutionary Process*, ed. J. Ziman, 52–65. Cambridge: Cambridge University Press.

Mole, K. F. and G. Bramley (2006) Making policy choices in nonfinancial business support: an international comparison. *Environment and Planning C-Government and Policy*, 24, 885–908.

Mole, K. F., M. Hart, S. Roper and D. S. Saal (2009) Assessing the Effectiveness of Business Support Services in England Evidence from a Theory-Based Evaluation. *International Small Business Journal*, 27, 557–582.

Mole, K. F. and M. Mole (2010) Entrepreneurship as the Structuration of Individual and Opportunity: A Response using a Critical Realist Perspective. Comment on Sarason, Dean and Dillard. *Journal of Business Venturing*, 25, 230–237.

Mønsted, M. (1995) Process and Structures of Networks: Reflections on Methodology. *Entrepreneurship and Regional Development*, 7, 193–213.

Morton, F. M. S. and J. M. Podolny (2002) Love or Money? The Effects of Owner Motivation in the California Wine Industry. *Journal of Industrial Economics*, 50, 431–456.

Mosakowski, E. (1998) Entrepreneurial Resources, Organizational Choices and Competitive Outcomes. *Organization Science*, 9, 625–643.

Mounce, H. O. (1997) *The Two Pragmatisms*. London: Routledge.

Murmann, J. P. (2003) *Knowledge and Competitive Advantage: The Co-evolution of Firms, Technology and National Institutions*. New York: Cambridge University Press.

Mutch, A. (2007) Reflexivity and the Historical Entrepreneur. *Organisation Studies*, 28 1123–1140.

Mutch, A. (2010) Technology, Organization and Structure – A Morphogenetic Approach. *Organization Science*, 21, 507–520.

Nelson, R. and S. Winter (1982) *Evolutionary Theory of Economic Change*. Cambridge, MA: Bellknap.

Newbert, S. L. (2007) Empirical Research on the Resource-Based View of the Firm: An Assessment and Suggestions for Future Research. *Strategic Management Journal*, 28, 121–147.

Nodoushani, O. and P. A. Nodoushani (1999) A Deconstructionist Theory of Entrepreneurship. *American Business Review*, 17, 45–49.

Nooteboom, B. (2006) Organization, Evolution, Cognition and Dynamic Capabilities. In *CentER Discussion Paper*, 1–23.

North, D. C. (1990) *Institutions, Institutional Change and Economic Performance*. Cambridge: Cambridge University Press.

O'Connor, E. (2002) Storied Business: Typology, Intertextuality and Traffic in Entrepreneurial Narrative. *Journal of Business Communication*, 39, 36–54.

O'Donnell, A., A. Gilmore, D. Cummins and D. Carson (2001) The Network Construct in Entrepreneurship Research: A Review and Critique. *Management Decision*, 39, 749–760.

Ogbor, J. O. (2000) Mythicising and Reification in Entrepreneurial Discourse: Ideology-Critique of Entrepreneurial Studies. *Journal of Management Studies*, 37, 605–635.

Ostgaard, T. A. and S. Birley (1994) New Venture Growth and Personal Networks. *Journal of Business Research*, 36, 37–50.

Outhwaite, W. (1998) Realism and Social Science. In *Critical realism: Essential Readings*, eds. M. S. Archer, R. Bhaskar, A. Collier, T. Lawson and A. Norrie, 282–296. London: Routledge.

Pages, E. and S. Garmise (2003) The Power of Entrepreneurial Networking. *Economic Development Journal*, Summer, 20–30.

Parker, M. (2002) *Against Management*. Cambridge: Polity Press.

Parker, S. (2006) *The Economics of Self-Employment and Entrepreneurship*. Cambridge: Cambridge University Press.

Patton, M. Q. (1990) *Qualitative Evaluation and Research Methods*. Thousand Oaks, CA: Sage.

Pawson, R. and N. Tilley (1997) *Realistic Evaluation*. London: Sage.

Penrose, E. T. (1959) *The Theory of the Growth of the Firm*. Oxford: Basil Blackwater.

Pentland, B. T. and M. S. Feldman (2005) Organizational Routines as a Unit of Analysis. *Industrial and Corporate Change*, 14, 793–815.

Perren, L. and P. L. Jennings (2005) Government Discourses on Entrepreneurship: Issues of Legitimization, Subjugation and Power. *Entrepreneurship Theory and Practice*, 29, 173–184.

Perren, L. and M. Ram (2004) Case-Study Method in Small Business and Entrepreneurial Research – Mapping Boundaries and Perspectives. *International Small Business Journal*, 22, 83–101.

Peteraf, M. A. (1993) The Cornerstones of Competitive Advantage: A Resource-Based View. *Strategic Management Journal*, 14, 179–191.

Peteraf, M. A. and J. B. Barney (2003) Unraveling the Resource-Based Tangle. *Managerial and Decision Economics*, 24, 309–323.

Pfeffer, J. and G. R. Salancik (1978) *The External Control of Organizations: A Resource Dependence Perspective*. New York: Harper and Row.

Phelps, R., R. Adams and J. Bessant (2007) Life Cycles of Growing Organizations: A Review with Implications for Knowledge and Learning. *International Journal of Management Reviews*, 9, 1–30.

Pihkala, T., E. Varamäki and J. Vesalainen (1999) Virtual Organization and the SMEs: A Review and Model Development. *Entrepreneurship and Regional Development*, 11, 225–349.

Pitt, M. (1998) A Tale of Two Gladiators: 'Reading' Entrepreneurs As Texts. *Organisation Studies*, 19, 387–414.

Plotkin, H. (1994) *Darwin Machines and the Nature of Knowledge*. Cambridge, MA: Harvard University Press.

Polkinghorne, D. (1988) *Narrating Knowing and the Human Sciences*. Albany, NY: State University of New York Press.

Porpora, D. (2007) On Elder-Vass: Refining a Refinement. *Journal for the Theory of Social Behaviour*, 37, 195–200.

Porter, M. E. (1980) *Competitive Strategy*. New York: The Free Press.

Porter, M. E. (1981) The Contribution of Industrial Organization to Strategic Management. *Academy of Management Review*, 6, 609–620.

Potter, J. and M. Wetherell (1987) *Discourse and Social Psychology*. London: Sage.

Powell, W. W. and J. A. Colyvas (2008) Microfoundations of Institutional Theory. In *The SAGE Handbook of Organizational Institutionalism*, eds. R. Greenwood, C. Oliver, K. Sahlin and R. Suddaby, 276–298. London: Sage.

Prahalad, C. K. and G. Hamel (1990) The Core Competence of the Corporation. *Harvard Business Review*, 68, 79–91.

Priem, R. L. and J. E. Butler (2001a) Is the Resource-Based 'View' a Useful Perspective for Strategic Management Research? *Academy of Management Review*, 26, 22–40.

Priem, R. L. and J. E. Butler (2001b) Tautology in the Resource-Based View and the Implications of Externally Determined Resource Value: Further comments. *Academy of Management Review*, 26, 57–66.

Procter, M. (2001) Measuring Attitudes. In *Researching Social Life*, ed. N. Gilbert, 105–122. London: Sage.

Pullen, A. and R. Simpson (2009) Managing Difference in Feminized Work: Men, Otherness and Social Practice. *Human Relations*, 62, 561–587.

Radkau, J. (2009) *Max Weber*. Cambridge: Polity Press.

Rainnie, A. (1989) *Industrial relations in small firms*. London: Routledge.

Ram, M. (1991) Control and Autonomy in Small Firms – The Case of the West Midlands Clothing Industry. *Work Employment and Society*, 5, 601–619.

—— (1994) Unravelling Social Networks in Ethnic Minority Firms. *International Small Business Journal*, 12, 42–53.

—— (1999a) Managing Consultants in a Small Firm: A Case Study. *Journal of Management Studies*, 36, 875–897.

—— (1999b) Managing Professional Service Firms in a Multi-Ethnic Context: An Ethnographic Study. *Ethnic and Racial Studies*, 22, 679–701.

—— (2001) Family Dynamics in a Small Consultancy Firm: A Case Study. *Human Relations*, 54, 395–418.

Ram, M. and R. Holliday (1993) Relative Merits – Family Culture and Kinship in Small Firms. *Sociology*, 27, 629–648.

Ram, M., N. Theodorakopoulos and T. Jones (2008) Forms of Capital, Mixed Embeddedness and Somali Enterprise. *Work Employment and Society*, 22, 427–446.

Ram, M. and K. Trehan (2010) Critical Action Learning, Policy Learning and Small Firms: An Inquiry. *Management Learning*, 41, 414–428.

Rauch, A. and M. Frese (2007) Born to be an Entrepreneur? Revisiting the Personality Approach to Entrepreneurship. In *The Psychology of Entrepreneurship*, eds. J. R. Baum, M. Frese and R. A. Baron, 41–65. Mahwah, NJ: Lawrence Erlbaum Associates Inc.

Read, S., S. Sarasvathy, R. Wiltbank and A. V. Ohlsson (2010) *Effectual Entrepreneurship*. New York: Routledge.

Reed, M. (2005a) Doing the Loco-motion: Response to Contu and Willmott's Commentary on 'The Realist Turn in Organization and Management Studies'. *Journal of Management Studies*, 42, 1663–1673.

Reed, M. (2005b) Reflections on the realist turn in organization and management studies. *Journal of Management Studies*, 42, 1621–1644.

Reed, R. and R. J. Defillippi (1990) Causal Ambiguity, Barriers to Imitation and Sustainable Competitive Advantage. *Academy of Management Review*, 15, 88–102.

Reid, G., L. Jacobson and M. Anderson (1993) *Profiles in Small Business: A Competitive Strategy Approach*. London: Routledge.

Rich, A. (1977) *Of Woman Born: Motherhood as Experience and Institution*. London: Virago.

Richerson, P. J. and R. Boyd (2005) *Not by Genes Alone: How Culture Transformed Human Evolution*. Chicago: University of Chicago Press.

Ricoeur, P. (1981) *Hermeneutics and the Human Sciences*. Cambridge: Cambridge University Press.

Riding, R. J. and S. G. Rayner (1998) *Cognitive Style and Learning Strategies*. London: Fulton.

Rivkin, J. (2000) Imitation of Complex Strategies. *Management Science*, 46, 824–844.

Robinson, P. B., D. V. Simpson, J. C. Huefner and H. K. Hunt (1999) An Attitude Approach to the Study of Entrepreneurship. *Entrepreneurship Theory and Practice*, 15, 13–31.

Robson, M. T. (1997) The Relative Earnings from Self and Paid Employment: A Time-Series Analysis for the UK. *Scottish Journal of Political Economy*, 44, 502–518.

Robson, M. T. and C. Wren (1999) Marginal and Average Tax Rates and the Incentive for Self-Employment. *Southern Economic Journal*, 65, 757–773.

Romanelli, E. (1989) Environments and Strategies of Organization Start-up: Effects on early survival. *Administrative Science Quarterly*, 34, 369–387.

Romanelli, E. and C. B. Schoonhoven (2001) The Local Origins of New Firms. In *The Entreprenurship Dynamic*, 40–67. Stanford: Stanford University Press.

Romijn, H. and M. Albu (2002) Innovation, Networking and Proximity: Lessons from Small High Technology Firms in the UK. *Regional Studies*, 36, 81–86.

Ronstadt, R. (1988) The Corridor Principle. *Journal of Business Venturing*, 3, 31–40.

Rose, N. (1992) Governing the Enterprising Self. In *The Values of Enterprise Culture*, eds. P. Heelas and P. Morris, 141–164. London: Routledge.

Roseneil, S. (2000) Queer Frameworks and Queer Tendencies: Towards an Understanding of Postmodern Transformations of Sexuality. *Sociological Research Online*, 5, 1–19. http://www.socresonline.org.uk/5/3/roseneil.html (last accessed 21 March 2011).

Rosenkopf, L. and A. Nerkar (1999) On the Complexity of Technological Evolution. In *Variations in Organization Science, In Honor of Donald T. Campbell*, eds. J. C. Baum and B. McKelvey, 169–183. New York: Sage.

Rotter, J. B. (1966) Generalized Expectancies for Internal Versus External Control of Reinforcement. *Psychological Monographs General and Applied*, 80, 1–27.

Rowbotham, S. (1992) *Hidden from History*. London: Virago.

Rumelt, R. P. (1984) Towards a Strategic Theory of the Firm. In *Competitive Strategic Management*, ed. R. Lamb, 556–570. Englewood Cliffs, NJ: Prentice-Hall.

Rumelt, R. P. (1987) Theory, Strategy, and Entrepreneurship. In *The Competitive Challenge: Strategies for Industrial Innovation and Renewal*, ed. D. J. Teece, 137–158. Cambridge, MA: Ballinger.

Salerno, J. T. (1993) Mises and Hayek Dehomogenized. *Review of Austrian Economics*, 6, 113–146.

Santos, F. A. and K. A. Eisenhardt (2005) Organizational Boundaries and Theories of Organization. *Organization Science*, 16, 491–508.

Sarasvathy, S. D. (2001) Causation and Effectuation: Towards a Theoretical Shift from Economic Inevitability to Entrepreneurial Contingency. *Academy of Management Review*, 26, 243–263.

Sarasvathy, S. D. (2004) Making It Happen: Beyond Theories of the Firm to Theories of Firm Design. *Entrepreneurship Theory and Practice*, 28, 519–531.

Sarasvathy, S. D. (2008) *Effectuation: Elements of Entrepreneurial Expertise*. Cheltenham: Edward Elgar.

Sayer, A. (2000) *Realism and Social Science*. London: Sage.

SBS. (2003) *A Strategic Framework for Women's Enterprise*. London: DTI Small Business Service.

——. (2004) A Government Action Plan for Small Business: Making the UK the Best Place in the World to Start and Grow a Business – The Evidence Base. London: HMSO.

Scherer, P. D., J. Adams, S. Carley and F. Wiebe (1989) Role Model Performance Effects on Development of Entrepreneurial Career Preference. *Entrepreneurship Theory and Practice*, 13, 53–81.

Schumacher, E. F. (1993) *Small is Beautiful: a Study of Economics as if People Mattered*. London: Vintage.

Schumpeter, J. A. (1934a) *History of Economic Analysis*. New York: Oxford University Press.

Schumpeter, J. A. (1934b) *The Theory of Economic Development*. Cambridge MA: Harvard University Press.

Schumpeter, J. A. (1942) *Capitalism, Socialism and Democracy*. New York: Harper and Row.

Schutz, A. (1967) *The Phenomenology of the Social World*. Evanston, IL: Northwestern University Press.

Scott, M. and R. Bruce (1987) Five Stages of Growth in Small Business. *Long Range Planning*, 20, 45–52.

Scott, M. G. and D. F. Twomey (1988) The Long Term Supply of Entrepreneurs. Student Career Aspirations in Relation to Entrepreneurship. *Journal of Small Business Management*, 26, 5–13.

Scott, W. R. (1995) *Institutions and Organizations*. Thousand Oaks, CA: Sage.

Selznick, P. (1949) *TVA and the Grass Roots*. Berkeley, CA: University of California Press.

Shane, S. (2000) Prior Knowledge and the Discovery of Entrepreneurial Opportunities. *Organization Science*, 11, 448–469.

Shane, S. (2001) Technology Regimes and Few Firm Formation. *Management Science*, 47, 1173–1190.

Shane, S. (2003) *A General Theory of Entrepreneurship: The Individual-Opportunity Nexus*. Cheltenham: Edward Elgar.

Shane, S. and D. Cable (2002) Network Ties, Reputation and the Financing of New Ventures. *Management Science*, 48, 364–381.

Shane, S. and S. Venkataraman (2000) The Promise of Entrepreneurship as a Field of Research. *Academy of Management Review*, 25, 217–226.

Shapero, A. and L. Sokol (1982) The Social Dimensions of Entrepreneurship. In *Encyclopedia of Entrepreneurship*, eds. C. Kent, D. Sexton and K. Vesper, 72–90. Englewood Cliffs, NJ: Prentice-Hall.

Shaver, K. G. (2003) The Social Psychology of Entrepreneurial Behaviour. In *Handbook of Entrepreneurship Research. An Interdisciplinary Survey and Introduction*, eds. Z. J. Acs and D. B. Audretsch, 331–357. Dordrecht: Kluwer.

Shaver, K. G. and L. R. Scott (1991) Person, Process, Choice: The Psychology of New Venture Creation. *Entrepreneurship Theory and Practice*, 16, 23–42.

Shaw, E., S. Marlow, W. Lam and S. Carter (2009) Gender and Entrepreneurial Capital: Implications for Firm Performance. *International Journal of Gender and Entrepreneurship*, 1, 25–42.

Shook, C. L., R. L. Priem and J. E. McGee (2003) Venture Creation and the Enterprising Individual: A Review and Synthesis. *Journal of Management*, 29, 379–399.

Short, J. C., T. W. Moss and G. T. Lumpkin (2009) Research in Social Entrepreneurship: Past Contributions and Future Opportunities. *Strategic Entrepreneurship Journal*, 3, 161–194.

Simons, H. A. (1957) *Administrative Behavior*. New York: Macmillan.

Sine, W. D. and R. J. David (2003) Environmental Jolts, Institutional Change, and the Creation of Entrepreneurial Opportunity. *Research Policy*, 32, 185–207.

Sine, W. D., R. J. David and H. Mitsuhashi (2007) From Plan to Plant: Effects of Certification on Operational Start-up in the Emergent Independent Power Sector. *Organizational Science* 18, 578–594.

Sine, W. D. and B. H. Lee (2009) Tilting at Windmills? The Environmental Movement and the Emergence of the US Wind Energy Sector. *Administrative Science Quarterly*, 54, 123–155.

Slotte-Kock, S. and N. Coviello (2010) Entrepreneurship Research on Network Processes: A Review and Ways Forward. *Entrepreneurship Theory and Practice*, 34, 31–57.

Soper, K. (1990) *Troubled Pleasures: Writings on Gender, Politics and Hedonism*. London: Virago.

Sorenson, O. and T. E. Stuart (2008) Entrepreneurship: A Field of Dreams? *Academy of Management Annals*, 2, 517–543.

Souitaris, V., S. Zerbinati and A. Al-Laham (2007) Do Entrepreneurship Programmes Raise Entrepreneurial Intention of Science and Engineering Students? The Effect of Learning, Inspiration and Resources. *Journal of Business Venturing*, 22, 566–591.

Spender, D. (1980) *Man Made Language*. London: Routledge.

Sperber, D. (1996) *Explaining Culture: A Naturalistic Approach*. Oxford: Blackwell.

Spicer, A., M. Alvesson and D. Karreman (2009) Critical Performativity: The Unfinished Business of Critical Management Studies. *Human Relations*, 62, 537–560.

Staber, U. and H. Aldrich (1995) Cross-national Similarities in the Personal Networks of Small Business Owners: A Comparison of two Regions in North America. *Canadian Journal of Sociology*, 20, 441–465.

Stark, D. (2009) *The Sense of Dissonance: Accounts of Worth in Economic Life*. Princeton, NJ: Princeton University Press.

Steyaert, C. (1998) A Qualitative Methodology for Process Studies of Entrepreneurship. *International Studies of Management and Organisation*, 27, 13–33.

Steyaert, C. (2007) 'Entrepreneuring' as a Conceptual Attractor? A Review of Process Theories in 20 years of Entrepreneurship Studies. *Entrepreneurship and Regional Development*, 19, 453–477.

Steyaert, C. and J. Katz (2004) Reclaiming the Space of Entrepreneurship in Society: Geographical, Discursive and Social Dimensions. *Entrepreneurship and Regional Development*, 16, 179–196.

Stiglitz, J. E. and A. Weiss (1981) Credit Rationing in Markets with Imperfect Information. *American Economic Review*, 71, 393–410.

Stinchcombe, A. L. (1965) Social Structure and Organizations. In *Handbook of Organizations*, ed. J. G. March, 153–193. Chicago: Rand-McNally.

Stinchcombe, A. L. (2005) *The Logic of Social Research*. Chicago: University of Chicago.

Stoelhorst, J. W. (2008) The Explanatory Logic and Ontological Commitments of Generalized Darwinism. *Journal of Economic Methodology*, 15, 343–363.

Storey, D. J. (1982) *Entrepreneurship and the New Firm*. London: Croom-Helm.

Storey, D. J. (1994) *Understanding the Small Business Sector* London: Routledge.

Storey, D. J. (2003) Entrepreneurship, Small and Medium Sized Enterprises and Public Policies. In *The Handbook of Entrepreneurship*, eds. D. B. Audretsch and A. Z., 473–511. London: Kluwer.

Storey, J., G. Salaman and K. Platman (2005) Living with Enterprise in an Enterprise Economy: Freelance and Contract Workers in the Media. *Human Relations*, 58, 1033–1054.

Storper, M. (1995) Regional Technology Coalitions – An Essential Dimension of National Technology Policy. *Research Policy*, 24, 895–911.

Streufert, S. and G. Y. Nogami (1989) Cognitive Style and Complexity. Implication for I/O Psychology. In *International Review of Industrial and Organizational Psychology*, eds. C. L. Cooper and I. Robertson, 93–143. Chichester: Wiley.

Sudbury, J. (1998) *Other Kinds of Dreams: Black Women's Organisation and the Politics of Transformation*. London: Routledge.

Suddaby, R., K. D. Elsbach, R. Greenwood, J. W. Meyer and T. B. Zilber (2007) Academy of Management Journal Special Research Forum Call for Papers: Organizations and Their Institutional Environments: Bringing Meaning, Culture, and Values Back In. *Academy of Management Journal*, 50, 468–469.

Szarka, J. (1990) Networking and Small Firms. *International Small Business Journal*, 8, 10–22.

Taylor, S. and S. Marlow (2009) Engendering Entrepreneurship: Why can't a Women be more like a Man? In *Paper to the 26th EURAM Conference*. Liverpool.

Teece, D. J. (1986) Profiting from Technological Innovation. *Research Policy*, 15, 286–305.

Teece, D. J. (2007) Explicating Dynamic Capabilities: The Nature and Microfoundations of (Sustainable) Enterprise Performance. *Strategic Management Journal*, 28, 1319–1350.

Teece, D. J., G. Pisano and A. Shuen (1997) Dynamic Capabilities and Strategic Management. *Strategic Management Journal*, 18, 509–533.

Thompson, E. R. (2009) Individual Entrepreneurial Intent: Construct Clarification and Development of an Internationally Reliable Metric. *Entrepreneurship Theory and Practice*, 33, 669–694.

Thornton, P. H. (2004) *Markets from Culture: Institutional Logics and Organizational Decisions in Higher Education Publishing*. Stanford, CA: Stanford University Press.

Thornton, P. H. and W. Ocasio (2008) Institutional Logics. In *The SAGE Handbook of Organizational Institutionalism*, eds. R. Greenwood, C. Oliver, K. Sahlin and R. Suddaby, 276–298. London: Sage.

Timmons, J. A. (1986) Growing up Big: Entrepreneurship and Creation of High Potential Ventures. In *The Art and Science of Entrepreneurship*, eds. D. Sexton and R. Smilor, 223–239. Cambridge, MA: Ballinger.

Tkachev, A. and L. Kolvereid (1999) Self-employment Intentions among Russian Students. *Entrepreneurship and Regional Development*, 11, 269–280.

Tolbert, P. S. and L. G. Zucker (1983) Institutional Sources of Change in the Formal Structure of Organizations: The Diffusion of Civil Service Reform, 1880–1935. *Administrative Science Quarterly*, 28, 22–39.

Tooby, J. and L. Cosmides (1992) The Psychological Fundations of Culture. In *The Adapted Mind: Evolutionary Psychology and the Generation of Culture*, eds. J. H. Barkow, L. Cosmides and J. Tooby, 19–136. Oxford: Oxford University Press.

Tracey, P. (2011) Neo-Institutionalism and Entrepreneurship. In *Perspectives in Entrepreneurship: A Critical Approach*, eds. K. F. Mole and M. Ram. Basingstoke: Palgrave Macmillan.

Tracey, P., N. Phillips and O. Jarvis (2011) Bridging Institutional Entrepreneurship and the Creation of New Organizational Forms: A Multilevel Model. *Organization Science*, 22(1): 60–80.

Tsoukas, H. (1994) What is Management? An Outline of a Metatheory. *British Journal of Management*, 5, 289–301.

Tsoukas, H. and R. Chia (2002) On Organizational Becoming: Rethinking Organizational Change. *Organization Science*, 13, 567–582.

Turner, J. H. (2005) A New Approach for Theoretically Integrating Micro and Macro Analysis. In *The Sage Handbook of Sociology*, eds. C. Cahoun, C. Rojek and B. Turner, 405–422. London: Sage.

Tushman, M. L. and P. Anderson (1986) Technological Discontinuities and Organizational Environments. *Administrative Science Quarterly*, 31, 439–465.

Uzzi, B. (1996) The Sources and Consequences of Embeddedness for the Economic Performance of Organizations: The Network Effect. *American Sociological Review*, 61, 674–698.

Uzzi, B. (1997) Social Structure and Competition in Interfirm Networks: The Paradox of Embeddedness. *Administrative Science Quarterly*, 42, 35–67.

Uzzi, B. and J. J. Gillespie (2002) Knowledge Spillover in Corporate Financing Networks: Embeddedness and the Firm's Debt Performance. *Strategic Management Journal*, 23, 595–618.

Uzzi, B. and R. Lancaster (2003) Relational Embeddedness and Learning: The Case of Bank Loan Managers and their Clients. *Management Science*, 49, 383–399.

van Dijk, T. A. (1999) On Context. *Discourse and Society*, 10, 291–292.

van Maanen, J. (1988) *Tales of the Field: On Writing Ethnography*. Chicago: University of Chicago Press.

van Praag, C. M. and P. H. Versloot (2008) The Economic Benefits and Costs of Entrepreneurship: A Review of the Research. *Foundations and Trends in Entrepreneurship*, 4, 65–154.

Van Stel, A. J. and D. J. Storey (2004) The Link Between Firm Births and Job Creation: Is There a Upas Tree Effect? *Regional Studies*, 38, 893–909.

Vaughan, D. (1999) The Dark Side of Organizations: Mistake, Misconduct and Disaster. *Annual Review of Sociology*, 25, 271–305.

Venkataraman, S. (1997) The Distinctive Domain of Entrepreneurship Research: An Editor's Perspective. In *Advances in Entrepreneurship*, eds. J. Katz and R. Brockhaus, 119–138. Greenwich: JAI Press.

Venkataraman, S. (2004) Regional Transformation through Technological Entrepreneurship. *Journal of Business Venturing*, 19, 153–167.

Vincent, S. (2008) A Transmutation Theory of Inter-Organizational Exchange Relations and Networks: Applying Critical Realism to Analysis of Collective Agency. *Human Relations*, 61, 875–899.

Vygotsky, L. S. (1981) The Genesis of Higher Mental Functions. In *The Concept of Activity in Soviet Psychology*, ed. J. V. Wertsch, 189–240. Amronk, NY: M.W. Sharpe.

Ward, H. (2002) Rational Choice. In *Theory and Method in Political Studies*, eds. D. Marsh and G. Stoker, 65–89. London: Palgrave Macmillan.

Watson, T. J. (1995) Entrepreneurship and Professional Management: A Fatal Distinction. *International Small Business Journal*, 13, 33–45.

Watson, T. J. (2002) *Organising and Managing Work: Organisational, Managerial and Strategic Behaviour In Theory And Practice*. Harlow: FT Prentice-Hall.

Watson, T. J. (2006) *Organising and Managing Work: Organisational, Managerial and Strategic Behaviour in Theory and Practice*. Harlow: FT Prentice-Hall.

Watson, T. J. (2008) Managing identity: Identity work, personal predicaments and structural circumstances. *Organization*, 15, 121–143.

Watson, T. J. (2009) Entrepreneurial Action, Identity Work and the Use of Multiple Discursive Resources The Case of a Rapidly Changing Family Business. *International Small Business Journal*, 27, 251–274.

Watson, T. J. (2011a) Entrepreneurial Action and the Euro-American Social Science Tradition: Pragmatism, Realism and looking beyond "The Entrepreneur". *Submitted to Entrepreneurship and Regional Development.*

Watson, T. J. (2011b) Entrepreneurship in Action: Studying Entrepreneurial Action in its Individual, Organisational and Institutional Context. *Submitted to Entrepreneurship and Regional Development.*

Watson, T. J. (2011c) Ethnography, Reality, and Truth: The Vital Need for Studies of 'How Things Work' in Organizations and Management. *Journal of Management Studies*, 48, 202–217.

Weber, M. (1947) *The Theory of Social and Economic Organization*. Glencoe, IL: The Free Press.

Weber, M. (1949) *The Methodology of the Social Sciences*. Glencoe, IL: The Free Press.

Weick, K. (1995) *Sensemaking in Organisations*. Sage: Thousand Oaks, CA.

Weick, K. E. (1979) *The Social Psychology of Organising*. Reading, MA: Addison-Wesley.

Weldon, F. (2003) Look What We Have Done. *Daily Mail* (23 November 2003), 12–13.

Wennekers, A. R. M. and A. R. Thurik (1999) Linking Entrepreneurship and Economic Growth. *Small Business Economics*, 13, 27–55.

Wernerfelt, B. (1984) A Resource-based View of the Firm. *Strategic Management Journal*, 5, 171–180.

Westhead, P., D. Ucbasaran and M. Wright (2005) Decisions, Actions and Performance: Do Novice, Serial and Portfolio Entrepreneurs Differ? *Journal of Small Business Management*, 43, 393–417.

Winter, S. G. (2000) The Satisficing Principle in Capability Learning. *Strategic Management Journal*, 21, 981–996.

Witt, U. (2004) On the Proper Interpretation of 'Evolution' in Economics and its Implications for Production Theory. *Journal of Economic Methodology*, 11, 125–140.

Wittgenstein, L. (1953) *Philosophical Investigations*. Oxford: Basil Blackwell.

Wooten, M. and A. J. Hoffman (2008) Organizational Fields: Past, Present and Future. In *The SAGE Handbook of Organizational Institutionalism*, eds. R. Greenwood, C. Oliver, K. Sahlin and R. Suddaby, 130–148. London: Sage.

Wren, C. and D. J. Storey (2002) Evaluating the Effect of Soft Business Support upon Small Firm Performance. *Oxford Economic Papers-New Series*, 54, 334–365.

Yin, R. K. (2009) *Case Study Research: Design and Methods*. Thousand Oaks, CA: Sage.

Zafirovski, M. (1999) Probing into the Social Layers of Entrepreneurship Outlines of the Sociology of Enterprise. *Entrepreneurship and Regional Development*, 11, 351–372.

Zahra, S. A. (2007) Contextualizing Theory Building in Entrepreneurship Research. *Journal of Business Venturing*, 22, 443–452.

Zeleny, M. (2001) Autopoiesis (self-production) in SME Networks. *Human Systems Management*, 20, 201–207.

Zilber, T. B. (2006) The Work of The Symbolic in Institutional Processes: Translations of Rational Myths in Israeli High Tech. *Academy of Management Journal*, 49, 281–303.

Zott, C. and Q. N. Huy (2007) How Entrepreneurs Use Symbolic Management to Acquire Resources. *Administrative Science Quarterly*, 52, 70–105.

Zucker, L. G. (1977) The Role of Institutionalization in Cultural Persistence. *American Sociological Review*, 42, 726–743.

Author Index

Acedo, F.J., Barroso, C. and Galan, J.L., 121, 178

Adegbesan, A.J., 125, 133, 178

Adkins, L., 59, 178

Adome, Kwame, 41, 178

Ahl, H., 7, 59, 61, 63–70, 72, 73, 178

Ahlstrom, D. and Bruton, G.D., 103, 178

Ahmadjian, C.L. and Robinson, P., 103, 178

Ajzen, I., 29–31, 34, 178

Akerlof, G.A., 13, 16–17, 178

Aldrich, H. and Sakano, T., 81, 178

Aldrich, H. and Zimmer, C., 76, 178

Aldrich, H., Reese, P.R., Dubini, P., Rosen, B. and Woodward, B., 81, 178

Aldrich, H.E. and Fiol, M.C., 97, 105, 114, 178

Aldrich, H.E. and Martinez, M.A., 109, 178

Aldrich, H.E. and Ruef, M., 6, 8, 107–109, 114, 117, 119, 178

Aldrich, H.E. and Wiedenmayer, G., 8, 178

Aldrich, H.E., Hodgson, G.M., Hull, D.L., Knudsen, T., Mokyr, J. and Vanberg, V.J., 115, 178

Aldrich, H.E., Rosen, B. and Woodward, W., 80, 178

Allinson, C.W. and Hayes, J., 28, 179

Alvarez, S.A. and Busenitz, L.W., 131, 179

Alvesson, M. and Skoldberg, K., 42, 51–52, 179

Alvesson, M. and Due Billing, Y., 62, 179

Alvesson, M. and Willmott, H., 150, 179

Alvesson, M., Bridgman, T. and Willmott, H., 149, 179

Anderson, A.R., Jack, S.L. and Dodd, S.D., 7, 84, 179

Anderson, Drakopoulou Dodd and Jack, 91

Arauzo, J.M. and Manjon, M.C., 6, 179

Archer, M., Bhaskar, R., Collier, A., Lawson, T. and Norrie, A., 8, 148, 179

Archer, M.S., 137, 139–141, 143–148, 179

Arend, R.J., 126, 179

Armington, C. and Acs, Z.J., 4, 179

Armitage, C.J. and Connor, M., 31, 179

Armstrong, C.E. and Shimizu, K., 126, 179

Armstrong, P., 156–157, 160, 179

Atkinson, P., 52, 179

Audretsch, D.B. and Keilbach, M., 4, 6, 179

Badham, R., Garrety, V., Morrigan, V., Zanko, M. and Dawson, P., 154, 179

Baker, T. and Pollock, T.S., 133, 179

Bandura, A., 30, 31, 179

Barley, S.R., 101, 179

Barney, J.B., 117, 123–125, 129–130, 133, 179

Barnhart, R.K., 167, 180

Baron, R.A., 27, 29, 32–33, 110, 114, 180

Bates, T., 90, 180

Battilana, J., Lok, J. and Powell, W.W., 101, 180

Battilana, leca and Boxembaum, 105

Baum and Rowley, 111

Baum, J.A.C. and Singh, J., 114, 180

Baum, J.R., Frese, M. and Baron, J.A., 27, 39, 180

Baum, J.R., Frese, M., Baron, J.A. and Katz, J.A., 33, 180

Bauman, R. and Briggs, S.L., 49, 50, 180

Bauman, Z., 141, 143, 180

Baumol, W.J., 15, 22, 26, 130, 180

Baygan, G. and Freundenberg, M., 20, 180

Beck, U., 60, 180

Becker, M.C., 109–110, 117, 180

Beesley, V., 61–62, 180

Bennett, R., 22, 180

Bennett, R. and Robson, P., 21, 180

Bennett, R.J. and Smith., C., 4, 180

Bennett, R.J., Bratton, W.A. and Robson, P.J.A., 4, 180

Benson, J.K., 150, 180

Berger, P. and Luckmann, T., 43, 101, 164–165, 180

Berglund, K. and Johansson, A.W., 47, 180

Bester, H., 18, 180

Bevir, M. and Rhodes, R.A.W., 44, 180

Bhaskar, R., 8, 9, 140, 148, 165, 180

Biggiero, L., 85, 181

Bird, B., 29, 30, 181

Birley, S., 76, 81, 109, 181

Birley, S., Cromie, S. and Myers, A., 81, 181

Blaikie, N., 2, 3, 181

Blanchflower, D.G. and Oswald, A.G., 4, 5, 22, 23, 26, 138, 181

Blumer, H., 147, 181

Blyler, M. and Coff, R.W., 126, 181

Boisot, M. and Cohen, J., 83, 85, 181
Boje, D.M., 48, 181
Bolton, S.C. and Houlihan, M., 170, 181
Bouwen, R., 52, 181
Bowden, P. and Mummery, J., 59, 61–62, 64, 181
Boyd, N.G. and Vozikis, G.S., 30, 181
Bracker, J., 176, 181
Bradley, H., 59–60, 63–64, 70–71, 181
Brandstätter, H., 28, 181
Braverman, H., 146, 181
Breslin, D., 108–110, 112, 114–118, 176, 181
Brittain, J.W. and Freeman, J.H., 108, 109, 181
Brock, W.A. and Evans, D.S., 176, 181
Brockhaus, R.H. and Horwitz, P.S., 28, 181
Brockhause and Horwitz, 36, 181
Bruderl, J. and Preisendorfer, P., 78, 181
Bruner, J., 43, 181
Bruni, A., Gherardi, S. and Poggio, B., 68, 73, 181
Brush, De Bruin and Welter, 73
Buenstorf, G., 115, 181
Burchell, G., 153, 182
Burgelman, R.A., 109, 112–113, 118, 132, 182
Burr, V., 55, 182
Burrell, G. and Morgan, G., 9, 182
Burrows, R., 176, 182
Burt, R.S., 78–79, 91, 182
Busenitz, L.W. and Barney, J.B., 29, 110, 114, 182
Butler, J., 59–60, 62, 71, 73, 182
Bygrave, W.D. and Minnitti, M., 83, 182
Bygrave, W.D. and Zackarakis, A., 4, 182

Camagni, R., 83, 182
Campbell, D., 107, 111, 182
Capelleras, J-L. and Mole, K.F., 19, 182
Capelleras, J-L., Mole, K.F., Greene, F.J. and Storey, D.J., 10, 15, 182
Capron, L. and Shen, J-C., 125, 182
Carroll, G.R. and Hannen, M.T., 8, 182
Carroll, G.R. and Swaminathan, A., 112, 182
Carter, S. and Jones-Evans, D., 5, 182
Carter, S. and Shaw, E., 65, 72, 182
Casson, M. and Wadeson, N., 121, 182
Casson, M.C., 148, 182
Chandler, G.N. and Hanks, S.H., 27, 182
Chell, E. and Tracey, P., 10, 182
Chen, C.C., Greene, P.G. and Crick, A., 30, 176, 182
Chia, R., 52, 182
Chrisman, J.J., McMullan, E. and Hall, J., 21, 183
Chua, J. H. Chrisman, J.J. and Steier, L.P., ix

Churchill, N.C. and Lewis, V.L., 114, 183
Clark, G.L., Palaskas, P., Tracey, P. and Tsampra, M., 7, 183
Clark, T. and Salaman, G., 47, 183
Clegg, S.R., 41, 183
Code, L., 64, 183
Coff, R.W., 126, 183
Cohen, M.D. and Bacdayan, P., 109, 183
Cohen, W.M. and Levinthal, D.A., 124, 183
Collins, R., 146, 183
Conner, K., 129, 183
Contu, A. and Willmott, H., 146, 183
Cooper, A.C., 28, 183
Cooper, A.C., Gimenogascon, F.J. and Woo, Y.C., 27, 183
Cooper, A.C., Woo, Y.C. and Dunkelberg, W.C., 28, 183
Cordes, C., 115–116, 183
Cornelissen, J.P. and Clarke, J.S., 97, 183
Cranny-Francis, A., Waring, W., Stavopoulos, P. and Kirkby, J., 60, 183
Crook, T.R., Ketchen, D.J., Combs, J.G. and Todd, S.Y., 126, 183
Cruickshank, J., 140, 142, 183
Curran, J., Jarvis, R., Blackburn, R.A. and Black, S., 77, 81, 183
Cyert, R.M. and March, J.G., 109, 183
Czarniawska, B., 48, 183
Czarniawska-Joerges, B., 53, 184

Dachler, H.P., Hosking, D.M. and Gergen, K.J., 52, 55, 184
Dacin, 95
Danermark, B., Ekstrom, M., Jacobsen, L. and Karlsson, J.C., 141–143, 148, 184
Darwin, C.R., 107, 184
Davidsson, P., 35–37, 184
Davidsson, P. and Wiklund, P., 35, 114, 184
Davies, B. and Harré, R., 52, 184
Dawkins, R., 107–108, 184
De Beauvoir, S., 64, 184
De Koning, A.J., 78, 184
Deakins, D. and Freel, M., 5, 18, 19, 26, 184
Delacroix, J. and Carroll, G.R., 108, 112, 184
Delacroix, J. and Rao, M.V., 109, 184
Delgado, M., Porter, M.E. and Stern, S., 4, 184
Delmar, F. and Shane, S., 109, 184
Demsetz, H., 121, 184
Dennett, D., 107, 114, 184
Denrell, J., Fang, C. and Winter, S.G., 125, 130, 133, 184
Denzin, N.K., 40–41, 43, 51, 184
DePropris, L., 78, 83, 85, 184
Dess, G.G. and Lumpkin, G.T., 132, 185
Dick, B. and Morgan, G., 46, 185

Dierickx, I. and Cool, K., 124, 185
DiMaggio, P.J., 96, 100, 185
DiMaggio, P.J. and Powell, W.W., 94, 176, 185
Dimov, D., 4, 10, 185
Dobbs, M. and Hamilton, R.T., 114, 185
Dodd, S.D. and Anderson, A.R., 4, 6, 185
Doolin, B., 154, 185
Down, S., 44, 55, 185
Downing, S., 55, 185
Drakopoulou Dodd, S. and Patra, E., 81, 185
Drakopoulou Dodd, S., Jack, S.L. and Anderson, A.R., 76, 81, 90, 185
Drucker, P., 150, 185
Du Gay, P., 154–155, 160, 170, 176, 185
Du Gay, P. and Salaman, G., 153, 185
Du Gay, P., Salaman, G. and Rees, B., 154, 185
Durham, W.H., 107, 114, 185

Economist, The, 19, 185
Eisenhardt, K.M., 5, 10, 99, 185
Eisenhardt, K.M. and Graebner, M.E., 10, 186
Eisenhardt, K.M. and Martin J.A., 127, 186
Ellis, C. and Bochner, A., 51–52, 186
Emirbayer, M. and Mische, A., 144, 186
England, K.V.L., 51, 186
Evans, D. and Jovanovic, B., 17, 22, 23, 175–176, 186

Fairclough, N., 153, 186
Felin, T. and Foss, N.J., 110, 186
Fenwick, T.J., 170, 186
Fitzgerald, M.A. and Muske, G., 172, 186
Fleck, J., 117, 186
Fleetwood, S. and Hesketh, A., 137, 140, 148, 186
Fletcher, D.E., 44, 49, 52, 55, 66, 186
Fletcher, D.E. and Watson, T.J., 53, 186
Forbes, D.P., 114, 186
Foreman-Peck, J., 14, 186
Foss, N.J., 133, 186
Foss, N.J. and Lyngsie, J., 133, 186
Foss, N.J. and Stieglitz, 133, 186
Foss, N.J. and Knudsen, T., 123, 186
Foucault, M., 63, 186
Fournier, V., 154, 156, 186
Fournier, V. and Grey, C., 151, 186
Fraser, S., 18, 187
Fraser, S. and Greene, F.J., 24, 187
Fraser, S., Greene, F.J. and Mole, K.F., 23, 187
Fraser, S., Storey, D., Frankish, J. and Roberts, R., 10, 187
Freemans, R.E., 168, 187
Freidan, B., 62, 187

Freund, J., 164, 187
Friedland, R. and Alford, A.A., 105, 187
Friedman, M., 14, 187

Garfinkel, H., 101, 187
Gartner, W.B., 28, 44, 66, 110, 187
Gartner, W.B. and Carter, N.M., 130, 187
Gartner, W.B., Carter, N.M. and Hills, G.E., 44, 187
Garvan, T.N. and O'Cinneide, B., 38, 187
Gatley, S., Lessem, R. and Altman, Y., 75, 187
Gavetti, G. and Levinthal, D.A., 127, 187
Geertz, C., 51, 187
Gehlen, A., 166, 187
Gergen, K.J. and Gergen, M.M., 43, 52, 187
Gergen, K.K., 43, 52, 55, 187
Giddens, A., 50, 60, 137, 143, 187
Gilad, B. and Levine, P., 27, 187
Gist, M.E., 30, 187
Gnyawali, D.R. and Fogel, D.S., 4, 188
Goffman, E., 43, 170, 188
Goldthorpe, J.H., Lockwood, D., Bechhofer, F. and Platt, J., 169, 188
Goss, D., 157, 176, 188
Granovetter, M., 24, 75, 77, 79, 91, 188
Grant, P. and Perren, L., 5, 9, 177, 188
Greene, F. and Mole, K., 3, 188
Greene, F.J., Mole, K.F. and Storey, D.J., 5, 19, 188
Greenwood, R. and Hinings, C.R., 95, 188
Greenwood, R. and Suddaby, R., 145, 188
Greenwood, R., Oliver, C., Sahlin, K. and Suddaby, R., 94–95, 102–103, 105, 188
Greiner, L.E., 114, 188
Greve, A., 81, 188
Greve, A. and Salaff, J., 85, 188
Grix, J., 2, 3, 23, 71, 148, 177, 188
Guardian, 174, 188

Habermas, J., 150, 188
Halford, S. and Leonard, P., 170, 188
Hamilton, E., 47, 188
Hanna, V. and Walsh, K., 85, 188
Hannan, M.T. and Freeman, J., 108, 188
Hargadon, A.B. and Douglas, Y., 97–98, 188
Hargrave, T.J. and Van de Ven, A.H., 102, 188
Harper, D.A., 130, 188
Hart, M., 138, 188
Hartmann, H., 62, 189
Hartsock, N., 70–71, 189
Hartwig, M., 142–143, 189
Haveman, H.A. and David, R.J., 105, 189
Hayek, F.A., 128, 189

Heelas, P. and Morris, P., 153, 189
Helfat, C.E. and Peteraf, M.A., 127, 189
Helfat, C.E., Finkelstein, S., Mitchell, W., Peteraf, M.A., Singh, H., Teece, D.J. and Winter, S.G., 127, 189
Hiatt, S.R., Sine, W.D. and Tolbert, P.S., 97, 189
Hillman, A.J., Withers, M.C. and Collins, B.J., 168, 189
Hills, G.E., Lumpkin, G.T. and Singh, R.P., 78, 189
Hirdman, Y., 60, 189
Hisrich, R., Langan-Fox, J. and Grant, S., 37, 189
Hitt, M.A. and Ireland, R.D., 132, 189
Hitt, M.A., Ireland, R.D., Camp, S.M. and Sexton, D.L., 132, 189
Hoang, H. and Antonic, B., 76, 91, 189
Hodgson, G.M. and Knudsen, T., 107, 109–110, 114, 117, 119
Hollis, M., 5, 9, 189
Holmes, M., 60, 73, 189
Holmwood, J., 146, 189
hooks, b., 62, 189
Hoopes, D.G. and Madsen, T.L., 126, 189
Hughes, A., 140, 189
Hull, D.L., 108, 189
Human, S. and Provan, K., 85, 189
Hurst, E. and Lusardi, A., 18, 23, 189
Hwang and Powell, 105

Iakovleva T. and Kolvereid, L., 37, 190
Ingham, G., 46, 190
Ireland, R.D., Hitt, M.A., Camp, S.M. and Sexton, D.L., 132, 190
Ireland, R.D., Kuratko, D.F. and Covin, J.G., 132, 190
Irigaray, L., 62, 190
Isaksen, E., 39, 190

Jack, S.L., 78, 91, 190
Jack, S.L. and Anderson, A.R., 10, 49, 190
Jagose, A., 60, 190
Jeanes, E., 60, 190
Jennings, P.L., Perren, L. and Carter, S., 5, 10, 190
Joas, H., 162, 166, 190
Johannisson, B., 49, 55, 78, 166, 190
Johannisson, B. and Mønsted, M., 76–77, 83, 89, 190
Johannisson, B. and Nilsson, A., 81, 190
Johannisson, B., Ramirez-Pasillas, M. and Karlsson, G., 49, 190
Jones, C. and Spicer, A., 5, 157, 160, 190
Jones, S., 69, 190
Josselson, R. and Lieblich, A., 48, 190
Jovanovic, B., 16, 25, 190

Kahneman, D., Slovic, P. and Tversky, A., 23, 191
Karatas-Ozkan, M. and Murphy, W.D., 5, 191
Karra, N., Tracey, P. and Phillips, N., 7, 191
Katz, J.A., 28, 36, 191
Keat, R. and Abercrombie, N., 153, 191
Keat, R. and Urry, J., 141, 191
Keeble, D., 4, 191
Keeble, D., Lawson, C., Moore, B. and Wilkinson, F., 4, 191
Kemp, S. and Holmwood, J., 146, 191
Kenney, M. and Patton, D., 7, 191
King, A., 146–147, 191
King, G., Keohane, R.O. and Verba, S., 177, 191
Kirzner, I.M., 4, 110, 113, 128, 133, 191
Klyver, K. and Hindle, K., 90, 191
Knight, F.H., 6, 121, 129, 191
Knott, A.M., Bryce, D.J. and Posen, H.E., 125, 191
Kogut, B. and Zander, U., 127, 191
Kolvereid, L., 31, 39, 191
Kolvereid, L. and Åmo, B.W., 38, 191
Kolvereid, L. and Isaksen, E., 36–37, 191
Kor, Y.Y. and Mahoney, J.T., 121, 191
Kristeva, J., 62, 191
Krueger, N.F., 29–30, 34, 37, 191, 192
Krueger, N.F. and Brazeal, D.V., 30–31, 191
Kuhn, T.S., 9, 111–112, 192

Lafuente, E., Vailliant, Y. and Rialp, J., 147, 192
Langlois, R.N., 127, 192
Larson, 91
Larson, A. and Starr, J.A., 84, 192
Law, S., 59, 192
Lawrences, T.B. and Suddaby, R., 93, 96, 100, 192
Lawrences, T.B., Suddaby, R. and Leca, B., 100, 192
Lawson, T., 141, 146, 148, 177, 192
Leca, B. and Nacceche, P., 138, 192
Lechner, C. and Dowling, M., 83–84, 91, 192
Lee, D.Y. and Tsang, E.W.K., 28, 192
Lee, R. and Jones, O., 138, 192
Levitt, S.D. and Dubner, S.J., 13, 192
Lewis, P.A., 73, 148, 192
Linan, F. and Chen, Y.W., 37, 192
Lincoln, Y.S. and Guba, E.G., 55, 192
Lindgren, M. and Wåhlin, N., 44, 192
Lippman, S.A. and Rumelt, R.P., 123, 125, 133, 192
Littunen, H., 27, 192
Loadsby, B.J., 110, 192
Locke, E.A. and Baum, J.R., 38, 192

Lounsbury, M. and Glynn, M.A., 97, 192
Lumpkin, G.T. and Dess, G.G., 24, 128, 132, 193

MacDonald, G. and Ryall, M.D., 126, 193
MacDonald, R. and Coffield, F., 5, 176, 193
MacPherson, A. and Holt, R., 114, 193
Maguire, S., Hardy, C. and Lawrence, T.B., 96, 193
Makadok, R., 122, 125, 193
Makadok, R. and Barney, J.B., 125, 130, 193
Malthus, 116
March, J., 113, 193
Marlow, S. and Patton, D., 73
Marlow, S., 65, 70, 73, 193
Marlow, S., Carter, S. and Shaw, E., 72, 193
Marlow, S., Henry, C. and Carter, S., 65, 71, 193
Marsh, D. and Stoker, G., 6, 193
Marsh, D. and Furlong, P., 3, 193
Martin, J., 60, 193
Mason, C. and Harrison, R., 20, 193
Matthews, C.H. and Moser, S.B., 28, 193
May, T., 141, 193
McAdam, M. and Marlow, S., 66, 193
McAnulla, S., 137, 139, 193
McClelland, D.C., 6, 28, 165, 193
McGuiness, S. and Hart, M., 21, 193
McKelvey, B., 117, 193
McRobbie, A., 59–60, 63, 194
Mead, G.H., 43, 194
Menzies, T.V., 38, 194
Meyer, J.W., 94, 194
Meyer, J.W. and Rowan, B., 7, 94–95, 101, 194
Miettinen, O., Mazhelis, O. and Luoma, E., 10, 194
Mills, C.W., 162, 164, 173, 194
Minitti, M., Arenius, P. and Langowitz, N., 72, 194
Mirchandani, K., 66, 194
Mises, L.V., 121, 194
Mitchell, R., Busenitz, L., Lant, P., MacDougall, P., Morese, E. and Smith, C., 28, 194
Mokyr, J., 117, 194
Mole, K.F and Bramley, G., 21, 194
Mole, K.F. and Mole, M., 8, 138–139, 148, 194
Mole, K.F., Hart, M., Roper, S. and Saal, D., 21, 194
Mønsted, M., 80–81, 194
Morton, F.M.S. and Podolny, J.M., 14, 194
Mosakowski, E., 129, 131, 194
Mounce, H.O., 162, 194
Murmann, J.P., 109, 114, 116–117, 119, 194
Mutch, A., 138–139, 143–145, 148, 194

Nelson, R. and Winter, S., 107, 109, 114, 117, 127, 194
Newbert, S.L., 121, 194
Nodoushani, O. and Nodoushani, P., 50, 194
Nooteboom, B., 115–116, 195
North, D.C., 96, 195

O'Connor, E., 47, 195
O'Donnell, A., Gilmore, A., Cummins, D. and Carson. D., 76, 195
Ogbor, I.O., 5, 50, 68, 79, 73, 154, 195
Ostgaard, T.A. and Birley, S., 78, 195
Outhwaite, W., 141, 195

Pages, E. and Garmise, S., 83, 195
Parker, M., 151, 195
Parker, S., 26, 195
Patton, M.Q., 55, 195
Pawson, R. and Tilley, N., 138, 141–142, 148, 195
Penrose, E., 114, 121, 195
Pentland, B.T. and Feldman, M.S., 109, 117–118, 195
Perren, L. and Jennings, P.L., 103, 154, 195
Perren, L. and Ram, M., 10, 195
Peteraf, M.A., 123–124, 131, 133, 195
Peteraf, M.A. and Barney, J.B., 122–123, 195
Pfeffer, J. and Salancik, G.R., 168, 195
Phelps, R., Adams, R. and Bessant, J., 114, 195
Phillips, N. and Tracey, P., 105
Pihkala, T., Varamäki, E. and Vesalainen, J., 83, 195
Pitt, M., 47, 195
Plotkin, H., 107, 114, 195
Polkinghorne, D., 48, 195
Porpora, D., 140, 195
Porter, M.E., 122, 195
Potter, J. and Wetherall, M., 43, 195
Powell, W.W. and Colyvas, J.A., 101, 196
Prahalad, C.K. and Hamel, G., 133, 196
Priem, R.L. and Butler, J.E., 126, 196
Proctor, M., 24, 196
Pullen, A. and Simpson, R., 60, 196

Radkau, J., 163, 196
Rainnie, A., 46, 196
Ram, M. and Trehan, K., 5, 196
Ram, M., 10, 78, 90, 196
Ram, M., Theodorakopoulos, N. and Jones, T., 177, 196
Ram. M. and Holliday, R., 46, 176, 196
Rauch, A. and Frese, M., 33, 36, 196
Read, S., Sarasvathry, S., Wiltbank, R. and Ohlsson, A.V., 171, 174, 196

Reed, M., 146, 196
Reed, R. and Defillipi, R.J., 125, 196
Reid, G., Jacobson, L. and Anderson, M., 25, 196
Rich, A., 62, 196
Richerson, P.J. and Boyd, R., 107, 114, 196
Ricoeur, P., 43, 196
Riding, R.J. and Rayner, S.G., 28, 196
Rivkin, J., 125, 196
Robinson, P.B., Simpson, D.V., Huefner, J.C. and Hunt, H.K., 28, 36, 196
Robson, M.T., 14, 15, 16, 25, 197
Robson, M.T. and Wren, C., 25, 197
Romanelli, E., 176, 197
Romanelli, E. and Schoonhoven, C.B., 4, 197
Romijn, H. and Albu, M., 85, 197
Ronstadt, R., 34, 197
Rose, N., 153, 197
Roseneil, S., 60, 197
Rosenkopf, L. and Nerkar, A., 114, 197
Rotter, J.B., 28, 197
Rowbotham, S., 59, 197
Rumelt, R.P., 121, 123, 130, 197

Salerno, J.T., 128, 197
Santos, F.A. and Eisenhardt, K.M., 176, 197
Sarasvathy, S.D., 129, 133, 170, 176, 197
Sayer, A., 142–143, 197
SBS, 21, 26, 73, 197
Scherer, P.D., Adams, J., Carley, S. and Wiebe, F., 28, 197
Schumacher, E.F., 143, 197
Schumpeter, J.A., 3, 6, 109, 113, 130, 133, 197
Schutz, A., 43, 197
Scott, M. and Bruce, R., 114, 198
Scott, M.G. and Twomey, D.F., 28, 198
Scott, W.R., 106, 198
Selznick, P., 94, 198
Shane, S and Venkataraman, S., 3, 4, 50, 110, 114, 177, 198
Shane, S., 4, 34, 39, 129, 131, 133, 198
Shane, S. and Cable, D., 78, 198
Shapero, A. and Sokol, L., 28, 30, 198
Shaver, K.G., 27, 29, 198
Shaver, K.G. and Scott, L.R., 27–28, 198
Shaw, E., Marlow, S., Lam, W. and Carter, S., 72, 198
Shook, C.L., Priem, R.L. and McGee, J.E., 36, 198
Simons, H.A., 21, 198
Sine, W.D. and David, R.J., 97, 198
Sine, W.D. and Lee, B.H., 97, 198
Sine, W.D., David, R.J. and Mitsuhashi, H., 97, 198
Slotte-Kock, S. and Coviello, N., 76, 90, 198

Soper, K., 71, 198
Sorenson, O. and Stuart, T.E., 2, 6, 9, 176, 198
Souitaris, V., Zerbinati, S. and Al-Laham, A., 38, 198
Spender, D., 62, 198
Sperber, D., 116, 198
Spicer, A., Alversson, M. and Karreman, D., 151, 198
Staber, U. and Aldrich. H., 80–81, 198
Stark, D., 158, 199
Steyaert, C., 52, 53, 55, 166–167, 199
Steyaert, C. and Katz, J., 49, 199
Stiglitz, J.E. and Weiss, A., 17, 199
Stinchcombe, A.L., 24, 109, 199
Stoelhorst, J.W., 107, 199
Storey, D.J., 17, 21, 26, 140, 176, 199
Storey, J., Salaman, G. and Platman, K., 170, 199
Storper, M., 83, 199
Streufert, S. and Nogami, G.Y., 28, 199
Sudbury, J., 63, 199
Suddaby, R., Elsbach, K.D., Greenwood, R., Meyer, J.W. and Zilber, T.B., 101, 199
Szarka, J., 76–77, 199

Taylor, S. and Marlow, S., 65, 70, 74, 199
Teece, D.J., 125, 127, 199
Teece, D.J., Pisano, G. and Shuen, A., 127, 133, 199
Thornton. P.H., 105, 199
Thornton. P.H. and Ocasio, W., 105, 199
Timmons, J., 28, 199
Tkachev, A. and Kolvereid, L., 31, 32, 199
Tolbert, P. S. and Zucker, L.G., 4, 94, 200
Tooby, J. and Cosmides, L., 107, 114, 200
Tracey, P., 24, 114, 148, 200
Tracey, P., Phillips, N. and Jarvis, O., 4, 10, 97–98, 200
Tsoukas, H., 176, 200
Tsoukas, H. and Chia, R., 176–177, 200
Turner, J.H., 7, 200
Tushman, M.L. and Anderson, P., 109, 200

Uzzi, B., 7, 77–78, 86–89, 91, 200
Uzzi, B. and Gillespie, J.J., 78, 85, 200
Uzzi, B. and Lancaster, R., 85, 200

van Dijk, T.A., 50, 200
van Maanen, J., 52, 200
Van Praag, C.M. and Versloot, P.H., 25, 200
Van Stel, A. and Storey, D.J., 5, 200
Vaughan, D., 150, 200
Venkataraman, S., 90, 177, 200
Vincent, S., 148, 200
Vygotsky, L.S., 43, 200

Ward, H., 24, 200
Watson, T.J., 44, 52, 166–168, 171, 174, 176–177, 200, 201
Weber, M., 163, 201
Weick, K., 167, 201
Weldon. F., 59, 201
Wennekers, A.R.M. and Thurik, A.R., 129, 201
Wernerfelt, B., 123, 133, 201
Westhead, P., Ucbasaran, D. and Wright, M., 177, 201
Winter, S.G., 125, 201
Witt, U., 115, 201

Wittgenstein, L., 111, 115, 201
Wooten, M. and Hoffman, A.J., 106, 201
Wren, C. and Storey, D.J., 10, 201

Yin, 143

Zafirovski, M., 49, 201
Zahra, S. A., ix
Zeleny, 85
Zilber, T.B., 97, 201
Zott, C. and Huy, Q.N., 97–100, 175, 177, 201
Zucker, L.G., 94, 101, 201

Subject index

Achievement motivation, 28
Adoption of practices, 95
Adverse selection, 16, 20
Agency, 137, 176
Agent's knowledge, 143
Alert to opportunities, 128
Alternatives of building organizations, 160
Alternatives to positivist social science, 5
Analytic dualism, 140
Anti-foundationalism, 177
Applied CR study, 142
Archer's morphogenetic approach, 138, 143
    and analysis of institutional change, 138
    and entrepreneurship policy, 138
    and institutional entrepreneurship, 138
    and theory of entrepreneurship, 138
Asset mass efficiencies, 124
Asset stocks, interconnectedness in, 125
Asymmetric information, 22
    and small firm finance, 16–20
Attitude measurement, 31
    and self-employment, 31
Autonomous reflexives, 144
    and discontinuity, 145
    and institutional entrepreneurs, 144
    as society's strategists, 144

Bank lending to small firms, 17
Bargaining
    and resource mobility, 126
    and social capital, 126
    and value appropriation, 126
Barriers to entry, 122
Behavioural Science, 24
Behavioural science and anchoring, 23
Beliefs and preferences, 47
Bhaskar's RRREI(C) model, 142–143, 145
Biological analogies in social science, 115
Brewing, 143
British Social Attitudes Survey, 22
Building legitimacy
    as a discursive and symbolic process, 100
Bureaucracy, 141, 142
Business advisers
    see also business support, 47
Business ownership
    women's under-representation in, 73

Business start-ups, 172
Business support, 76, 140

Canada, 81, 82
Capital constraints, 22, 23
Case replication method, 99
Case studies, 46, 143, 144
Causal ambiguity, 125
Causes
    distant (distal), 35
    proximate, 35
Change
    from intended and unintended outcomes, 145
Changes in founding rates, 109
Co-preneurship, 172
Cognitive abilities, 176
Cognitive style index, 28
Collective routines, 117
Competences or 'comp's, 113, 117
Competing paradigms in evolutionary theory, 111
Competition
    high levels of, 100
Competitive imperfection in strategic management, 122
Complementary resources, 125
Concept of perspectives, 177
Constructed meaning, 40, 45, 46
Constructive perspective on institutions, 94
Contextualizing, 55
Corporate cultures, 155
Corporate entrepreneurial behaviour, 112
Corridor principle, The, 34
Counterfactual thinking, 143
Creativity and innovation, 28
Credit rationing, 17, 18
Critical knowledge, 150, 151
    and emancipation, 150
Critical management studies (CMS), 149, 150, 151
Critical Realism
    compared with positivist approach, 137
    the critique of, 146–147
    empirical work using, 148
    and entrepreneurship, 137–148
    its future in entrepreneurship, 147–148

Critical Realism – *continued*
    and quantitative methods, 146
    tenets of, 138
    and three levels of reality, 138
Critical research
    and empirical research, 142
Critical Theory, 5, 8, 149–160
Cross-national studies, 103
Cultural emergent properties (CEPs), 140
Culture of enterprise *see* Enterprise culture

Darker side of business life, The, 150
Darwinian principles, 107
Decision-making
    analysts *versus* intuitivists, 28
    and heuristics, 29
Deconstruction, 68
Deinstitutionalzation, 103
Demographic models, 36
Dependency culture, 5
Dewey, Charles, 9
Dewey, John, 162
Dialectical approaches
    call for, 90
Discourse, 43, 62, 146
    contradictory and complementary, 45
    embodying power and legitimacy, 68
    masculine, 63, 69
    prevailing, 71
    tension within, 152
Discourse of enterprise, 155, 170
    internalization of, 153
    reconfiguring, 153
Discourse of entrepreneurship
    challenged, 151
    in non-entrepreneurial contexts, 156
Discrimination, 59
Doing entrepreneurship, 44
Dominant epistemologies, 64
Due diligence, 20
Dynamic capabilities, 132
Dynamics
    of founding rates, 108
    and learning, 127
Dyson, James
    as designer not entrepreneur, 159

Economic approach, The, 5
Economic interactions, 75
Economic theory
    criticisms of, 86
Economic view of institutions, The, 96
Economics, 13–27
    industrial, 120
    of entrepreneurship, 120
Effectuation, 5, 129, 161, 170–171
Emancipatory knowledge, 152

Embedded ties, 88
Embeddedness, 7, 75, 77, 88, 91, 94
    and interfirm networks, 86
Emergence, 52
Emergent life orientations, 161, 169, 173
Employees
    as responsible risk-takers, 154
Employment choice
    predictions of, 33
Enterprise
    concept, language resources, 44
    the darker side of, 159
Enterprise culture, 5, 60, 153, 155, 156
Enterprise discourse
    affective dimension of, 157
    as coherent, 154
    contested, 155
    and ideation, 154, 156
    and neo-liberal policy, 154
    objections to, 156, 157
    and power relations, 156
    see also entrepreneurship discourse, 72,
        154–157
Enterprise ideology, 157, 170
Enterprise policy
    three decades of, 19
Enterprising discourse, 44, 50
Enterprising subjects, 153
Enterprising worker, The, 155–156
Entreprenerial labour process, 158
Entreprenerial phenomena
    differentiated, 49
Entrepreneur
    as occupational choice, 22
    skills and capabilities, 98
Entrepreneurial ability, 25, 175
Entrepreneurial action, 161, 167–169, 171,
    172
Entrepreneurial actor, The, 161
Entrepreneurial actors
    business competences, 170
    as creative force, 168
    as distinct from owner, 168, 169, 170
    and family circumstances, 170
Entrepreneurial behaviour
    and institutional forces, 99
    multi-level understanding of, 102
Entrepreneurial capital
    types of, 97
Entrepreneurial career performance, 35
Entrepreneurial characteristics, 154
Entrepreneurial choice, 27
Entrepreneurial decisions, 144
Entrepreneurial discourse
    challenging normative representations of,
        68
    discriminatory nature of, 50

gendered nature of, 64
persistence of, 70
Entrepreneurial economy, 25
Entrepreneurial identities, 154
Entrepreneurial identity and deception, 69
Entrepreneurial intention models, 27
Entrepreneurial intentions questionnaire,
    36–37
Entrepreneurial network benefits and
    drawbacks, 77–79
Entrepreneurial networks
    analysing the, 79
    see also networks, 75
Entrepreneurial Orientation, 132
Entrepreneurial resources, 131
Entrepreneurial society, 151
Entrepreneurial start-up, 107
Entrepreneurial teams, 118, 130
Entrepreneuring, 166
    and process thinking, 167
Entrepreneurs
    ambivalence towards, 168
    building legitimacy for ventures, 96, 100
    changing aspects of social, cultural and/or
        political life, 159
    demand and supply of, 22
    and discursive and symbolic action, 96
    embedded in socio-centric networks, 83
    encouraging and helping, 151
    explanations and reasonings of, 45
    and individual context, 49
    as innovative connectors, 157
    and institutional context, 49
    judgement of, 148
    and legitimation, 95
    marginalized, 158
    more research to identify key skills of, 37
    negative aspects of, 158
    personal characteristics as predictors of
        success, 33
    as a product of history and culture, 152
    real experiences of, 152
    and resource acquisition, 99
    and socio-economic context, 48, 49, 50
    social situatedness of, 48, 49
    social, emotional and aethetic labour of, 158
    socially positioned, 76
    supposed informational advantage, 120, 121
Entrepreneurs-low and high risk, 18
Entrepreneurship, 3–4, 128–129, 167,
        definition of
    affective dimensions of, 149
    attitudes towards, 38
    as a broader process of creating
        opportunities, 159
    critical theories of, 149–160
    and dominant economic approaches, 103

discipline of, 2, 5–7, 176
epistemological bias in, 64
exclusionary and discriminatory, 68
in emerging markets, 103
in established firms, 130
and individual-level variables, 33
and knowledge or insight, 128
meaning and vocabulary of, 44
methodological assumptions, 151
and microeconomics, 13
micro-level research, 114
as a multi-level process, 96
as not value-free, 150, 152
over-concentration on opportunity
    discovery, 5, 130
political presuppositions of, 150
power and domination, 149
and small business, 177
and small business management, 128
and strategic institutional change, 97
in society, 173
sociological and economic theories, 89
structural constraints on, 149
and training, 38
women's experience of, 65
Entrepreneurship as a discipline
    and legitimation, 176
    strategic management's takeover, 133
entrepreneurship discourse, 149, 177
Entrepreneurship policy
    and Archer's morphogenetic approach, 138
Entrepreneurship, study of
    as a broader undertaking, 161
    and entrepreneurial actors, 163
    human interests, 152
Environment, 110–111
Environmental analysis, 123
Epistemic Fallacy, 165
Epistemology, 146
    and the perpetuation of female
        subordination, 64
Equality, 59
Equity finance, 19, 20
Essentialism, 72
Ethnographic studies, 40, 46, 86, 89, 111,
    118, 155
Evolution and Entrepreneurship, 107–119
Evolution of habits, routines and heuristics,
    118
Evolution of knowledge, 112
Evolutionary approach, the, 8
    contribution to entrepreneurship research,
        113–115
    critiscisms of, 115–116
    epistemological and empirical methods, 111
    future directions, 116–118
    implications for entrepreneurs, 118

Evolutionary epistemology
    critical realist variant, 111
    interpretivist variant, 111
Evolutionary theory, 107–119
Evolving managerial behaviour, 114
Exchange relationship, 168
Experimental methods, 111, 118
Explanation and depth ontology, 139

Fallible knowledge, 143
Family background, 28
Family business, 40, 45, 46, 47, 172
Family culture in small firms, 45, 46, 47
Female entrepreneurship
    and context, 72
Female subordination *see* Gender-based
    subordination
Feminism
    as an emancipatory perspective, 71
    first wave, 61
    future directions of, 71–72
    and qualitative methods, 66
    second wave, 61
Feminist critique, The, 59
Feminist empiricist, 65
Feminist ontology and epistemology, 63
Feminist perspectives
    black feminism, 62
    radical feminism, 62
    socialist feminism, 62
Feminist theory, 7, 8
    and post-structural, 62
Fieldwork, 41, 46, 52
Firm resources, 121
Firm-specific
    advantages, 121
    capabilities, 125
Formal practices in organizations, 94
Founding stories, 47
Frankfurt School *see* CMS, 150
Freakeconomics, 13

Gardening culture, 141
Gender
    as constructed, 70
    as social practice, 60
Gender and Entrepreneurship, 59–74
Gender effect, 65
Gender trouble, 60
Gender-based subordination, 59–62, 68–69,
    73
Gendered characterizations, 69, 71
Gendered discourses, 63
Gendered management, 46
Gendered order
    challenged, 60
Generalists and specialists, 108

Generalized Darwinism, 8, 108, 110, 114, 115
Generative mechanisms, 145
Genotypes, 107, 108
Governance, 78
Graduate employment opportunities, 31
Graduates from business schools who have
    taken entrepreneurship courses, 38
Greece, 82

Habermasian forms of knowledge, 150
Habits and routines, 110, 111, 115, 117
Habits, routines and heuristics
    as socially constructed, 111
Hermeneutic-interpretive knowledge, 150
    and interpretivist studies, 150
Heuristics, 23, 111
Holocaust, The, 141, 142
Homophily, 80
How entrepreneurs think, 28
Human action, 166
Human beings
    as project-orientated, 169

Ideas and beliefs in interpretivist inquiry, 44,
    45
Identification, 143
Implementing entrepreneurial ideas (IEI),
    29, 30
Incentives, 14
Individual level intentionality and choice, 110
Individuality, 60
Industrial districts
    parallels with network literature, 83
Information, 78
Innovation, 95
Innovation systems, 78
innovative business models, 102
Institutional analysis
    and power and politics, 102
Institutional change
    and Archer's morphogenetic approach, 138
    and critical realism, 145
    the role of agency, 95
Institutional contexts, 95
Institutional entrepreneurs, 98, 143, 145, 148
Institutional entrepreneurship, 96, 98, 157
    and Archer's morphogenetic approach, 138
Institutional entropy, 103
Institutional innovation, 144
Institutional strategies, 105
Institutional theory
    explanation of Sir Andrew Barclay Walker's
        administrative innovation, 145
    implications for entrepreneurs, 104–105
    macro and micro, 101
    and micro aspect of, 104
    micro-level, 101

Institutional work, 96
Institutionalized scripts or logics, 94
Instrumental-technocratic knowledge, 150
Intel, 112
Intention models, 29–31
Intentionality, 115
Interactor, 108, 115
Interdisciplinary approaches, 72
Internal resource accumulation, 125
Internal selection criteria, 119
Interpretation, 47
    multiple levels of, 54
Interpretive and symbolic interactions, 40
Interpretive Ethnography
    principles of, 40
Interpretive methodology
    contrasted with positivism, 41–42
    and epistemological issues, 42
Interpretive orientations, 43
Interpretive processes, 50
Interpretive research
    attending to language in, 43
Interpretive research why we engage in, 42, 43
Interpretive sociology, 164
Interpretive work
    in Entrepreneurship, 40–55
    and macro and micro, 53, 54
Interpretivism, 161, 164, 175
    as an analytical device, 164
    and ethnomethodology, 41
    and hermeneutics, 41
    and linguistic, 43
    and narrative, 43
    and phenomenology, 41, 43
    and pragmatism, 41
    and social constructionist, 43
    and symbolic interactionism, 41, 43
Interpretivist approach to female
    entrepreneurship, 66
Interpretivist Evolutionary Epistemologists, 112
Interpretivist view, The, 6
Interpretivists see Interpretivism
Interviewing entrepreneurs, 47
Intraorganizational behaviour, 103
Intrinsic quality of ventures, 99
Ireland, 82
Irrational decision-making, 24
Isomorphism, 94, 95, 102
Italy, 82

James, William, 162
Japan, 81, 82

Kirznerian Entrepreneurship, 3, 4, 128
Knowledge, 117, 151, 162
    critical approach to, 151
    and human action, 162

Language game, The, 111
Language of enterprise, 153
Legimacy and new venture creation, 97
Legitimacy, legitimation, 7, 78, 94, 95, 104
Liability of newness, 97, 113
Limited liability, 140
Locus of control, 28
Longitudinal research, call for, 36, 90
Low barriers to entry, 100

Macro and micro, 110, 112, 116, 127, 161,
    164, 169, 173
    as objective and subjective, 164
Macro factors, 169
Macro views, 7, 8
Macro-level entrepreneurship discourses, 169
Macro-level institutional forces
    ignoring agency, 114
Managerial practices, 118
    and the evolutionary approach, 119
Market for lemons, 16
Marxism, 137
Material conditions of society, 147
Measurement
    attitudes concepts and intentions, 39
    perceived behavioural control, 32
    and subjective norms, 32
Mechanisms, 137, 138, 141, 142, 143, 163
    casual, 138, 141
    essential features of, 141
Mechanisms and powers
    as intellectual devices, 163
Mechanisms of variation, selection and
    retention, 111, 115–117
Memes, 108
Methodology
    participant observation, 51
    qualitative research, 40
    testing for attitudes, 37
Micro and meso structures, 89
Micro-level evolutionary scholars, 111
Model of change, 137
Models, 13
Moral hazard, 17, 20
Morphogenesis, 139, 140, 145
    as a framework for change, 139
    framework for entrepreneurship, 139
Multi-level research
    and the co-evolution of habits, routines
        and heuristics, 114
Multi-level work
    call for, 90
Myths of entrepreneurship, 159

Narrative, 48, 104, 175
Natural orders, 59
Need for autonomy, 33

Neo-institutional theory, 7, 93–106
  a cognitive approach, 93
  contribution to entrepreneurship research,
    96
  criticisms of, 100–102
  new wave and neglecting social structure,
    100
  overview, 93–96
  and social context, 93
Neo-institutional theory's agentic turn, 95
Network and joint problem solving, 88
Network approaches, 7, 75–92
Network centrality, 79
Network characteristics, 79
Network contacts per month, 82
Network density, 80, 82
Network diversity, 80
Network governance, 76
Network process, 76
Network size, 81
Network structure, 76
  reach, 81
Networking studies
  linking economic and sociological
    approaches, 76
  linking micro and macro, 76
Networks
  call for dialectical approach, 90
  and collective learning, 83
  contribution to the entreprenerial process,
    76, 77
  development through the entrepreneurial
    process, 83–85
  family friends and business ties, 82
  and fine-grained information, 88
  formal and informal, 76
  and innovation, 85
  and international homogeneity, 81
  and participantion in formal networks,
    85
  and SME knowledge and learning, 85
Networm content, 76
New business ventures
  emergence of, 47
New institutional theory see Neo-institutional
  theory
New organizational form, 98
New venture
  creation, 110
  strategies, 25
New ventures identity of, 97
Normative gendered social order
  see also gendered order, 68

Occupational identity, 155
Ontological and epistemological positions,
  176

Ontology, 2, 3, 42, 146, 175
  and anti-foundationalists, 3
  and epistemology, 175
  and foundationalists, 3
Ontology of becoming, 42
An ontology of relational becoming, 52
Opportunities
  and institutional change, 97
Opportunity, 48
  and dynamic capabilities, 127
  and the environment, 96
  and identifying changing social trends, 104
Opportunity cost, 25
Opportunity discovery, 34
Opportunity exploitation
  and Theory of Planned Behaviour, 33
Opportunity recognition, 27, 34
Organizational behaviour, 116
Organizational change
  evolutionary view of, 113
Organizational ecology, and r and
    K strategies, 109
Organizational form, 108, 109, 117, 160
  as replicator, 109
Organizational institutionalism, 94
Organizations study of, 94, 115
Outcomes
  and prediction, 14
Outsider, 145
Over-embeddedness
  see also under and over-embeddedness,
    88, 91
Overconfidence, 37

Paradigms
  see also perspectives, 112, 161
Path-dependent processes, 131
Peirce, Charles, 162
Performing ritualistically, 177
Personal emergent properties (PEPs), 140
Personal savings, 48
Personality traits, 28, 35, 38
Perspectives in entrepreneurship, 1, 6, 10,
    161, 175, 177, ix
  and the broad church, 177
  benefits of, ix
  and enhanced knowledge, 175
  micro and macro, 1
  ontological and epistemological
    assumptions, 177
  providing conceptual resources, 163
  variety of, 175
Peteraf framework, 131
Phenotype, 108
Political entrepreneurs, 157
Population density, 108
Population ecology, 108–109, 111, 115, 117

Population growth, 116
Porter's five-forces, 123
Positive Economics, 14
Positivist social science, 42
  and constant conjunctions, 140
  research aims of, 14, 24, 42, 140
Post-feminism, 63
Post-positivist explanation
  and quantitative methods, 146
Post-structuralism, 66, 67, 70, 73, 146, 155
Pragmatic philosophy
  and scientific knowledge, 162
Pragmatic Realism, 161–174, 162, 164
  and interpretive processes, 164
  useful to whom?, 172
Pragmatic thinking
  critiscism of, 171
Pragmatism
  and entreprenership, 161–174
  and judgement of knowledge, 172
  and Weber, 163
Pragmatist philosophy, 161
Pragmatist thinking, 173
Preference for employment, 38
Preference for self-employment, 28
Preferences, 14, 23
Prevailing ideologies of power
  challenging, 59
Private equity, 19, 20
Productive opportunities, and top
    management team
  see also opportunity, 121
Psychological approach
  contribution of, 33
Psychological approach, The
  cognitive approach, 39
  intention models, 34, 37
  methodology of, 39
  and traits, 39
Psychological studies
  mismatch between independent and
    dependent variables, 35
Psychological view
  and the cognitive approach, 27, 28
  traits, 27
Psychology of the Entrepreneur, The,
  6, 27–39
Public Policy, 20–21, 156, 175
  and cost-benefits analysis, 21
  and market failure, 20, 21
  and the means-ends rational model, 21
  and US Small Business Development
    Centers, 21
Public servants
  as entrepreneurs, 156

Qualitative research, 40, 94

Racism, 141
Radical innovation, 105
Rational choice, 6, 13–26, 175
  and assumptions of rationality, 23
  the critique, 23
  and future development of, 24
  implications for entrepreneurs, 24
Rational myths, 94, 95
Realism
  and social construction, 165
  see also Critical Realism, 164–165
Realist Evolutionary Epistemologies
  and explanation, 112
Reductionism, 165
Reflexive agency
  and internal conversations, 143, 144
Reflexive interpretation, 51
Reflexive knowledge, 152
Reflexives
  autonomous, 144
Reflexivity, 50–52, 66, 143–144
Regular occurences of events, 146
Relating micro and macro, 162
Relational networks, 75
Relationally responsive, 54
Replicator, 107, 109, 110, 115, 117
  routines as the, 109
Reputations, 78
Research
  pluralist view of, 5
Resource accumulation, 124
Resource base, 125
Resource dependant parties, 168
Resource organization, 131
Resource-based view
  and capabilities view of the firm, 127
  compared to evolutionary approach, 117, 121
  and creating strategic resources, 130
  and dynamic capabilities, 127
  and effectuation, 129
  and evolutionary theory, 127
  and exploration versus exploitation, 133
  few connections with entrepreneurship,
    129, 131
  and knowledge based view and, 127
  low church RBV, 127
  and managerial cognition, 132
  and managerial practice, 121
  and modest empirical track record, 126
  origins of, 121
  as a theory of outlier firms, 130
  as a theory of SCA, 123
Resource-based view, The, 8, 120–135
Resources
  organizational embeddedness of, 131
  relative immobility of, 124
  use of symbolic management to acquire, 98

Retention, 107, 109–110, 112
Rethinking the entrepreneur, 150
Retroduction, 141–142, 145–146
Risk-taking, 28
Role models, 28
Routines, 109–111, 116–117
   transmission of, 116
Routinization and creativity
   and balance between, 110
RRREI(C) model, 142–143, 145
   correction, 143
   elimination, 142
   identification, 143
   redescription, 142
   resolution, 142
   retroduction, 142

Schumpeterian Entrepreneurship, 3, 4,
   107, 128
Scotland, 82
SEE model of the entrepreneurial event, 30
Selection, 100, 107, 109, 112
   and cognitive bias, 110
Self-assertion, 28
Self-efficacy, 30–31, 34–35, 37–38
   and experience, 38
Self-employed
   happiness of, 22
   increase in the 1980s, 15
   occupational choice, 15
Sensemaking, 48
Signalling, 18, 25
Sir Andrew Barcley Walker, 143, 145
Situated creativity, 166, 169, 173
Small business, 46, 176
Small firm growth, 114, 118, 140, 142, 143
Social Capital, 88
Social construction of reality, 42, 43, 45,
   101, 164–165
Social constructionist thinking, 53
Social enterprise, 98, 148, 157, 158, 160
Social interaction, 145
Social mechanisms
   see also mechanisms, 141
Social movements, 96, 159, 160
   and opportunity creation, 96
Social norms, 7
Social practices, 45, 47, 55
Social psychology, 29
Social reality
   and depth ontology, 139
   a realist view, 138
Social structure
   defined, 140
   its role in explanation, 146
Social structure and personal milieu
   see also structure and agency, 163

Social structures
   in interpretive ontology, 147
   see also structure and agency, 137, 140,
     146–147
Social ties, 75, 77–80, 88, 91
Socially legitimate behaviour, 94
Specialists (in markets), 109
Stages of institutionalization, 103
Stakeholders, 104, 168
Start-up capital, 22, 48
Starting a business, 14
Storytelling
   see also narrative, 47
Strategic decision-making, 118
Strategic entrepreneurship, 131–132
Strategic factor markets, 125
Strategic groups, 122
Strategic initiatives
   autonomous, competing and induced,
     112–113
strategic management
   indebted to economics, 122
   and value creation, 120
stratgic investment flows, 124
Strong, special embedded ties, 88
Structural conditioning, 145
Structural elaboration, 145
Structural emergent properties (SEPs),
   140
Structural holes, 78–79, 79
Structural inertia, 115
Structural similarity, 99
Structure and agency, 100, 137–138, 140,
   145, 147
   in institutional analysis in institutional
     analysis, 100
Subordination, 60, 64, 71
   and common experiences denied, 71
   cultural/symbolic/physical, 60
   economic, 60
   social/political, 60
Support and advice, 78
Survey techniques, 111, 118
Sustainable comparative advantage (SCA)
   emergence of, 120
Sustainable comparative advantage
   (SCA), 120, 122–123, 130,
     132
Sweden, 82
SWOT framework, 123
Symbolic action, 96–97, 99
   four types of, 99
Symbolic management, 98
Symbols
   and culture in the legitimation of new
     ventures, 96
   and language, 94

Teaching entrepreneurship, 5
Templates for organizing, 102
The Feminine Mystique, 62
The sociological imagination, 163, 173
Theory development, 43
Theory of planned behaviour, 29, 31, 38
Theory-laden concepts, 175
Thick description, 50–52
    and ethnography, 51
    longitudinal research, 51
Thin description, 51
Time allocated to network activity, 82
Time compression diseconomies, 124
Toy Story, 66–69
Triggering mechanism, 30
Typical entrepreneur
    masculine form of, 61

Uncertainty, 100
Under- and over-embedded, 79
Underperformance thesis
    and family businesses, 65
    and women-owned firms, 65, 70, 72
Undervalued resources in the market
    see Strategic factor markets, 125

Universal or Generalized Darwinist
    Approach, 107
Untraded dependences, 83
USA, 21, 81–82
Utilitarianism, 14
Utility maximization, 14

Value creation, 120
Variation, 107–108, 110, 112
Variation, Selection and Retention
    processes of, 107–108
Venture Capital
    theory of, 20
Venture survival, 33
Victorian England, 143
VRIO or VRIN framework, 123–124, 126

Weber, Max, 9, 173
Weber's social action, 173
West Midlands region, 46
Women' contribution
    disregarded, 67
Women's Christian Temperance Union
    (WCTU), 97
Women's oppression, 62